MW01487788

The Presidential Republic

WITHDRAWN

The Presidential Republic

Executive Representation and Deliberative Democracy

GARY L. GREGG II

ROWMAN & LITTLEFIELD PUBLISHERS, INC.
Lanham • Boulder • New York • London

ROWMAN & LITTLEFIELD PUBLISHERS, INC.

Published in the United States of America
by Rowman & Littlefield Publishers, Inc.
4720 Boston Way, Lanham, Maryland 20706

3 Henrietta Street
London WC2E 8LU, England

Copyright © 1997 by Rowman & Littlefield Publishers, Inc.

An article adapted from this book, "The Deliberative Republic and the Compound
Theory of Representation in *The Federalist*," will be published in *Perspectives on
Political Science* 26, no. 1 (1997). Permission has been granted by the Helen Dwight
Reid Educational Foundation. Published by Heldref Publications, 1319 18th Street NW,
Washington, D.C. 20036-1802.

All rights reserved. No part of this publication may be reproduced,
stored in a retrieval system, or transmitted in any form or by any
means, electronic, mechanical, photocopying, recording, or otherwise,
without the prior permission of the publisher.

British Cataloging in Publication Information Available

Library of Congress Cataloging-in-Publication Data

Gregg, Gary L., 1967–
    The presidential republic : executive representation and
deliberative democracy / Gary L. Gregg II.
        p.   cm.
    Includes bibliographical references and index.
    ISBN 0–8476–8377–X (alk. paper). — ISBN 0–8476–8378–8
(pbk. : alk. paper)
    1. Presidents—United States. 2. Representative government and
representation—United States. 3. Democracy—United States.
I. Title.
JK516.G7   1997
320.473—dc20   96–33214

ISBN 0–8476–8377–X (cloth : alk. paper)
ISBN 0–8476–8378–8 (pbk. : alk. paper)

Printed in the United States of America

⊖™ The paper used in this publication meets the minimum requirements of American
National Standard for Information Sciences—Permanence of Paper for Printed Library
Materials, ANSI Z39.48-1984.

TK
516
G7
997

*In memory of Thomas E. Gregg,
agrarian, Christian gentleman, grandfather.
And to Jacob:
may he share some of the best traits of his great-grandfather.*

Contents

Preface

There is perhaps no more important concept in American public life than that of political representation. America was conceived by her Founders to be a republic—a free government in which representatives of the people would make the essential decisions of politics. The Constitution of 1787 established a representative government based on the principle of separation of powers and checks and balances. Such a system pits the people's servants against one another in several institutions in the name of good and non-tyrannical government.

In such a separated system, the president is to function as a representative just as much as the people's representatives assembled in Congress do. As the American political system has evolved over the last two centuries, the presidency has come to occupy a more central role in government than could have been imagined in Philadelphia in 1787 or at the subsequent ratifying conventions in the states. To a significant degree we retain our separated system laid out in the Constitution, and yet it is one that has become presidentially centered. If we are to retain republican government, we must come to grips with the issues raised by enhanced presidential power in a representative form of government. To that end I offer the following pages.

In response to the behavioralist dominance in the discipline of political science, a number of scholars have recently renewed the call for a more traditional science wedding empirical evidence with concerns of political theory. *The Presidential Republic* was inspired by the work of these authors, many of whom are cited in its pages. This book is both an exploration of the evolution of presidential power as well as an investigation of the very idea of executive influence within a representative form of government. As such, I think it will be of interest to political scientists and historians concerned with political development, American political thought, legislative politics as well as the study of the presidency itself.

If I have said anything of import in the pages that follow, it is only because I have had such tremendous assistance as I thought about this book and then wrote it over the last several years. For having inspired my interest in American political thought and issues of constitutional governance, I owe much to Marshall L. DeRosa. It is because of my old professor and friend's example and encouragement that this book was possible.

There were three men present at the moment *The Presidential Republic* was conceived as a dissertation project at Miami University. Steven DeLue read the entire manuscript in several formulations and was always there with ideas and words of encouragement. He was a model mentor and department chair. Herbert Waltzer lent his considerable learning and deft editorial hand to every page of the first incarnation of this research.

To no one do I owe more than I do to Ryan J. Barilleaux. Ryan was there at the conception of this project and patiently endured countless visits, phone calls, and e-mail messages over several years. It is no exaggeration to say that without his guidance this project would never have come to fruition.

Over the years this work has benefited from a number of people who have read portions of the manuscript or simply engaged its author in stimulating conversations on its subject matter. Here Randall Adkins, David Brooker, Thomas Chadwick, Michelle Deardorf, Andrew Dowdle, Augustus Jones, Solomon Obotetukudo, Kimberly Pace, Steven Piott, and Dave Turner all deserve mention. This book has also benefited from a number of more formal reviewers, some of whom remain anonymous. Among these reviewers, Louis Fisher proved to be most helpful. His dedication to the search of primary source material and his vast knowledge of foreign policy improved my arguments immeasurably.

Over the years I have also been blessed with fine technical, editorial, and research assistance. For their many favors large and small as I worked on this manuscript, thanks must go to Lana McClune, Dotti Pearson, Estella Wilkinson, and Ellen Yorty—the best in the business, all. Todd Eberly and Chad Kifer assisted in some research that contributed to my arguments.

Heather and Carol Gregg performed some of the most tedious work imaginable on these pages and I am thankful for their assistance.

Limited financial support of my research was provided by the Department of Political Science of Miami University and The College of Arts and Sciences of Clarion University. The Intercollegiate Studies Institute provided financial assistance in the form of a Richard M. Weaver Fellowship in 1992 and by naming me a Henry Salvatori Fellow the following year as I was working on this manuscript. Both for the financial assistance and for the confidence they showed in this author, I am most grateful.

To my family I owe a grand debt—a debt that I will never really be capable of repaying. For the example, tutelage, love, and support of my parents I am exceedingly grateful. A lucky man is he who has had parents like these.

But, having said all this, no one merits my gratitude more than does my wife, Krysten. Over the last several years she has had to endure many long hours with her husband cloistered in his office or hunched over his computer at home pecking out this book word by word, page by—at times seemingly endless—page. Through it all she has never failed to exhibit the twin virtues of an author's wife—a patient soul and an unwavering heart. For her understanding, companionship, and love, I am truly thankful.

Introduction

The presidency has come to occupy center ground in the American political system. We have invested an immense amount of power and prestige in the office in the hopes of placing it where it could do the most good for the nation. That is to say, we have gone far toward creating a presidential republic. Many have seen the president as a white knight doing battle with the forces of evil, both domestically and internationally, in the name of the American people and their values and beliefs.[1] Students of the office have also informed us that we can and should equate the health of the office with the general health of the nation. As the presidency goes, so goes the United States, or, as Richard Neustadt has put it, "what is good for the country is good for the president and vice versa."[2] And presidents themselves have encouraged us to see the office as one providing "moral leadership" for the nation, as well as the primary judge of the national interest. Though there have been those who have counseled us to beware of investing too much in "Caesar" and becoming too reliant on executive benevolence, the general trend over the last century has been in the opposite direction.[3]

Along with the prevalence of the "cult of the presidency," we are told by our presidents, our other elected and non-elected leaders, and our political culture, that we live in a democracy. We are part of a government "of the people, by the people, and for the people," according to our lore and heritage. Our fundamental law sounds the same theme in its opening line that begins "We the people" and continues with a list of the goals of that compacting people. We are a self-governing nation, a nation whose public philosophy encourages a democratic spirit and the mixture of freedom and equality that such a spirit necessitates.

And yet, can the two strains of a strong presidency and democratic self-rule be reconciled? If so, on what basis? Can a democracy long exist when the people have invested in one man, or in one office, the expectations and centrality of position like that now occupied by America's chief executive? A degree of tension appears to exist here in America's political culture. We tend to value, revere, and respect a powerful presidency as we equally value our democratic traditions and our cultural dedication to freedom and self-governance.

As a nation and a people we historically have stabilized and maintained this tension between presidential power and democratic accountability through the system of institutional representation established by the Constitution of 1787. Direct democracy was really never an option for national governance to the founding generation. Most saw representation as necessary both for logistical purposes to govern a scattered and growing nation and to encourage the development of proper laws. Even the Antifederalists argued for an improved system of representation and not for any type of direct democracy or popular participation in actual governance.

But what of the American presidency? Can a single executive elected over a diverse and extended nation be a representative? The easy answer we can offer is that in some fashion such an office must offer representation. I say this is the easy answer because, if we do not so respond, we are forced to admit that we have elevated an office to the heart of our political life as a nation that is alien to our roots in self-governance and liberal democracy. Such a conclusion we are loath to make.

A more critical answer to the question necessitates a serious and scholarly exploration of the very concept of representation and of representative government itself. It would involve a consideration of the idea of representation in political theory and in the American public philosophy, the various ideas on the possibility of executive representation and the forms it might take, as well as the intended and actual place of the presidency in the American regime. In this study I endeavor to undertake just such an interpretation of the meaning of the presidency for representative government.

Scholars of American politics, political commentators and pundits, as well as the American people in general have upheld at various times competing normative models of presidential activity. Some have argued for a restrained executive that is obedient to the wishes of the legislature, where, it has been argued, "real representation" takes place. Others have urged that the presidency actively lead the other political institutions and the public—to "synthesize" the separated government with one will. And still others have argued for models of presidential activity between these two extremes. In accordance with these models we have evaluated our presidents and, by so doing, rendered judgment on the American regime itself. But, the Constitution established a representative form of government of separated institutions, and we lack the development of the concept of representation according to which we can then evaluate presidents in a more meaningful manner.

The place of the American presidency in the government and in society offers the occupant of that office a unique position from which to both actively represent the nation in the public policy process and to exercise symbolic representation of that nation. The president serves as the primary agenda setter for national affairs and is also seen as the living symbol of the people and the nation. And yet, despite the centrality of the office of the presidency to the process of self-governance in America today and the important place of the idea of representation in American political history, there has been precious little scholarly interest expressed in the idea of presidential representation.

This despite the fact that presidents themselves have been among the most fervent supporters of the idea that the president occupies a role as a representative in American democracy. This presidential assertion should not be surprising. Especially since the start of the "democratization" of American politics that has continued by fits and starts since the early days of the Republic, presidents have understandably wanted to be considered "representatives of the people." With democratization comes the legitimation of political institutions based on their perceived popular character. If presidents were not to assert their role as representatives they would run the risk of holding an office of questioned legitimacy. In an era when "democracy" has become so much the primary recognized ground of political legitimacy, the occupant of an institution that was not considered to somehow wield governmental power in a "democratic" or "representative" way would occupy a considerably weakened office with a narrowed scope of legitimate behavior.[4]

In his famous "Farewell Address" President Washington recognized the Constitution as having divided political power into different depositories, including the presidency, and thereby made "*each* the Guardian of the Public Weal."[5] And at least since Thomas Jefferson presidents have claimed to represent a distinctly national constituency or national interest—usually in contradistinction to members of the legislature whose representative positions do not "command a view of the whole ground," and who might, "condemn what they would not if seen in all its parts."[6]

The idea of the president as the direct representative of the American people is most associated with the presidency of Andrew Jackson. In 1828 Jackson became the first president since George Washington to be chosen without the involvement of Congress either through nomination of the candidate or through outright election in the House of Representatives, as was the case with Jefferson in 1801 and with John Quincy Adams after the electoral deadlock of 1824. For this reason it has been said that Jackson may have been the first popularly elected president in U.S. history.[7] As president, Jackson convulsed the congressional whigs by asserting that, "The President is the direct representative of the American people," and he is "elected by the people and responsible to them."[8]

The presidency of Andrew Jackson marked a significant revolution in the American system of free government. Following Jackson's presidency and his espousal of his doctrine concerning the direct link between the people and their president, subsequent presidents continued to adhere to Jackson's view of the office.[9] James K. Polk, for example, wrote of the president representing "in the executive department the whole people of the United States, as each member of the legislative department represents portions of them."[10]

Theodore Roosevelt also advocated and asserted a representational function for the presidency. Roosevelt asserted that "the executive is or ought to be peculiarly representative of the people as a whole." He went on, "As often as not the action of the executive offers the only means by which the people can get the legislation they demand and ought to have."[11] Roosevelt's "stewardship theory" of executive power was also based on an understanding of the president as the "embodiment of all of the people."[12] He wrote, "My view was that every executive officer, and above all every executive officer in high position, was a steward of the people bound actively and affirmatively to do all he could for the people, and not to content himself with the negative merit of keeping his talents undamaged in a napkin."[13] Woodrow Wilson put it this way, "No one else represents the people as a whole, exercising a national choice . . . the nation as a whole has chosen him, and is conscious that it has no other political spokesman. His is the national voice in affairs."[14]

Closer to the present day, presidents and presidential candidates have continued to claim a representational role for the presidency. In a campaign speech in 1960, then Senator John F. Kennedy claimed "only the president represents the national interest. And upon him alone converges all the needs and aspirations of all parts of the country, all departments of government, all nations of the world."[15] In 1976 presidential candidate Jimmy Carter was quoted as saying, "The president is the only person who can speak with a clear voice to the American people and set a standard of ethics and morality, excellence and greatness."[16]

Moving beyond individual presidents, Barbara Hinckley has recently shown how presidential rhetoric has become institutionalized around certain elements of symbolic politics. Among her findings is that each modern president tends to emphasize in his public speeches the president's centrality in the political process and life of the nation. Presidents tend to identify themselves with the American people and with the nation—to use "we" to create a "symbolic equivalence" among the three. The president thereby not only represents the nation and the people, but *becomes* them. Presidents also rhetorically paint a picture of government that ignores or diminishes the other branches of government as almost "non-actors." Such institutionalized rhetorical symbolism by presidents shows clearly the place they feel they occupy as *the* representatives of the people.[17]

Presidents, however, have not been the only governmental officials to assert the representational role of the presidency. The Supreme Court, the so-called "final arbiter" of the Constitution, has also asserted this position of the executive. For example, in *U.S. v. Curtiss-Wright Export Corporation* (1936) the Court declared that at least in regard to the international arena, "with its important, complicated, delicate and manifold problems, the president alone has the power to speak as a representative of the nation."[18] Twentieth century presidents have ridden such assumptions to levels of presidential power unparalleled in American history.

Despite these public assertions and their consequences for the American political system, the scholarly community has virtually ignored this important concern. In the literature that does mention such a representational conception of the office, the tendency has been to simply assert the role. Such declarations usually come with little or no supporting evidence and generally take the form of self-evident and undisputed dogma. Writing of the limitations that he found placed on the presidency toward the close of the last century, James Bryce nonetheless added that "his office retains a measure of solid independence in the fact that the nation regards him as a direct representative and embodiment of its majesty."[19] Clinton Rossiter recognized the president as "the leading formulator and expounder of public opinion in the United States,"[20] and "the American people's one authentic trumpet," possessing "no higher duty than to give a clear and certain sound."[21] Similarly, Edward S. Corwin called the presidency the "sole representative of the nation as a whole,"[22] and said that it is "the natural and responsible, because the sole, representative of that citizenship" which is "independent in its affiliation of either labor or capital."[23]

When asserting the representative nature of the office of chief executive most recent scholars have done so by contrasting its characteristics with those they find in Congress. This comparison has almost universally taken the form of a contrast between the parochialism that characterizes legislative representation and the more unified and national focus of presidential representation.[24] We might also make mention of the considerable literature that seems to contain *implicit assumptions* about the role of the president as a representative in the American regime. For instance, the presidocentric conceptions of the system that puts the office of the presidency at the center of the governmental process contain an implicit assumption about presidential representation. To wit, those like Richard Neustadt who have come to interpret the health of the regime in terms of the president getting his way with Congress and the bureaucracy assume a view of representation that holds the president to be the proper representative of the nation as a whole.[25] In this view congressional representation is assumed to be inadequately energetic, overly parochial, or democratically less legitimate than the representation of one man elected by the country at large.

The opposite, yet still largely implicit, assumption is found in the work of those who have resisted what some have referred to as the "hero worship" of the presidency and maintained a congressionally-centered view of the proper operation of the political system. Such a view is underlaid by the assumption that political representation is properly exercised through an assembly containing numerous locally elected men and women. This also seems to be the assumption of most who have taken political representation under consideration as they have routinely applied the concept to elected legislatures while virtually ignoring elected executives. We cannot be satisfied with this existing state of the literature on the relationship between political representation and the presidency. The logic of the constitutional system of separated institutions and checks and balances necessitates the president function as a representative, lest the office be alien to the republican principles upon which the system was founded. Presidents themselves have claimed such a role and students of the office have asserted it without adequate consideration or development. What we lack is a scholarly and sustained treatment of the topic.[26]

In such an effort, a theoretical foundation must be established for conceiving the office as a representative one, and we must also explore the actual operation of the office and its impact on representative government in the United States. Developing such a conceptualization of the office will not only improve our understanding of the presidency as an institution, but it will enable us to evaluate the behavior of individual presidents and the overall health of the American regime according to some standard(s) of representation.

Outline of the Book

To undertake such a study, we must first come to grips with the concept of political representation and the central issues surrounding it. Representation has been an ambiguous concept in the history of political ideas and has generated a considerable amount of disagreement and controversy. In the first chapter I discuss the idea of political representation with the objective of arriving at some understanding of the term that will be useful as we apply it to the study of the American presidency. Central to any discussion of representation is the perennial "mandate-independence" controversy and the differentiation between symbolic and active forms of representation. They are among the central concerns of this chapter.

Having established much of the groundwork for a theory of executive representation, I next turn to the question of the place of the presidency in the political system established by the Constitution of 1787. In chapter 2 I explore the concept of representation found in *The Federalist Papers*. Madison, Hamilton, and Jay's collection of essays are some of the most important writings ever produced on the topic of democratic self-government, and they contain an important and sophisticated understanding of political representation that directly bears upon our concern.

In Publius' essays we can see the "systematic" view of representation that was intended for the American regime. Rather than taking the presidency as an isolated institution, as has too often been the flaw of such studies, I take a regime-level approach and explore the general understanding of representation that was the basis of Publius' work. Such an enquiry requires a consideration of such topics as Publius' stand on the "mandate-independence" controversy, the place of virtue, passion, and reason in government, and the effects of the extended republic on political representation in America.

We see in *The Federalist* an understanding of representative government in which each political and constitutional institution holds a share of representation and plays a central role in a stable representative democracy. The American presidency, as one of the central political institutions of the fledgling republic, had an important role to play in the system of government outlined and defended in Publius' essays. This interpretation culminates in an understanding of Publius' "deliberative republic" model for the American system of government and the compound theory of representation that supports it. These concepts of "deliberative democracy" and institutional non-partisanship provide the normative structure for the chapters that follow.

Though this was the intention of the authors of *The Federalist Papers*, it has not always held sway in American political history and in the political science literature. In chapter 3 I discuss two other opposing views on the idea of the president being a representative. The first is found in the more "whiggish" view that only in an elected and numerous assembly that is close to the public can the people be truly represented. This view has its corollary in the political science literature in which the concept of representation has been almost exclusively the bastion of students of legislatures. Underlying this view is a particular conception of representation that, when applied to an office such as the presidency, finds that office lacking in representative characteristics.

The second understanding, the one that has dominated a considerable part of the literature on the American presidency this century, I term the "presidentialist" or "modern" view. According to the conception of representation on which it is based, only the president, who is elected by all the people, can be the true representative of "the nation as a whole." I trace the popularization and systematization of this view to the mature thought of Woodrow Wilson, although it cropped up from time to time before him.[27] As such, I explore Wilson's thought on this topic and the "presidocentric" literature in political science that follows from it—such as is classically represented in the work of Richard Neustadt.[28]

Both these views bring with them a certain conception of government and what government should be and what it should do. These views have not only influenced political science, but they have had important impacts on the operation of the presidency and the way the American people look at that institution. As such, they hold implications for democratic politics in contemporary America that are worthy of exploration. In essence, I find that both these views are only partial explanations of modern representative government in a system of separated and shared powers and that both hold unhealthy implications for stable self-governance in a constitutional democracy.

In the next two chapters I move on to explore the operation and practice of the modern presidency with regard to the issues of representation and representative government that I have developed in previous chapters. With the depression- and war-era administrations of Franklin Roosevelt came a new presidency with important implications for representative government in America. What we see in FDR is the institutionalization of the presidocentric view of representation previously developed theoretically by Woodrow Wilson.[29]

When considering the operation of the American presidency as an institution of representation, there are two major topics that must be considered. The first is the question of the relationship between the representative and the represented—the president and the people. This is the concern of chapter 4. The second topic that presents itself for consideration is the place of the modern presidency within the system of representative government outlined in the Constitution. Chapter 5 is devoted to this question.

In chapter 4 I explore the modern presidential office in regard to its relationship with the American public. I consider the changing nature of presidential election campaigns, the decline of political parties as representational "filters," presidential rhetoric, and the impact of public opinion polls on the presidency and the wider American polity. What we see is the contemporary presidency linked directly to the American people in a plebiscitary relationship that is far from what the Founding Fathers intended.

In chapter 5 I take up the presidency's relationship with the rest of the federal government in the modern era. A once weak office has been transformed into the vital center of public life in America today. From agenda setting to prerogative powers, the modern presidency is a powerful player in American politics and government. Contemporary presidents have been delegated grand representational responsibilities and have also been given important representational resources (such as an institutionalized White House staff) in the twentieth century. The center of gravity of representative government in America has shifted over the years from Congress to the presidency. This shift has brought with it some benefits but also many reasons for concern.

I conclude in chapter 6 with an overview of the concept of executive representation and what it means for the future of the American Republic. Here I am particularly concerned with the needs and values of deliberative democracy and the presidency's relationship to such a framework for representative government. For citizens of a democratic republic, few concerns should be more important than the health of the representational relationship. This is the fundamental concern that guides this study.

Notes

1. I borrow the term "white knight" from Philippa Strum, *Presidential Power and American Democracy* (Pacific Palisades, Calif.: Goodyear Publishing Company, 1972), ix.

2. Richard Neustadt, *Presidential Power and the Modern Presidents: The Politics of Leadership from Roosevelt to Reagan* (New York: The Free Press, 1990), 156.

3. Though the tendency to fear presidential power has been with us throughout our history as a nation, it resurfaced most powerfully in recent years as a response to the perceived abuses of the office by Presidents Johnson and Nixon with regard to the Vietnam War and Watergate.

4. For instance, note the nature of the attacks made by many this century against an activist Supreme Court. Even those espousing "original intent" as the justification of their positions on restricting the freedom of the court to legislate have found it necessary to argue that the court is "undemocratic" and "oligarchical"—the intended effect being the delegitimation of the Court as a policy-making institution. See Robert Bork, *The Tempting of America* (New York: Basic Books, 1990).

5. George Washington, "Farewell Address," in *George Washington: A Collection*, William B. Allen, ed. (Indianapolis: Liberty Fund, 1988), 521.

6. Thomas Jefferson, "First Inaugural Address," in *The Portable Thomas Jefferson*, Merrill D. Peterson, ed. (New York: Penguin Books, 1977), 294. The address was delivered in the Senate chamber on March 4, 1801.

7. Wilfred E. Binkley, *President and Congress*, Third Edition (New York: Vintage Books, 1962), 83.

8. This quotation is from Jackson's "Protest" message to the Senate (April 15, 1834). *Register of Debates in Congress*, 1st Session of the 33rd Congress, 1833-1834, Part 2 (Washington, D.C.: Gales and Seaton, 1834), 1334.

9. See Binkley, 1962, Chapter V, "The Jacksonian View of the Presidency Prevails," 105-132, for a solid analysis of Jackson's affect on the office beyond his eight-year tenure.

10. From James K. Polk's "Fourth Annual message," in James D. Richardson, *A Compilation of the Messages and Papers of the Presidents 1789-1897* (Washington, D.C.: Government Printing Office, 1897), Volume IV, 665.

11. Theodore Roosevelt, *Autobiography*, 306.

12. Quoted in Marcus Cunliffe, *American Presidents and the Presidency* (New York: American Heritage Press, 1972), 255.

13. Reprinted in Robert S. Hirschfield, ed., *The Power of the Presidency: Concepts and Controversy*, Second Edition (Chicago: Aldine Publishing Company, 1973), 82.

14. Woodrow Wilson, *Constitutional Government* in *The Papers of Woodrow Wilson*, Vol. 18, Arthur S. Link, ed. (Princeton, N.J.: Princeton University Press, 1974), 113-114.

15. Quoted in Thomas Cronin, *The State of the Presidency* (Boston: Little, Brown, and Company, 1980), 75.

16. Quoted in an interview published in *The National Journal*, August 7, 1976, 993.

17. Barbara Hinckley, *The Symbolic Presidency: How Presidents Portray Themselves* (New York: Routledge, 1990). On this note, see especially, 38-64.

18. *United States v. Curtiss-Wright Export Corporation* 81 L.Ed. 299 (1936).

19. James Bryce, *The American Commonwealth*, Second Edition (New York: MacMillan, 1891), Vol. I, 278.

20. Clinton Rossiter, *The American Presidency,* Revised Edition (New York: Mentor, 1960), 29.

21. Rossiter, 1960, 31.

22. Edward S. Corwin, *The President: Office and Powers*, 4th Edition (New York: New York University Press, 1957), xi-xiii.

23. Woodrow Wilson, *Divisions and Reunion 1829-1909* (New York: Longmans, Green and Co.,́ 1909), 356. Prepared by Edward S. Corwin.

24. See for example, Grant McConnell, *The Modern Presidency*, 2nd Edition (New York: St. Martin's Press, 1976), 42; Richard Rose, *The Postmodern President: George Bush meets the World*, 2nd Edition (Chatham, N.J.: Chatham House, 1991), 5; Ruth P. Morgan, *The President and Civil Rights: Policy-Making by Executive Order* (New York: St. Martin's Press, 1970), 84; and, Kenneth M.

Curtis, "The Presidency—An Imperfect Mirror," *Presidential Studies Quarterly* (Winter 1981), 28.

25. See Neustadt, 1990 as the prime example of this school of literature which was originally published in 1960.

26. For one of the very few scholarly attempts to address the representative role of the president see, Kathy B. Smith, "The Representative Role of the President," *Presidential Studies Quarterly* (Spring 1981), 203-213. See also, Alfred DeGrazia, *Public and Republic: Political Representation in America* (New York: Alfred A. Knopf, 1951) and David J. Vogler and Sidney R. Waldman, *Congress and Democracy* (Washington, D.C.: Congressional Quarterly Press, 1985).

27. I take Wilson's "mature thought" to be that found in his expressions while in the presidency, but most importantly for us here, also that found in *Constitutional Government* in *The Papers of Woodrow Wilson*, Vol. 18, Arthur Link, ed. (Princeton, N.J.: Princeton University Press, 1974). I call this his "mature thought" as this work and the place of the presidency in it are in marked contrast to that found in his first book, *Congressional Government* (New York: The World Publishing Company, 1967) published originally as a graduate student in 1885.

28. Neustadt, 1990.

29. Recently, several scholars have come along to offer dissenting views on the generally accepted idea that in the twentieth century we have a new edition of the presidency that is qualitatively different from the "traditional" edition that went before. As will become clear in the pages that follow, I generally do not share this reconsideration but see the "modern" presidency to be different in important ways that justify it being set apart as a distinct version of the office. See, David K. Nichols, *The Myth of the Modern Presidency* (University Park, Pa: The Pennsylvania State University Press, 1994) and Andrew Dowdle, *The Protomodern Presidency*, Unpublished dissertation (Oxford, Ohio: Miami University, 1995). For a related and rather extraordinary recent exploration of similar topics, see Charles O. Jones, *The Presidency in a Separated System* (Washington, D.C.: The Brookings Institution, 1994).

1

Political Representation and the Presidency

Amerian presidents have long been considered to function as political representatives. But what does such a characterization of the office and its incumbents really mean? How would such a view of our chief executive affect the questions we ask about the institution and about the behavior of individual presidents? Answers to such questions necessitate a consideration of the concept of political representation itself. To that end, this chapter explores the idea of political representation, introduces some of the central questions that have been raised by political theorists and statesmen who have considered such issues, and makes a preliminary attempt to apply the term to the presidency.

What Is Political Representation?

Etymologically, the literal meaning of representation is to "make present something that is not in fact present,"[1] or to "present again."[2] Today we seem everywhere to take it for granted that genuine representative political institutions are possible and desired. In fact, we routinely consider the governmental institutions of the United States and the West to constitute "representative democracy" or simply "democracy"; this despite the extended size of the American nation (the paradigmatic "democracy") that centralizes great power in legislatures, executive institutions, and courts that are composed of a very small number of people in comparison with the actual population. How is a legislator to "present again" the interests or views of five hundred thousand citizens, or is the chief executive to "make present" a nation of 250 million? The question begs a number of others: Is the mere election of government officials enough to constitute "representation"? With the growth in the size of the nation-state, have we rendered the term a hollow shell of what it once symbolized? From the other end of the issue, there has also surfaced considerable empirical data showing the American people to be "apathetic" to political issues, with a "low level of public knowledge"[3] and some have questioned if the *vox populi* is even capable of being "an intelligible guide to a policy maker who wishes to heed public opinion."[4]

The term representation has numerous contexts in the modern English language. We, however, are here concerned only with "political representation." Political representation can be loosely defined as the "representing" of a constituency and its power as a collective social unit by an individual or group smaller than the original. Here of course we are concerned with strictly political power and not theological, interrelational, or any lesser power that exists in any social situation. I use *power* in this definition rather than some other concept like "will," "interest," or "opinion" because it seems to be the only ingredient essential to all concepts of political representation. According to liberal democratic theory, "the people" are the source of all power. As politics cannot exist without power, or so the modern political scientists tell us, this power somehow must be transferred (for a temporary period or indefinitely) to the representative who is then empowered to act according to the terms and limits of societal power set by law and custom.

All conceptions of political representation can be found within this simple definition—a feat that cannot be accomplished if we substitute "will," "opinion," or "interest" as the element being transferred and represented. But, we must also realize that political representation has eluded a myriad of attempts to develop a single, comprehensive definition. For instance, competing normative evaluations cut to the very heart of any definition dealing with representation as a function, activity, or status; without agreements on the normative concerns, there can be no agreement on defining representation.

A political system is composed of a series of activities and institutions that are related to one another functionally and have some continuity in time.[5] This complex of activities hint that there may be more than a single type of representative in a representative government. The logic of representative democracy would even seem to point to the fact that all political activities within the system that were not directly carried out by the people would thereby (being a "democracy") have to fall to some sort of representatives. Barring a consideration of any such specifics, there are two primary types of political representation: representation as the symbolization of another or another's characteristics or values, and representation as "acting for" another. The American president, as both chief executive and chief of state, uniquely fulfills both types of representation in the American polity.

Active Representation:
Representation as "Acting For"

The most common meaning of representation is that of "acting for," or acting in place of, another person or group. The modern concept of politics as a power relationship or "the authoritative allocation of values in society,"[6] places an emphasis on the activity of politics and such an emphasis also has been placed on representation as an active enterprise. Despite its prevalence, there has been no serious analytical attempt to define representation explicitly centering on the *activity* of representing—such a definition has been taken for granted, however, in the great bulk of the literature on representation.[7] This seems to be the case because the varying descriptions and normative evaluations on the subject make it nearly impossible to come to any agreement on what the proper conduct of representatives would be or on how their offices should be constituted.

Because of the variety of normative positions on how a public official should act in his role as a representative, any simple, and generally agreed upon, definition seems illusive. However, we can, in the most general terms, lay down a preliminary definition of a political (active) representative as: *a person who, through election, tradition, or some other way seen as legitimate in the eyes of the general populace, holds a position in society to which the society has invested its power of self-government. Said person then **acts** as a representative as he or she performs these functions (and only these functions) that are invested in the office through custom, constitution, law, or public acceptance.*

So conceived, it is not members of the legislature alone that function as active political representatives, but other members of government also have important representative roles to play.[8] How then does the American presidency provide such active representation? *Official* presidential actions can be organized around three types of activities that provide a good framework toward answering such a question. These three types of activities are the executive, legislative, and special magisterial duties of the presidency.[9]

Legislative bodies are not equipped to perform certain tasks that are necessary to governance. At other activities, though they may be able to perform them tolerably well, they would not be as suited to the task as would an institution structured like the presidency. The American Founding Fathers, under the experience of the Articles of Confederation, had learned well the lesson that legislative bodies alone could not make for effective governance. The American chief magistracy that emerged from the Constitutional Convention in 1787 was based on an understanding of the need for an effective and energetic executive coupled with the assumption that such an office could be made republican and consistent with the needs of representative democracy.

The American presidency was given, and continues to exercise, three broad categories of powers and responsibilities in the fulfillment of which the officer performs active representation. First, Article II, Section 1 of the Constitution vests the executive power of the nation in the presidency and Section 3 charges the person in that office to "take care that the laws be faithfully executed." The president is also given the executive power of nominating for Senate confirmation or otherwise appointing on his own accord the lower executive officials that are likewise charged with carrying out the laws of the nation. In these executive capacities the president would represent the nation by acting for it in a way that it is unable to do itself and which a legislative body could not do effectively. As the nation's chief executive, the president is also its representative—to contend otherwise is to accept the existence of an unrepublican force at the center of our government and politics.

The Constitution also gives the presidency certain special magisterial roles to play. The president, for example, is commander in chief; he has the power to make treaties, receive ambassadors, grant reprieves and pardons, and convene both houses of Congress in certain circumstances. These functions are neither completely executive nor completely legislative in nature. They are special roles given to the president to perform in the name of the American people and their fundamental compact. An important example is the president's foreign policy powers and responsibilities that make the incumbent the nation's special representative in the international arena. In these special ways, the president also acts as a political and constitutional representative.

Even more important for understanding presidential representation is the third type of presidential activity sanctioned by the Constitution—that which is legislative in nature. It is well known that the Constitution of 1787 established a bicameral legislature; what is less well documented, however, is that the Constitution also established a *tricameral* legislative authority. Two constitutional provisions give the president an important share of the legislative process of the national government.

One constitutional source of the president's participation in the legislative aspects of government is the Recommendation Clause of Article II, Section 3. The president "shall from time to time give to the Congress information on the state of the Union, and recommend to their consideration such measures as he shall judge necessary and expedient." As Terry Eastland has pointed out, this is a *duty* of the president to be part of the legislative process, it is not simply a *right* he may choose to exercise or not to exercise as he would.[10]

The Recommendation Clause is the constitutional basis for much of the modern presidency. Upon that constitutional ground has been erected in this century what some scholars have called "The Legislative Presidency."[11] To a significant degree, Congress has come to rely on presidents to set the legislative agenda by forwarding proposals for legislation and then seeking to build support for them with the public as well as with individual legislators. Indeed, as Robert Spitzer has pointed out, Congress has systematically given primary responsibility for agenda setting and policy coordination to the president.[12] It is through this constitutional provision and the delegation of responsibility from Congress to the presidency in this area over the past several decades that the president is most able to exercise *positive* political representation in the legislative arena.

The Constitution also gives the president a qualified veto over legislation. The legislative nature of this power is obvious as it is found not in Article II, but Article I, which establishes the legislative authority of government. The Presentment Clause (Article I, Section 7), in which is found the president's veto, places the executive near the end of the legislative process, but nonetheless still in the position of being an important player in the development and passage of legislation. He may return with objections any bill of which he does not approve and thereby force Congress to reconsider the legislation in light of the objections he puts forward.

The veto power is primarily a negative one. It is the power to say "no" to legislation passed by both branches of the legislature. It is true that the use of the veto may "positively" cause a reinvigorated and healthy debate within the legislature as legislators attempt to override the president's veto or amend the legislation in line with his objections. Still, the essence of the veto power is negative. It is through the use of the veto that the president is able to provide *negative* political representation—to say "no" as one of the people's officers in the legislative process.

But this is not the whole story with regard to the president's veto power and his role as a representative in the legislative process of government. Where the actual *use* of the veto is a negative act, the *threat* of that use can be a method through which a president can act positively to shape legislation in Congress.[13] By threatening to veto a proposed piece of legislation before Congress unless certain changes are made to it, the president can pressure the bill's supporters into making concessions in order to avert the threatened veto. Of course, a veto threat does not always result in the president getting what he would like, but it has been an important legislative tool of modern presidents, especially those facing "divided government."[14]

Together these two constitutional provisions give the presidency an important share of the legislative power that was entrusted by the people to their representatives. They make the president a central player in the deliberative process of republican self-government. As such a player, the president acts as much a political representative as do those in Congress who may act upon his proposals or react to his use or threat to use the veto.

In none of these three types of presidential action does the officer act as a private citizen. All that he does is done in the name of the people or in the name of their fundamental law. In this way his doings transcend his person and he acts as a representative of things larger than himself. To have it otherwise would mean that we have empowered at the center of our government a force alien to the genius of our constitutional democracy. In his various capacities to act officially, the American president provides representation to a diverse people under one government and one constitutional tradition.

Symbolic Representation

Political symbolism, as such, does not necessitate the representative to act or even to have the capacity to act. The Stars and Stripes symbolically represents the United States government and her people, though it cannot act. The presidential seal with its majestic eagle represents the office, majesty, and current occupant of the office of President of the United States. And the coat of arms of a Scottish clan represents the current Highlanders along with their ancestors and posterity. As symbolic representatives of larger groups or forces, these inanimate objects symbolize the internal connection and cohesion of these groups, persons, or institutions, and also function as "links" with other forces found outside the symbolized group or institution. That is, the American flag represents the American people in all their *pluribus* as well as in their essential *unum* to themselves and to the wider world as a coherent and established political society existing at a certain time in history.

But human beings themselves also can be symbolic representatives of greater political entities. This type of representation has less to do with what the person actually does than with *who* they are (personal characteristics) and/or the position held. For instance, Thurgood Marshall was seen as a symbolic representative of the black community because of his personal characteristics (being black himself and being associated with the cause of civil rights) and his position as a justice of the Supreme Court. His being a symbol was not necessarily dependent on how he performed (substantively) his duties. Or witness 1992's "year of the woman" in American politics when the greatest emphasis was placed on the female candidates for the House and Senate *being* women and the high positions they would hold, while concern for how they would *act* in office was more of a subsumed issue—at least symbolically. These women were considered to be symbolically representing the women of the entire nation (not merely those in their state or district).

The monarchy and the monarch in a parliamentary democracy or other political system is an important example of a symbolic representative—in this case the representative of the nation as a whole. He or she "stands for" the nation as it exists in his or her own time and as it has existed previously. Note that such a role does not require any particular character elements or any substantive activity by the monarch. The Antifederalist pamphleteer The Federal Farmer noted the importance of having an individual standing as the symbolic representative for the internal cohesion and unity of any large group of people. "In every large collection of people," he said, "there must be a visible point serving as a common center in the government, toward which to draw their eyes and attachments."[15] The presidency serves this function in the contemporary American political system. As Attorney General Stanberry argued before the Supreme Court in the 1867 case of *Mississippi v. Johnson*, "He (the president) represents the majesty of the law and of the people as fully and as essentially, and with the same dignity, as does any absolute monarch or head of any independent government in the world."[16] An incumbent in the office is the focal point of the American polity as he is both chief of government and chief of state.[17]

Where in many other modern nations these two roles of chief of government and chief of state are separated and distinct, in the United States they are inescapably fused into one office. This indeed seems to have been the intention of the Founders of the presidency. It was this understanding that inspired men like John Adams and Alexander Hamilton to urge that the trappings of royalty be placed in the office.[18] While the Senate originally wished to refer to the president as "His Highness the President of the United States, and Protector of the Rights of the Same," they eventually compromised with the House to settle upon the simple but still respectful "Mr. President."[19] It was an understanding of the awesome symbolic potential of the office that made the election of George Washington as the nation's first president all the more important. As Forrest McDonald has recounted the understanding of Washington's presidency:

> As a man idolized by the people—almost all the people, whatever their station in life—he could make it possible for them to indulge their habitual adulation of a monarch without reneging on their commitment to republicanism. As a symbol of the Union, he could stimulate, at least for a time, the emotional attachment to the Nation that normally requires centuries in the building.[20]

The presidency was and has remained much more than a political institution. As James David Barber has said, it is "the focus for the most intense and persistent emotions in the American polity."[21] In Michael Novak's phrase, the presidency is a "carrier of meaning."[22] All that a president does in some way holds symbolic import. His actions do not always mean the same things to different interpreters and yet there is little doubt that what a president does and how he does it hold important meanings beyond the immediate material and political consequences of his efforts. Thus Novak has called the presidency "the nation's most central religious symbol."[23]

> The President of the United States is one of the great symbolic powers known to human history. His actions seep irrepressibly into our hearts. He dwells in us. We cannot keep him out. That is why we wrestle against him, rise up in hatred often, wish to retch—or, alternatively, feel good, feel proud, as though his achievements were ours, his wit the unleashing of powers of our own. . . Hands are stretched toward him over wire fences at airports like hands extended toward medieval sovereigns or ancient prophets.[24]

Seven Levels of Presidential Symbolism

We can note at least seven different ways in which presidents can be understood to function as symbolic representatives in the American political system. The list is not exhaustive. Indeed, no list of such a nature could ever truly exhaust all the possibilities as long as so many individuals continue to so personally relate to the office. It should also be noted that those listed do not necessarily always fit neatly into a self-contained box; "meaning" often has a way of slipping through the cracks of our best efforts to contain and isolate specific elements of cultural and political symbolism. The list, however, is illustrative of the place of the office in the American culture, political system, and individual psyches of the American citizenry. I arrange the list here from most specific and personal to the widest in scope and most fundamental in meaning.

Presidents as Personal Symbols. First, an incumbent president often functions as a personal symbol to people. In this way Eisenhower was said to be a father-figure, a benevolent caretaker who gave a sense of reassurance during times of trouble. This was perhaps the case with President Reagan as well. While he remained personally a very popular president throughout most of his term in office, such personal attachments to the "Gipper" did not uniformly translate into support for his actions or legislative agenda. Barbara Hinckley has recently put this relationship like this, "As Children sleep better when a trusted parent is watching over them, adults, in childlike fashion, place the president in a parental role."[25] Those who have studied political socialization in America have noted how this understanding of the presidency stems from early childhood education and experiences.[26]

Machiavelli wanted his prince to have the capabilities and knowledge to overcome and tame the powerful forces of fortune in life. The American people seem to hold out this same vision for their own prince. Murray Edelman writes, "Because it is apparently intolerable for men to admit the key role of accident, of ignorance, and of unplanned processes in their affairs, the leader serves a vital function by personifying and reifying the processes. As an individual, he can be praised and blamed and given 'responsibility' in a way that processes cannot."[27] Particularly important on this level is a president's ritualistic willingness to take personal responsibility for the actions and mistakes of his subordinates. One thinks especially of Harry Truman's dictum, "The buck stops here." "Each time this stylized manifesto appears," says Edelman, "everyone involved experiences a warm glow of satisfaction and relief that responsibility has been assumed and can be pinpointed. It once again conveys the message that the incumbent is the leader, that he knows he is able to cope, and that he should be followed."[28] In a dangerous and unpredictable world, presidents may serve as symbols of reassurance and confidence.

Presidents as Cognitive Aids. In a related vein, presidents tend to function as what Fred Greenstein calls a "cognitive aid," allowing citizens to come to terms with the complexity of modern government through the symbolic representation of the person in the office.[29] In this way the president symbolizes the national government in Washington to the people of the nation. On a larger level, the presidency also serves as a shorthand way of understanding our own history as a nation. Important events, important periods, influential ideas, all become associated in the nation's mind with certain presidencies. From "Jeffersonian democracy" to "Jacksonian democracy," from "Camelot" to "the Reagan-Bush years," the history of the presidency provides us with the mental boxes through which to understand our own history as a nation.

Presidents as Symbols of the Nation. On a level of even more importance to the national community, individual presidents, as well as the institution of the presidency itself, are wellsprings of meaning. According to Eric Voegelin, societies erect symbols as part of their "self-interpretation." Such symbolic representation is essential to all human societies because it enables members to "experience it as more than an accident or a convenience; they experience it as of their human essence." The symbols also express the experience "that man is fully man by virtue of his participation in a whole which transcends his particular existence."[30]

These symbols represent the whole of which each individual is but a part and facilitate a given society having an understanding of itself.

With Voegelin's observations in mind, then, we can note that on a third level incumbent presidents exist as symbols of the nation. As the only nationally elected official, the president stands as a symbolic representative of the American people—allowing for their transcendence from pluralism, diversity, and parochial concerns to a more truly national identity; a cosmion, to appropriate Voegelin's word.[31] This is especially true during times of national crisis when the nation tends to rally around its central figure—supporting the president as well as finding the comfort of a national community.

The Presidency as Symbol of National Understanding. Indeed, in another related way, the office of the presidency itself has been an important symbol of the nation. Note that in the Articles of Confederation, that document that loosely bound together different and disparate political communities, there was no single executive officer resembling the president. This lack of a central figure within the government was more important than most commentators and historians have noticed. The government under the Articles was part of how the people of the 1770s and 1780s thought of themselves—as Virginians and Pennsylvanians first and foremost. Such a loose association of sovereign and essentially independent communities can best be symbolized and represented in a numerous and pluralistic legislature, such as the one in existence under the Articles. The Constitutional Convention's decision to establish a unitary executive office at the center of government marked a major break in America's interpretation of itself. The unitary office symbolizes the existence of a national community that exists in conjunction with the smaller political communities found in the individual states. Many of those who have at one time or another called for the replacement of the unitary presidency with a plural executive, such as John C. Calhoun in the nineteenth century, seem to have understood the symbolic importance built into the structure of the office itself.[32]

Presidents themselves have also actively done their part on this score. Through their actions, but perhaps most importantly through their rhetoric, presidents have articulated and interpreted America's understanding of itself as one nation. Through a study of presidential inaugural addresses, Dante Germino has found that the central idea in presidential rhetoric has been, not surprisingly given what has been said, "the nation." Early presidents were gravely concerned with preserving the Union and strove to do so through the articulation of an understanding of the nation as a transcendent political community deserving preservation and respect. Though the content of later presidential rhetoric changed, the centrality of the idea of "one nation" has not wavered.[33]

The Presidency as Symbol of the Regime. Much like the rest of the nation, the presidency has not been static over the course of the past two centuries. We can note that the changing nature and power of the presidential office itself has symbolized an important aspect of America's interpretation of itself. Just as it may be said that inanimate objects like the Declaration of Independence and the Bill of Rights are part of the American political tradition's "basic symbols,"[34] the office of the presidency can also be seen as a symbol of the American polity. The once weak office that symbolized the nation became, with the change in American public life in the twentieth century, a powerful, central office at the heart of a newly enlarged central government. The changing nature of the presidency itself has been a symbol—an existential representative of the polity as it reflects the basic idea that informs it.[35]

The weak and limited office of the nineteenth century adequately symbolized the nation's understanding of itself and what it was about—limited, constitutional national government, a nation of local connections and interests, a republic without world ambitions. With the earth-shattering changes of the twentieth century, the limited office of the traditional presidency was not adequate in symbolically representing the new idea that was coming to the fore in America. This new self-understanding, centering on America's emergence as a world force, the explosion in people's expectations from the national government, and the new ethic of democratization that fueled the movement toward the morality of mass national democracy, necessitated a symbolic office that would adequately represent it. The modern presidency, with its plebiscitary relationship to the mass national public, its expanded powers and responsibilities, and its cloak of protector from Armageddon that nuclear weapons brought to the office, offered the twentieth century American polity a vital symbol of itself.

The President and Outside Observers. The president is also a symbolic representative of the nation and the government on the level of outside observers. The president or his direct delegates represent the nation at funerals, coronations, and other important events occurring outside the United States. On a more substantive level, it is the president's ability to act as commander in chief and as chief diplomat of the United States that enhances his position as the one man distillation of the American public when it comes to relations with foreign peoples.

Presidents as Partisans. The symbolic roles of American presidents and the presidency that have been mentioned to this point all emphasize the essential unity of the American people and their self-understanding as a society organized for action in history. We must now make note of a seventh way in which presidents function as symbolic representatives; this last their role as divisive rather than unifying symbols in American politics. Early in American history presidents and presidential candidates became the central figures around which the political parties understood themselves and were understood by the American people. As Alexis de Tocqueville observed, "political parties in the United States are led to rally round an individual in order to acquire a more tangible shape in the eyes of the crowd, and the name of the candidate for the Presidency is put forward as the symbol and personification of their theories."[36] As Andrew Jackson was the symbol of the Democratic party during Tocqueville's visit to the United States in the 1830s, so Ronald Wilson Reagan became the embodiment of Republican theories and principles of government in the 1980s.

Each president since the advent of the political party system early in our history has lived in a universe of symbolic tension. They have occupied the seat through which national unity is symbolized; they have also been seen to be the central embodiment of their particular political faction. Symbolically, presidents are expected to be *above party* while still being *of party.* This tension becomes particularly strained during national election cycles when the nation is charged with partisanship amidst the quest of candidates and their supporters for public office. The tension, however, remains always beneath the surface of any presidency. The cynic or diehard partisan of the out of power party is always willing to attribute to the incumbent motivations based on electoral incentives rather than the long-term public good. The president's stature as national, non-partisan symbol tends to prevail primarily during times of national and international crises when partisanship may be overawed by love of country or a deference to communal harmony.

Although there are those who dismiss symbolism in politics as non-empirical nonsense, or even brand it the tool of oppression by the powerful through the quiescence of the powerless, symbolism is critically important to the office. To recognize this is to recognize the subtle but pervasive impact that the office has had upon each citizen and each generation since George Washington took the oath in 1789. As Robert Denton has said, "To describe the President as Priest, Prophet, and King is to acknowledge the respect, expectations, hopes, and values of the American people."[37]

The Intersection between Action and Symbolism

Public figures also attempt to wield society's inanimate symbols in efforts to enhance their own power or representational capacity by capturing their inherent "magic." Witness George Bush's use of the "flag-issue" in his 1988 bid for the White House or Ronald Reagan's masterful use of important language symbols like "freedom," "liberty," "God," or "the evil empire." As Hugh Duncan has noted of public people, "The resonance of symbols, the sensuous as well as intellectual attention evoked, supplies the individual with means by which he can enlarge or intensify his sphere of power."[38] So especially with the presidency.

It is particularly the presidency's dual role as home of the head of the government as well as chief of state, our chief national figure, that affords presidents the opportunity of being our most powerful definers and manipulators of political symbolism. Part of the need for presidents to wield and manipulate symbols stems from the plebiscitary nature of today's office. To govern, presidents have come to rely on the support of public opinion and to garner this support, to increase their ratings in public opinion polls, presidents increasingly have come to use one or another strategy of "going public."

Samuel Kernell has defined going public as "a class of activities in which presidents engage as they promote themselves and their policies before the American public."[39] Such efforts at promotion inevitably involve political symbolism, and presidents have never been shy about invoking them. National presidential addresses are themselves encased in symbolism of the highest order in American politics. Most come beamed into our living rooms direct from our national palace, the White House, and most of them from the Oval Office, where, the public is invited to imagine, some of the most fateful decisions in our history were made. Presidents are not shy to invoke the mantle of their revered predecessors who once walked the halls they themselves stroll. Other important speeches are delivered at the majestic national Capitol in front of Congress, the Cabinet, the Joint Chiefs of Staff in full uniform, the Justices clothed in their solemn black robes, and foreign officials. The stages are set for presidential appeals to the public with no sparing of the symbols of history and national unity that lend legitimacy to the man and the message.

Presidents also tend to rely heavily on symbolic invocations in their rhetoric itself. Barbara Hinckley, for instance, has shown how modern presidents have manipulated language symbols to rhetorically unite the nation and the people with themselves through the symbolic term "we."[40] Presidents thus place themselves squarely in the center of all symbolic and active representation in the American polity—no one comes between themselves and the people and no other political actor can better claim to know the national interest. Presidents also rhetorically invoke values and mores that are perceived to be an important part of the national heritage. Craig A. Rimmerman, writing particularly about the presidency of Ronald Reagan, has referred to this as a "values approach to government," in which presidents attempt to be seen as the "chief proponent of the values associated with American exceptionalism."[41]

Presidents regularly perform symbolic actions in their life as ceremonial head of the nation. They symbolically represent the nation and invoke political and cultural symbolism almost daily as they host U.S. Olympic Teams, honor heroes from everyday life and military campaigns, and present special honors and awards. Presidents also perform this function through their words expressed at particularly opportune moments in history. Presidents have always played this rhetorical role of ceremonial leader and moral agent. Lincoln's address at Gettysburg is the seminal example of such political and moral rhetoric. Recently, Ronald Reagan was a master of such appeals to the nation's heart and soul. From his memorable speech delivered overlooking Omaha Beach in 1984 to commemorate the Normandy invasion to his address to the nation on the occasion of the Space Shuttle *Challenger* disaster on January 28, 1986, Reagan seemed to relish his performance of this role.

These are a regular and inescapable part of the office. Acting in these capacities, presidents generally appear as non-partisan, non-political representatives of the people of the United States. We shouldn't dismiss easily such "non-substantive" activities. As a routine part of the office it is likely that any president who would balk at such ceremony would incur the wrath of thwarted public expectations. Likewise, by performing such activities in front of the television cameras, presidents have the opportunity to curry favor with the public and further solidify their trust in his person and policies.

Incumbent presidents and the power of the office itself clearly benefit from being recognized as the symbolic representative of the nation. For instance, during times of international crisis presidents benefit from the American people's tendency to "rally" around the sitting president and the flag. This effect occurs regardless of whether or not the president has taken positive action of his own. For instance, Carter's poll numbers jumped twenty points after the Iranians seized the hostages and the Soviets invaded Afghanistan. Such rallying also occurs when an administration makes serious blunders, such as Kennedy's Bay of Pigs fiasco.[42]

But presidents don't always benefit from being the objects of the nation's attention and the focus of its feelings and hopes. Dramatic events that do not serve to unify the nation but to emphasize its problems, divisiveness, and conflicts reduce public support for the president.[43] Whether or not the incumbent had anything to do with the problems or had the power to do anything about the situation, the president is held responsible as the chief living symbol of the nation. For instance, it is debatable how much influence over the economy any president is able to exercise by himself and yet there is little question that the American people hold presidents responsible for the economic condition of the nation. The presidency's place in the American mind provides incumbents both with resources with which public policy influence can be developed and with the position to be held responsible for events that may be completely out of their control.

Representation through Activity:
The Mandate-Independence Controversy

Philosophers, statesmen, and scholars who have turned their attention to political representation over the last several centuries have been concerned with one perennial question above all others: What is the proper nature of the relationship between a representative and the represented? What are the rights and duties of each? Who draws the bounds of the relationship? Where does sovereignty actually lie? Answers to these questions have tended to cluster around two opposed positions. The one emphasizing the rights of the represented to control the representative and the other emphasizing the representative's essential independence from the mandates of the people.

Hanna Pitkin has summarized the question at issue in the mandate-independence controversy as "should (must) a representative do what his constituents want, and be bound by mandates or instructions from them; or should (must) he be free to act as seems best to him in pursuit of their welfare?"[44] The central ethical issue involved in such a question is no less essential to democratic theory than the question who is the proper repository of governmental decision-making power: the mass electorate or the representatives elevated from and by that electorate? Should the representative view himself as being elevated in order to act according to his own judgment and conscience or should he view himself and his role as that of faithfully following "instructions" from his constituents? The latter alternative seems to value representative institutions solely for their quantitative and practical element; i.e., because direct democracy would be logistically impossible over any area approaching the size of a modern state. The former, however, contains a qualitative value assumption; representatives free to exercise their own intelligence and abilities and to follow their own conscience will be more likely to make just and proper decisions than those bound by their constituent's opinions.

Trustee-Independence

British statesman Edmund Burke provides the classic expression of the independence position of representation. Burke saw the representative as a "trustee" intrusted to act according to his own best judgment of what is in the best interest of the community. Burke outlined his trustee approach in a letter written to the sheriffs of the city of Bristol in 1777. "Your representative owes you," Burke wrote, "not his industry only, but his judgment; and he betrays, instead of serving you, if he sacrifices it to your opinion." The trustee is not to sacrifice "his unbiased opinion, his mature judgment, his enlightened conscience" to the people's will or mandate.[45] Rather, as "government and legislation are matters of reason and judgment," policy is to proceed from the discussion of uninstructed and independent statesmen in the representative body. To Burke, it makes no sense for a representative to follow the opinions and wishes of his constituency who may be hundreds of miles away from the parliamentary debate where the arguments were heard. Independence can here be referred to as the "style"of representation in the Burkean tradition.

A second important element of the Burkean trustee model is the question of "focus."[46] In essence, Burke held that the representative was not the particular representative of the interest and opinions of the people of his constituency, but of the long-term interests of the country as a whole.[47] "Parliament is not a congress of ambassadors from different and hostile interests; which interests each must maintain, as an agent or advocate, against other agents or advocates; but parliament is a deliberative assembly of one nation, with one interest, that of the whole; where not local purposes, not local prejudices ought to guide, but the general good resulting from the general reason of the whole."[48]

According to Burke's model, the representative is to maintain his or her independence, both from the opinion of constituents as well as from the narrow interests of a given constituency. It is the representatives' job to use their own best judgment and forward only public programs that they find to be in the interest of the whole nation.

Delegate-Mandate

As we have done with independence's relation to the Burkean trustee, we can similarly label mandate the "style" of representation exhibited by the representative as delegate. The delegate approach requires the officeholder to be highly responsive to the opinions and wishes of his or her constituents. The metaphor of the *mirror* is often invoked as a description of this side of the controversy because the representative is seen to be merely a reflection of the constituent's views.[49] This position is probably the most familiar one in democratic thought.[50] The representative is to act in the stead of his or her constituents or, "as they would have acted, had they been able to participate themselves."[51] In other words, the representative's only legitimate guiding will is to act as his constituents would act if they were themselves assembled.

Defenders of the delegate approach tout it as the only legitimate view of representation that remains consistent with democratic norms and values. The people can participate in the formation of legislation and governmental policy by issuing instructions that their servants (representatives) are to carry out. As would seem to logically follow, the "focus" of the delegate is not the national interest as a whole (as it is with the Burkean trustee) but rather the interest of his or her local constituency. Why else would they be elected locally?, one might ask. This is not to say, however, that mandate theorists are unconcerned with the interest of the nation as a whole. Generally, it is their view that the true national interest is only the sum of the interests of the local constituencies. Hence, the national interest will be forwarded as instructed delegates pursue the interests and obey the mandates of their local constituencies.

Though these two positions represent the classic thinking about this controversy that has dominated political thought on the subject, there have been other attempts at the development of a third position or of compromise positions. One argument holds that the representative is really the representative of his or her political party and so has the duty to support that party. Such a position is based on the assumptions of "party government" and the perceived desirability to have specifically outlined rival party programs for the electorate to consider, one of which would be implemented after a given election.[52] Such a view of representation based on partisanship is particularly important when considering the president's representational role as he most often is the chief formulator of his party's program.

Others have developed a "politico" view or compromise position in which the representative acts on some combination of his own judgment and the wishes of his constituents.[53] As a candidate for the Illinois legislature in 1836, Abraham Lincoln outlined such a compromise position: "While acting as their representative," he said, "I shall be governed by their will on all subjects upon which I have the means of knowing what their will is, and upon all others I shall do what my own judgment teaches me will best advance their interests."[54]

The mandate-independence debate became an important one almost immediately after the Constitution was established and has remained so in the minds of many politicians, scholars, and pundits.[55] During the House debate on James Madison's Bill of Rights in 1789, Representative Thomas Tudor Tucker of South Carolina moved to add to the Constitution the right of the people "to instruct their representatives." Some, such as Massachusetts's Elbridge Gerry, spoke in favor of such a right of the people to instruct and bind their representatives as the only position consistent with popular sovereignty.[56] Others did not agree. "Sir," said Pennsylvania's Thomas Hartley, "I have known within my own time so many inconveniences and real evils arise from adopting the popular opinions of the moment, that although I respect them as much as any man, I hope this Government will particularly guard against them, at least that they will not bind themselves by a Constitutional act and by oath to submit to their influence."[57] Under the leadership of James Madison, the father of the Bill of Rights, the Congress did not so bind itself to the opinions of the people on that day in April. The question, however, has remained a contentious one in democratic theory and American political history.

Mandate-Independence and the Presidency

And how does this classic debate affect the institution of the American presidency? Like any political representative, presidents must confront the question of how much influence they will give to others' wishes and how much they will stand with their own convictions. The creators of the American presidency gave considerable thought to this perennial dilemma of free government. One of the major concerns at the Constitutional Convention was the problem of how to elect an individual to the presidency and make him at once democratically dependent while remaining sufficiently independent of others to adequately perform his duties.

Traditionally, the strongest and most fundamental links between officials and others in the political community have been elections. In democratic theory it is by this process that the masters choose their servants; that the electorate choose their representatives. Concerned about both the logistics and the morality of democratic methods, the Founding Fathers intensely debated the modes of electing public officials. None more so than the method by which the nation would choose its chief magistrate.

Various modes of electing the president were proposed during the Constitutional Convention, each with varying degrees of independence assumed in its structure. Indeed, the subject of the method to be used to elect the president was taken up in more than thirty distinct votes on twenty-one different days during the course of that hot summer in 1787 in Philadelphia.[58] As a recent commentator has written, "No other constitutional provision gave them so much difficulty in its formulation."[59] Should the chief executive be elected by the national legislature, by some other popularly elected officers, the people themselves, or some other popular body established for that purpose? The answer to this question would go far in determining the nature of the relationship between the president and the people as well as between the president and the rest of the government.

Among the most recurrent proposals, favorably accepted by the delegates on several occasions, was to have the executive elected by the national legislature. Such a proposal was a feature of both the Virginia plan and the New Jersey plan. This idea, however, suffered from the major flaw that it violated the independence necessary for the executive to properly function in a system of separated powers. How could a president be independent of the will of the legislature if he was dependent upon that same body for election and reelection? James Madison was one of the delegates who spoke firmly against any such role of the national legislature in choosing the executive.

> If it be essential to the preservation of liberty that the Legisl:Execut: & Judiciary powers be separate, it is essential to a maintenance of the separation, that they would be independent of each other. The Executive could not be independent of the Legislature, if dependent on the pleasure of that branch for a re-appointment . . . .In like manner a dependence of the Executive on the Legislature, would render it the Executor as well as the maker of laws; & then according to the observation of Montesquieu, tyrannical laws may be made that they be executed in a tyrannical manner.[60]

As an attempt to obviate such problems involving independence of the executive from the legislature, the delegates repeatedly made legislative appointment contingent upon the president not being eligible for reelection. The legislature, it was believed, would thereby have little control over the president once he had been appointed because they could not reward him with reelection to his post.[61]

But what of the electoral relationship of the president to the people? A number of delegates, including some of the most fervent supporters of a strong and independent magistrate, advocated the direct election of the executive by the American people. Pennsylvania's James Wilson was one of the earliest and most important supporters of such a popularly elected executive. One of the strongest arguments for such a scheme was that it secured the needed independence of the officer from the legislature. As Gouverneur Morris told his colleagues on July 17th, 1787:

> He will be the mere creature of the Legisl: if appointed & impeachable by that body. He ought to be elected by the people at large, by the freeholders of the country . . . . If the people should elect, they will never fail to prefer some man of distinguished character, or services . . . of continental reputation. If the Legislature elect, it will be the work of intrigue, of cabal, and of faction.[62]

Not all, however, were enthusiastic about the possibilities of the people themselves having their hand directly in the process of electing the nation's chief executive officer. Roger Sherman of Connecticut found, "The sense of the Nation would be better expressed by the Legislature, than by the people at large."[63] Others felt such a scheme would render representation a mere shred of what it should be, the nation being too large for the people to adequately judge candidates.[64] Perhaps the most recurrent objection to popular election was simply logistical; it would be unreasonable to expect such a diverse and scattered people to arrive at agreement on one man to be placed at the head of the executive department of the federal government. At least one delegate, Elbridge Gerry of Massachusetts, spoke out regularly against the "ignorance of the people," which should preclude them from sharing in any such power. In particular, Gerry feared that if the election was left to the people, the appointment would in actuality fall into the hands of a few men organized and dispersed throughout the Union, such as existed in the Order of the Cincinnati.[65] Rather than a representative of the nation produced by popular elections, the president would be chosen by, and bound to, small groups of men.

The method of electing the president that would eventually develop in the Brearley Committee on Unfinished Parts may be understood as a compromise position between direct election by the people and the appointment of the executive by the legislature. The electoral college method that emerged from the Convention would hold important implications for the representative nature of the office.

Among its primary advantages, the new method removed the choice from the legislature, thus helping to insure the president's independence from the other political branch of government. By so doing, the president was afforded the "space" necessary to acting on his own judgment for the good of the nation. It also made the president the independent representative of the constitutional order: able to act to defend himself and the forms of the Constitution against legislative encroachments. By placing the election of the president in a temporary institution closer to the people, most of those who favored direct election by the people were also satisfied with its popular character.

Perhaps most importantly for the success of the whole scheme in getting through the Convention, the electoral college itself was created to be nearly an exact mirror of the legislature. That is to say, the electoral method applied the representational scheme of the Connecticut Compromise to the method of choosing the president. Each state would have just as many votes in the electoral college as it had in the national legislature. This was palatable to both large and small states alike; both slave states who would benefit from the three-fifths rule and non-slave states could live with such a scheme of representation. "In effect," as Shlomo Slonim has noted, "the electoral college was simply a special congress elected to choose a president, without the shortcomings of the real Congress."[66]

The delegates in Philadelphia had effectively created a president with a dual representational link to the American people; neither of which was direct but both of which were central to the officer's place as a political representative. As noted above, the traditional link between constituency and representative has been elections. The electoral college method of selecting the president maintained this traditional link by making it the choice of a chosen body elevated out of the people themselves for that limited and express purpose. The other representational link forged by the Convention flowed directly through the nation's fundamental law. Through the Constitution the president was connected to the transcendent majority of the American people. In this connection the president is not meant to be subject to immediate popular mandates but to those emanating from the public's express agreement in the various state ratifying conventions which thereafter has been tacitly agreed to. In this way he is particularly to defend his office from the passions of the moment, especially those found in Congress.

Perhaps in no other way has the representational nature of the presidency changed more over the course of American history than with regard to its "links" with the American public. The indirect mode of election of the Founders has evolved into a de facto direct popular election. The democratization of the nomination processes of the two parties in the 1960s and 1970s has further forged this direct electoral link. Presidents themselves and technological developments have also created new and unpredicted linkages between the people and their representative in the Oval Office. Presidents, through mass rhetoric and "going public," have established a whole new system of tethers securing the people and the incumbent in a way unpredicted by the founding generation and that cannot be matched by any other political representatives in America.[67] Technological developments of the twentieth century, most notably the invention and proliferation of radio and television, have fueled the development of these new representational relationships—as has the expansive use of public opinion polling. As a result, the presidency today stands closer to the people than it did in the 1790s—a situation that is further discussed in the chapters that follow.

Political parties have also become very important to presidential elections and governance. As was mentioned earlier, presidents have become their political party's chief spokesman and symbol. Indeed, many of our most notable presidents have acted in office as highly partisan advocates of party programs and interests. Jackson, Theodore and Franklin Roosevelt, Woodrow Wilson, and Lyndon Johnson were such presidents. With the possible exception of Eisenhower, all presidents in the twentieth century have been eminently party men. In fact, our very conception of democracy itself has come to be closely associated with the tugs and pulls of rival political parties and the "partisan" presidency has been an inescapable element in this understanding. John Kennedy captured this conception of the presidency's importance to modern party-oriented democracy:

> No President, it seems to me, can escape politics. He has not only been chosen by the nation—he has been chosen by his Party. And if he insists that he is President of all the people and should, therefore, offend none of them—if he blurs the issues and differences between the parties—if he neglects the party machinery and avoids his party's leadership—then he has not only weakened his political party; . . . *he has dealt a death blow to the democratic process itself.*[68]

Such a conception of the presidency as a place of partisan leadership has not been one that has always prevailed. The founding generation denounced nearly unanimously the spirit of party and faction. The authors of *The Federalist* realized factious impulses and tendencies were an inescapable part of man's very nature; however, the structure of the political system was in part designed to control such tendencies and their most destructive effects. George Washington made a similarly realistic assessment in his Farewell Address in September 1796 when he noted that the spirit of party and faction "is inseparable from our nature, having its root in the strongest passions of the human Mind." But such a spirit remained for Washington one of the greatest enemies of free government and it would always be "in the interest and the duty of a wise People to discourage and restrain it."[69]

The five presidents who followed Washington shared with the father of their country a general distrust of the party spirit and his ideal of non-partisan executive leadership. According to Ralph Ketcham, each of these first presidents, "sought to 'escape politics,' abhorred the idea of 'party leadership,' and hoped to end the 'differences between the parties'."[70] They saw the need for the president to stand above party, to exercise moral leadership for the whole nation, and to provide general non-partisan guidance in the nation's march into its future. They, in short, saw the need for a patriotic leadership such as outlined in Bolingbroke's *Idea of a Patriot King* that would remain closely bound within strict republican limits. Ketcham has called this non-partisan presidency the nation's first version of our presidential office. In 1829 Andrew Jackson came to occupy the presidency and thus transformed it into something far different from what his predecessors had envisioned; it became an office of party leadership and party warfare. The office and the American polity were transformed forever.

Representation as Resemblance

In addition to the two types of representation I have made note of so far, representation as "acting for" and representation through symbolism, some theorists have noted a third use of the term representation that is applicable to politics: representation as resembling some other entity. Such a conception of representation focuses less on what the representative or representative body does than on what it looks like—to what degree does it accurately reflect what it is to represent. For instance, at the time of the American Revolution John Adams said of a representative legislature that it "should be an exact portrait, in miniature, of the people at large, as it should think, feel, reason, and act like them."[71] John Stuart Mill held a similar standard for representative bodies. According to Mill each should be "an arena in which not only the general opinion of the nation, but that of every section of it, and as far as possible of every eminent individual whom it contains, can produce itself in full light and challenge discussion; where every person in the country may count upon finding somebody who speaks his mind."[72] Such an understanding of representation has been best developed in more recent years by advocates of proportional representation.

Is such a conception of representation applicable to the presidency? How closely have presidents resembled the American people? Though Jimmy Carter went to efforts to reduce the trappings of the office and to appear more like an everyday American with his cardigan sweater and occasionally carrying his own luggage, most presidents have not been shy to make use of the "imperial" trappings of the office. Carter's attempts at levelling the office notwithstanding, presidents have generally not been of the average stuff of the nation. In their person and background, in many ways, they have tended not to resemble those whom they are called upon to represent as the central officer of the nation.

The formal constitutional qualifications for being president are very few and quite easy for an average citizen to meet. They are but three: a candidate must be at least thirty-five years of age, a "natural born citizen," and a resident of the United States for at least fourteen years. But on top of these minimalist qualifications, a whole series of informal, extraconstitutional qualifications have been erected that the system seems to seek in presidential candidates. These informal qualifications have tended to make the presidency, and perhaps with very good reason, an "unrepresentative" institution. It has tended to be an office filled with men "uncommon" in their times and in many ways unlike the American people.

Though presidents have come from diverse backgrounds, from birth in log cabins to the highest places of the American social ladder, they have most often been recruited from the upper-classes of society. Indeed, nearly half of all presidents have come from socially and politically prominent families, with just four families alone accounting for nearly one in five of our chief executives.[73] Geographically, presidents have come disproportionately from certain states. Five states alone have produced twenty-four chief executives—New York, Ohio, Virginia, Massachusetts, and Tennessee—while more than thirty states still await their first occupant in the White House.

Occupationally, presidents have tended to be equally uncommon. More than half of the presidents have practiced law at some point in their lives. Others have been military leaders, educators, and gentlemen farmers, although there have been a few from more modest occupations. Truman had been a railroad timekeeper and a small farmer, Andrew Johnson was a tailor. Educationally, the presidential crop has been more elite still. Only nine presidents have lacked formal college or university training and only Harry Truman did so in the twentieth century. Presidents have counted among their alma maters the most prestigious institutions in America: Harvard alone has produced five presidents (John and John Quincy Adams, the two Roosevelts, and John Kennedy); Princeton (Madison and Wilson), Yale (Taft, Bush, and Clinton), Stanford (Hoover), the military academies

(Grant, Eisenhower, Carter), and a wide variety of smaller but still very prestigious institutions have had more than their share of alumni as the nation's chief executive.[74] In such ways presidents have tended not to look like the average American citizen.

But we must not lose sight of the fact that in other less specific but no less important ways, the American people have tended to entrust office to those like themselves. Ideologically, for instance, the American people have tended to reward the center. Serious candidates scramble to occupy the ideological middle ground and realize that they fail to do so at their own peril—the White House is no place for the radical ideologue of either the left or the right. Ethnically, much like the general population historically, presidents have overwhelmingly been decendents of the British Isles (England, Wales, Scotland, and Ireland)—all but five sharing such an ancestry. Religiously, only one president has not been a Protestant Christian, the Roman Catholic John Kennedy. Though dispropotionately from the Episcopalian, Presbyterian, and Unitarian churches, only men who have met the implicit religious test of a predominantly Christian nation have made it to the presidency.

In short, in many ways presidents have tended to resemble those whom they would represent while in other ways they have not—this being particularly the case in their social, educational, and economic backgrounds. There has never been a woman in the Oval Office, never a black occupant of the executive mansion, never a Jewish commander in chief. But such a standard of representation is one that probably makes little sense to apply to any unitary officer in a pluralistic republic such as the United States. And, indeed, it is perhaps a mark of the good sense of the American people that they have tended to choose men unlike themselves in many ways. Whatever the reasons, it is clear that the American people have developed other criteria for judging whom they would like to see as their representatives in the executive branch of their government.[75]

The Separation of Powers and Political Representation

One last question dealing with the concept of political representation and its relation to the American presidency deserves a brief mention here. Although it is of central concern to this study, it only garners a small comment in the present chapter as it is more properly explored and developed in the chapters that follow. In a system of separated powers and the built-in conflict such a system engenders between the chief political institutions, questions will inevitably develop as to the proper place of each institution within the polity. Which provides representation better, Congress or the presidency? Which institution should lead the public policy process and which should follow? Which institution is closer to the true wishes of the American people and which to the nation's true interests? What is the proper function of the legislature and what is the role of the president in American public life? Questions such as these have set the stage for much of the branch battles that have been commonplace since the earliest days of the Republic, and they are in many ways inevitable when discussing the norms, values, and needs of political representation within a governmental system of separated powers.

In many ways traditional understandings of political representation excluded it from the realm of executive institutions. As we have seen, the American presidency created by the Constitution of 1787 and further developed over our history as a nation is the great exception. In the United States all national power is delegated by the people to their representatives to wield in their interest. The presidency, especially the contemporary presidency, is the holder of a considerable portion of that delegated authority and power. This fact necessitates that the American public consider the presidency an office of political representation and that they apply the questions and values that come with it to that institution, just as has always been the case with legislative bodies.

The presidential office and its occupants stand as important carriers of meaning in the American political culture. Presidents stand as America's chief of state. They are our chief living symbolic representatives. Presidents also occupy an active, central place in the American system of representative government. Presidents are at the center of the legislative process through their task of agenda setting for Congress as well as through their constitutional authority to veto legislation. Presidents also occupy the central place in the administrative aspects of government. In these ways presidents are as much political representatives as is any member of the national legislature. The ways in which presidents have performed these representational roles, the place of the presidency in regard to the American people who are represented by incumbents, and the relationship between America's chief representational institutions are all essential questions that must be raised if we are to understand the office and its place in the American Republic.

Notes

1. Carl J. Friedrich, *Constitutional Government and Democracy* (Boston, 1950), 267.

2. John A. Fairlie, "The Nature of Political Representation," *American Political Science Review* (April and June 1940), 236.

3. Russell W. Neuman, *The Paradox of Mass Politics* (Cambridge, Mass.: Harvard University Press, 1986).

4. Robert Weissberg, *Public Opinion and Popular Government* (Englewood Cliffs, N.J.: Prentice Hall, 1976).

5. A. H. Birch, *Representation* (New York: Praeger, 1971), 19.

6. See David Easton, *The Political System* (New York: A.A. Knopf, 1953). Max Weber, *The Theory of Social and Economic Organizations*, translated by A.M. Henderson and Talcott Persons (New York: Oxford University Press, 1947), 145-154.

7. Hannah Pitkin makes this point and attempts to arrive at a definition through a consideration of the analogies found in the literature. See Hannah Fenichel Pitkin, *The Concept of Representation* (Berkeley: University of California Press, 1967), 112-143.

8. For a similar understanding see, J. Roland Pennock, "Political Representation: An Overview," in *Nomos X: Representation*, J. Roland Pennock and John W. Chapman, eds. (New York: Atherton Press, 1968), 3-27.

9. I use the term *official* here to differentiate the activities a president must carry out due to constitutional, statutory, or common law mandates from those activities that are not so based, such as speechmaking, campaigning, and presiding at official state functions. Though the presidential responsibilities of being "chief of state" certainly are "official," they are more symbolic than active. It is for this reason that I do not discuss them here but consider this role of the president under the consideration of symbolic representation below.

10. Terry Eastland, *Energy in the Executive: The Case for the Strong Presidency* (New York: The Free Press, 1992), 19-20.

11. Stephen J. Wayne, *The Legislative Presidency* (New York: Harper & Row, 1978).

12. Robert J. Spitzer, *President & Congress: Executive Hegemony at the Crossroads of American Government* (New York: McGraw-Hill, 1993), 40-86.

13. Of course, the mere threat of the veto can also function as a *de facto* use of the veto by deterring Congress from moving on a piece of legislation the president does not support—thus making the threat of the veto as much of a negative power as the actual use of that authority.

14. See Spitzer, 1993, 75-76.

15. Herbert Storing, ed., *The Complete Anti-Federalists* (Chicago: University of Chicago Press, 1981) Volume II, Number VIII, p. 178. John Adams makes a similar argument in his *Defence of The Constitutions of the United States* in *Works*, 285-292; 585.

16. Quoted in Clinton Rossiter, *The American Presidency*, Revised Edition (New York: Mentor, 1960), 16.

17. See Ryan J. Barilleaux, "Toward an Institutionalist Framework for Presidency Studies," *Presidential Studies Quarterly* (Spring 1982), 154-158.

18. For instance, John Adams wrote in 1790, "Take away thrones and crowns from among men, and there will be an end of all dominion and justice." Quoted in Michael Novak, *Choosing Our King: Powerful Symbols in Presidential Politics* (New York: MacMillan, 1974), 21.

19. Spitzer, 1993, 20.

20. Forrest McDonald, *The Presidency of George Washington* (Lawrence, Kans.: University Press of Kansas, 1973), 25.

21. James Barber, *Presidential Character* (Englewood Cliffs, N.J.: Prentice Hall, 1972), 4.

22. Novak, 1974, 8.

23. Novak, 1974, xiv.

24. Novak, 1974, 5.

25. Barbara Hinckley, *The Symbolic Presidency: How Presidents Portray Themselves* (New York: Routledge, 1990), 10.

26. See Robert D. Hess and Judith V. Torney, *The Development of Political Attitudes in Children* (Garden City, New York: Anchor Books, 1967); David Easton and Jack Dennis, *Children in the Political System: Origins of Political Legitimacy* (New York: McGraw Hill, 1969).

27. Murray Edelman, *The Symbolic Uses of Politics* (Urbana, Ill.: University of Illinois Press, 1964), 78.

28. Edelman, 1964, 79.

29. Fred Greenstein, "What the President Means to Americans," in *Choosing the President*, James David Barber, ed. (New York: American Assembly, 1974), 130-131.

30. Eric Voegelin, *The New Science of Politics* (Chicago: University of Chicago Press, 1952), 27-28.

31. See Voegelin, 1952.

32. See my discussion of the ideas for a plural executive in chapter 3.

33. Dante Germino, *The Inaugural Addresses of American Presidents: The Public Philosophy and Rhetoric* (Lanham, Md.: University Press of America, 1984).

34. Willmoore Kendall and George W. Carey, *The Basic Symbols of the American Political Tradition* (Baton Rouge: Louisiana State University Press,

1970).

35. I borrow the basis of this understanding from Eric Voegelin, 1952.

36. Alexis de Tocqueville, *Democracy in America* (New York: Vintage Classics, 1990), Volume I, 135.

37. Robert E. Denton, Jr. *The Symbolic Dimensions of the American Presidency: Description and Analysis* (Prospect Heights, Illinois: Waveland Press, 1982), 121.

38. Hugh D. Duncan, *Language and Literature in Society* (Chicago, 1953), 107.

39. Samuel Kernell, *Going Public: New Strategies of Presidential Leadership* (Washington, D.C.: CQ Press, 1986), viii.

40. Hinckley, 1990.

41. Craig A. Rimmerman, *Presidency by Plebiscite: The Reagan-Bush Era in Institutional Perspective* (Boulder, Colo.: Westview Press, 1993), 42-43.

42. Paul Brace and Barbara Hinckley, *Follow the Leader: Opinion Polls and the Modern Presidents* (New York: Basic Books, 1992), 27.

43. Brace and Hinckley, 1992, 27.

44. Pitkin, 1967, 145.

45. Burke, 1963, 187.

46. See Roger H. Davidson, *The Role of the Congressman* (New York: Pegasus, 1967), 115. Davidson asserts the Burkean trustee position "confuses" the issue of *style* and *focus* and finds them conterminous.

47. Burke has been considered here to be restating the views of Algernon Sidney in his *Discourses on Government* (1688). See Fairlie, 1940, 241.

48. Burke, 1963, 187.

49. The metaphor of the mirror was a favorite of the Anti-Federalists to contrast their dedication to a more participatory democracy with those supposedly elitist views of the Federalists. Speaking to the New York ratifying convention, Melancton Smith captured this view, "the idea that naturally suggests itself to our minds, when we speak of representatives, is that they resemble those they represent. They should be a true picture of the people..." In *The Debates of the State Conventions on the Adaptation of the Federal Constitution*, J. Elliot, ed.(Philadelphia, 1866), II, 246.

50. See Pitkin, 1967, 144.

51. Carl Friedrich. "Representation and Constitutional Reform," *Western Political Quarterly* (June, 1948), p. 127. Or, as James Hogan put it, "the representative acting as if the constituents were present," *Election and Representation* (Cork University Press, 1945), 141.

52. See Birch, 1971, 97-100, and Donald E. Stokes, "Political Parties in the Normative Theory of Representation," in *Nomos X: Representation*, J. Roland Pennock and John W. Chapman, eds. (New York: Atherton Press, 1968), 150-154.

53. See Roger H. Davidson. 1967. Davidson, in fact, found a plurality of the Congressmen sampled to adhere to this "politico" position.

54. Quoted in Robert Luce, *Legislative Principles* (Boston: Houghton Mifflin, 1930), 471. Such a position, we should note, gets us no closer to a definition of active political representation. How are we to define how each individual representative "has the means of knowing" his constituents' will? Would he not also be using his own judgment in determining what he "knows" to be their will?

55. See, for instance, John F. Kennedy's inspiring defense of the independence position in *Profiles in Courage* (New York: Harper & Brothers, 1956).

56. Elbridge Gerry, *Annals*, 1st Congress, 1st session, April 15, 1789, 737.

57. Thomas Hartley, *Annals*, 1st Congress, 1st session, April 15, 1789, 734.

58. Shlomo Slonim, "Designing the Electoral college," in *Inventing the American Presidency*, Thomas E. Cronin, ed. (Lawrence, Kans.: University of Kansas Press, 1989), 33.

59. Slonim, 1989, 33.

60. James Madison in *Records of the Federal Convention*, Max Farrand, ed. (New Haven: Yale University Press, 1966), II, 34.

61. This is a central piece of evidence virtually ignored by all those who have come to view the electoral college as a jerry-rigged compromise designed to fail and inevitably send the election of the president into the House of Representatives. In the original Constitution the president was to serve four-year terms and be eligible for reappointment as often as he wished. The Framer's concern for the independence of the executive therefore denies that they intended the House to regularly make the appointment of the president. Otherwise the executive would be the mere creature of the legislative majority. For the classic expression of the view that the Framers intended the electoral college to fail, see John P. Roche, "The Founding Fathers: A Reform Caucus in Action," *American Political Science Review* (December 1961), Volume LV, No. 4, 810-812.

62. Farrand, 1966, 29.

63. Farrand, 1966, 29.

64. See George Mason, in Farrand, 1966, p. 31. See also, Cecelia M. Kenyon, "Men of Little Faith: The Anti-Federalists on the Nature of Representative Government," *William and Mary Quarterly* 12 (January 1955), 13.

65. Farrand, 1966, Volume II, 114.

66. Slonim, 1989, 50.

67. See James Madison's comments in *Federalist* No. 49 on executives always being at a disadvantage *vis-à-vis* the legislature when it comes to enlisting public opinion.

68. Quoted in, Ralph Ketcham, *Presidents Above Party: The First American Presidency, 1789-1829* (Chapel Hill: The University of North Carolina Press, 1984), 225-226 Emphasis added.

69. Washington's "Farewell Address," reprinted in W.B. Allen, *George Washington: A Collection* (Indianapolis: Liberty *Classics*, 1988), 519-520.

70. Ketcham, 1984, 228.

71. John Adams, "Letter to John Penn," *Works* (Boston, 1852-1865), IV, 205.

72. John Stuart Mill, *Utilitarianism, On Liberty, Considerations on Representative Government*, H.B. Acton, ed., (London: J.M. Dent & Sons, 1972), 258-259.

73. These presidents include: John and John Quincy Adams and James Madison and Zachory Taylor who shared the same grandparents; Benjamin Harrison and his grandfather William Henry Harrison; and Theodore and Franklin Roosevelt.

74. The information in the previous two paragraphs is based on Richard A. Watson and Norman C. Thomas, *The Politics of the Presidency*, Second Edition (Washington, D.C.: CQ Press, 1988), 117-133.

75. We nonetheless might recall then-Candidate Bill Clinton's pledge during the 1992 presidential race to have an administration that "looks more like America." The candidate seemed to be operating according to a standard of representation based on the given body's (in this case his administration's) resemblance to the various elements of the nation. Clinton's very slow rate of filling vacancies in the first months of his administration was reportedly due to his insistence on finding qualified minority, women, and gay and lesbian candidates to better "balance" the look of the government.

2

Representation and the Presidency in *The Federalist*

M any leading Antifederalists had argued that a popular and locally elected legislature could be the only legitimate representative institution. This contention has found its way into contemporary political science where the concept of representation has almost exclusively been the bastion of legislative scholars. Others at the time of the American founding held celebratory views toward monarchy and executive power while distrusting popular assemblies. This view has also had its corollary in twentieth century American politics and in the scholarly community.

In contrast to both these perspectives, by considering the concept of representation in *The Federalist*, it becomes evident that the president was to be *a* representative in the American system but not *the* representative as some partisans of the institution would have it. Thus, the constitutional morality of *The Federalist* is balanced and without the type of institutional partisanship that has so often been a part of American political history.

To understand the conception of presidential representation in these important essays, we must first examine the more general theory of representation found there. By properly understanding Publius' thought on the nature and needs of representation, we will be able to see how the executive power in the Constitution meets these requirements.[1] Also, by understanding the place of the office in the larger political system explicated in *The Federalist*, we will be able to see the outline of presidential representation as it was envisioned.

The first part of this chapter takes up the task of expounding the theory of political representation in *The Federalist*. By interpreting the essays through the lens of the traditional "mandate-independence" controversy in political theory, we will see that the elements Publius is concerned with are ones that particularly can be found in the presidency, as well as the more traditional home of representation, the legislature. In the second part of the chapter, I offer an interpretation of the separation of powers scheme in which is embedded Publius' conception of representative government. I concentrate here particularly on the representative role intended for the American presidency while still maintaining a "systematic" account of representation. Representation in *The Federalist* was seen to be a "system" of representation in which both the president and the legislature participate; it was not reserved to one institution or branch of government. Taking such a "systematic" approach will help us understand the place of the presidency in the American system of representative democracy.[2] Representation, after all, is "the pivot on which" the American republic moves (63:372).[3]

The Concept of Representation in *The Federalist*

As we discussed in the previous chapter, the nature of the relationship between the representative and the represented constitutes one of the central controversies in the history of representative government. The basic arguments are worth repeating here. Hanna Pitkin has summarized the question at issue in this mandate-independence controversy as "should (must) a representative do what his constituents want, and be bound by mandates or instructions from them; or should (must) he be free to act as seems best to him in pursuit of their welfare."[4] The central ethical issue involved in such a question is no less essential to democratic theory than that of, who is the proper repository of governmental decision-making power: the mass electorate or the representatives elevated from that electorate? Should the representative view himself as being elevated in order to act according to his own judgment and conscience, or should he view himself and his role as faithfully following "instructions" from his constituents? The latter alternative seems to value representative institutions solely for their quantitative and practical element; i.e., because direct democracy would be logistically impossible over any area approaching the size of a modern nation-state. On the other hand, the former contains a qualitative value assumption; i.e., representatives free to exercise their own intelligence and abilities and to follow their own conscience will be more likely to make just and good decisions. It is by keeping these competing value systems in mind that we can best explore the idea of representation in the essays written by Hamilton, Madison, and Jay.

Publius on Representation: The Filter

If the aim of the Constitution, as Publius instructs us, is "to obtain for rulers men who possess most wisdom to discern, and most virtue to pursue, the common good of society"(57:343), one may ask: What use could be made of these special (clearly seen to be unrepresentative) qualities of the elected representatives if they were to simply mirror the opinions and wishes of their electors? If the representatives were meant to be compliant delegates of constituency will there would be no need for the Constitution to aim at obtaining rulers with the special characteristics Publius mentions. Rather, it would be the first object of the Constitution to acquire representatives with characteristics that would facilitate their being "mere" agents of public opinion or subordinate substitutes for the electors.

To enable us to cast a clearer demarcation between this "delegate" view and Publius' view, we can think of the former in terms of a metaphor of the "funnel." The representative as "funnel" is simply to act as a facilitating device for the people to bring their opinions to government. The funnel's main value to government is quantitative—taking the opinions and views of many and reflecting them as one. Opposed to the view of representatives as funnels, we can conceptualize Publius' intent by using the metaphor of the "filter". The filter is not a passive recipient and reflector of electoral opinion but serves to "filter out" those that his "wisdom and virtue" find inconsistent with the "common good of society." The ethical value of Publius' representative is thus qualitative—to change (where necessary) and improve the public voice in government. The particular benefit of such a filtering process is that it works to "*refine* and *enlarge* the public view by passing them through the medium of a chosen body of citizens, whose wisdom may best discern the true interest of their country and whose patriotism and love of justice will be least likely to sacrifice it to temporary or partial considerations" (10:126—emphasis added).

One should notice the important implication of this passage. Publius seems to say that if representatives weren't to employ their "wisdom," "patriotism," and "love of justice" as independent trustees to "refine" and "enlarge" the public view, the policies of such mandate-beholden delegates might very well tend to sacrifice "the true interest of their country" to "temporary or partial considerations."[5] Under such a filter arrangement of refining and enlarging the public view, however, "it may well happen that the public voice, pronounced by the representatives of the people, will be more consonant to the public good than if pronounced by the people themselves convened for the purpose" (10:126).[6]

Publius has clearly made a content distinction here between the policies that the mass public would pursue if they were themselves convened to conduct governmental business (and by extension those of representatives beholden to public mandates) and those policies emanating from a chosen body of citizens elected for the purpose of passing laws. Though Publius clearly favors the latter, it is not easily discernable from the above discussion on what criteria Publius makes such a value judgment. By looking more closely at the passage from *Federalist* 10, however, we can see fairly clearly two fundamental content differences between the laws willed by the public at large and those favored by the representatives of the people.

First, we see that the representatives as members of a "chosen body" can discern the "*true* interest of their country" and so are not subject to sacrificing it to "*partial*" (read local or parochial) considerations. Publius seems here to equate constituency opinion (referred to as "the people themselves") with local interests (*vis-à-vis* the true national interest) and sees the remedy in the representative "enlarging" that view in accordance with the common good. Like Edmund Burke, Publius here outlines a theory of representation in which the representative's primary ethical obligation is to look after the interest of the whole nation and to resist the impulses of parochialism.[7]

The second content differentiation Publius makes is one between the "temporary" considerations to which others may sacrifice the common good and the more permanent and well reasoned interests by which the people's representatives would conceivably be guided. This reading is consistent with the dichotomy Publius makes between *passion* (equated here with "temporary" considerations) and *reason* (the more permanent interests the representatives' wisdom facilitates).[8] Here Publius' differentiation closely resembles the one made by Edmund Burke between "reason and judgement" and "inclination."[9] Starting with the passion-reason dichotomy, it will be useful to explore further the two content differences Publius alludes to between the voice of the people expressed in a direct fashion and the public voice that has been filtered by the "chosen body of citizens."

Style: Passion and Reason

"If government were a matter of will upon any side, yours [electors as opposed to representatives]," Edmund Burke wrote, "without question ought to be superior. But government and legislation are matters of reason and judgement, and not inclination."[10] To Burke, governmental policy was to be arrived at through a process of discussion between the representatives of the people combined in a deliberative assembly. This process would arrive at "reason and judgement" while the product of mere majority will, expressed through compliant and subservient representatives, would be merely a matter of "inclination"—something inappropriate as a basis for governmental action. We have seen how Publius seems to share Burke's view of the content of the public voice as expressed directly from the people, and we have extended that to the public voice as funneled through instructed delegates compared to that expressed by those representatives acting independently with "wisdom," "patriotism," and "love of justice." Having established this comparison, let us now turn to considering the place of reason and passion in *The Federalist* focusing on which should prevail in government.

Despite Martin Diamond's assertions to the contrary, Publius did not base the American republic on a reliance on passions and "less than reasoned" opinions.[11] In fact, in a number of essays, Publius clearly and unmistakably disparages the effects of passion in the halls of government. In discussing why constitutional conventions aren't adequate to maintain the separation of powers, Publius finds in them a "danger of disturbing the public tranquility by interesting too strongly the public passions" (49:314). Again in essay number 50, Publius speaks of the unfortunate nature of Pennsylvania's experience with a council of censors because "passion, not reason, must have presided over their decisions" (50:317). And a reason given for limiting the numbers in the House of Representatives was to keep it from becoming a multitude because in "all very numerous assemblies, . . . passion never fails to wrest the scepter from reason" (55:336).

The political system expounded by Publius was not based on a free-for-all of passions, as some have contended. Rather, as Harvey Mansfield has put it, "[t]he Constitution is designed to make reason paramount over the passions."[12] Indeed, Publius says that "it is the reason, alone, of the public that ought to control and regulate the government. The passions ought to be controlled and regulated by the government" (49:315). It is particularly the function of the people's representatives to ensure that it is reason and not passion that holds the scepter of power. One would be hard-pressed to see how, acting as mandate-beholden delegates, they could possibly perform their function of expressing the reasoned public voice when that is not found in the voice of the people themselves. Though it is true that Publius intended the deliberate sense of the community to govern the actions of representatives, this "does not require an unqualified complaisance to every sudden breeze of passion" (71:409). In fact, Publius directly lauds the service of Burkean representatives who have historically "saved the people from very fatal consequences of their own mistakes" (71:410). In *Federalist* 71 it is made perfectly clear what representative style is to be followed in the American Republic: "When occasions present themselves in which the interests of the people are at variance with their inclinations, it is the duty of the persons whom they have appointed to be guardians of those interests to withstand the temporary delusions in order to give them time and opportunity for more cool and sedate reelection" (71:410).

Focus: The Common Good and Local/Parochial Interests

The prevailing interpretation of *The Federalist* in modern times tends to underplay the role of virtue in government officials. In consequence, it also tends to ignore the role of the common national good. Generally stated, the dominant contemporary interpretation of *The Federalist* on this point is that Publius in Number 10 views representation as interest or "faction" based. It has been held that factions, represented by elected officials, were to meet in the combative arena of competing and rival interests that composed the representative body, with the end result being "deadlock," a "non-tyrannical republic," or "inaction and stability." Adherents to this reading thus see Publius' intention as that of effectively making positive governmental action virtually impossible. Many also have claimed that enhancing this stalemate is the true role of the separation of powers as outlined by Publius. In such a system, how could the "common good" be promoted by government if it was designed for inaction and deadlock? The answer seems fairly clear: it cannot.

One of the most influential of such interpretations of *The Federalist* is found in Robert Dahl's *A Preface to Democratic Theory*.[13] Here Professor Dahl explicates what he finds to be the "Madisonian Model" of democratic theory: a system intended primarily, if not exclusively, to inhibit majorities from forming in government and thereby to frustrate action and protect the minorities of "wealth and power." There is no place for the active promotion of the public good, rather, the major goal of such a system is purely negative—a non-tyrannical republic.[14]

Hanna Pitkin has explicated a similar interpretation of *The Federalist*, finding in Publius' theory of representation an expression of "liberalism," which she defines as "representing people who have interests."[15] She finds this to be a "far cry from the Burkean view."[16] Pitkin maintains that Madison did not hold representatives to be capable of knowing the interests of the people any better than the people did themselves; "if anything, he in this respect is roughly their equal."[17] Thus, "Politics is not a realm of knowledge and reason for Madison as it is for Burke. It is much more a realm of pressures and opinion."[18] A representative is not to be "the right kind of man" but is simply to "pursue the factious interests of his constituency."[19] Is there, then, no place in such a system for the active promotion of the common good of society? Is the federal government simply a meeting place for hostile and competing interests that prohibit action by balancing opinions against opinions and passions against passions? Both Dahl and Pitkin think so, but their arguments are based on incomplete readings of the theory of the extended republic in *The Federalist*.[20]

To wit, both of these interpretations seriously underrepresent the place of the government's function of the promotion of the common good in *The Federalist*. This point is important to us because, as we have seen, the promotion of the common good (as a single "whole" interest) versus the delegated representation of local units is a central question in the mandate-independence controversy that directly impacts our study. If we take Pitkin's and Dahl's interpretations at their word, such a faction-based conception of representation would leave no room for the presidency to exercise representational functions. By denying virtue and knowledge to Publius' representatives, along with the denial of a concern for a common national good, these interpretations logically deny to the presidency the office's important role as a representative in the political system. According to such an interpretation, only locally elected individuals who would meet in a pluralistic free for all in the legislature could be deemed representatives. As we will see, these revisionist era interpretations of the Founders' views on representation ignore the central importance of a concern for the common good and the special virtue and knowledge intended for the representatives.[21]

Like Dahl, those adherents of revisionist era interpretations refuse to accept Publius at his word on the centrality of the common good as an end of the political system. "[T]he public good, the real welfare of the great body of the people," wrote Publius, "is the supreme object to be pursued; and that no form of government whatever has any other value than as it may be fitted for the attainment of this object" (45:293). Clearly the promotion of the common good was a central ethical goal in Publius' thought. Dahl finds the central Madisonian goal to be the avoidance of tyranny, the pursuit of which he finds to make the pursuit of the public good impossible. Looking at the text, however, one would be surprised to find that Publius, in numerous passages, lists *both* the common good and the avoidance of tyranny as ends of government (and often in that exact order). We see that, "To secure the public good and private rights . . . is then the great object to which our inquiries are directed"(10:125). In his definition of the important concept of faction, we find Publius to understand one to be a number of citizens "who are united by a common impulse of passion, or of interest, adverse to the rights of other citizens, or to the *permanent and aggregate interests of the community*" (10:123—emphasis added).[22] And further we find it hard to reconcile those who argue that the system was devised for "deadlock and inaction" with Publius' admonition that

> we are apt to rest satisfied that all is safe, because nothing improper will be likely *to be done*; but we forget how much good may be prevented, and how much ill may be produced, by the power of hindering that which is necessary from being done and of keeping affairs in the same unfavorable position in which they may happen to stand at particular periods (22:181).

The active promotion of the common good was a central goal in Publius' political theory, not merely obfuscation.[23]

Virtue, Distance, and the Extended Republic

On what grounds does Publius base his distinction between independent representatives and compliant delegates? The answer is twofold. First, there arc the characteristics Publius finds in the representatives themselves. Generally speaking, we can categorize these qualities under the general term of *virtue*. Second, there is the process by which the representatives in government would arrive at public policy decisions. This process we can understand as the deliberative function of representation.

Virtue

Contrary to the views represented by Dahl and Pitkin, Publius was concerned that republican officeholders should possess a degree of virtue uncharacteristic of the population as a whole. Publius lauds the members of the convention that drafted the Constitution for their virtue in *Federalist* 2. They were "highly distinguished by their patriotism, virtue, and wisdom," Publius tells us (2:92). But what about those who are to follow in governing the Republic? Does he expect them to be as noble?

Martin Diamond believed that Publius did not. While Diamond noted the special qualities of the Founders, he argued that *The Federalist* "had no necessary place and makes no provision for men of the founding kind."[24] Diamond not only contends that men as virtuous as the Founders are not needed, but goes on to contend that the system relies on officeholders as interested advocates of the causes they determine and on their "passions" rather than their "reason." Under Diamond's interpretation of Publius' system, representatives could not be, at least due to an assumption of virtue, independent statesmen. Nor could they be free or have the requisite qualities to deliberate about the common good of the political community. Instead, the institutions of the Republic would channel and arrange the passions and interests of representatives in a "durable and self-perpetuating" system.[25]

Despite Diamond's contention to the contrary, Publius repeatedly lauds the virtues of future office holders. In discussing the benefits of having one national government he asserts that, "One government can collect and avail itself of the talents and experience of the ablest men in whatever part of the Union they may be found" (4:99). Publius makes similar arguments in defense of the extended republic in number 10. The most prevalent reading of this essay centers on Publius' argument that "by extend[ing] the sphere you take in a greater variety of parties and interests," thereby making less probable the threat of one faction dominating in the majority at the expense of the common good or rights of the minority (10:122). This interpretation is correct as far as it goes; however, a full understanding of number 10's implications for representation cannot be reached without due consideration of the place of virtue in the extended republic. By extending the territory over which republican government operates, the chances improve that men of superior virtue will be elected representatives.[26] It is true that Publius recognizes that, "Enlightened statesmen will not always be at the helm" (10:125). However, a crucial benefit of the extended republic is that enlightened statesmen are *more likely* to be at the helm than in a smaller republic.[27]

> [As] each representative will be chosen by a greater number of citizens in the large than in the small republic, it will be more difficult for unworthy candidates to practice with success the vicious arts by which elections are too often carried; and the suffrages of the people being more free, will be more likely to center on men who possess the most attractive merit and the most diffusive and established characters (10:127).

Publius calls these representatives "a chosen body of citizens, whose wisdom may best discern the true interest of their country and whose patriotism and love of justice will be least likely to sacrifice it to temporary and partial considerations" (10:126). Though "men of factious tempers" may gain office through "intrigue," "corruption," or other means, the extended republic makes it more likely that representatives will possess a degree of virtue unrepresentative of the population at large and under such a situation the public voice may very well be more consonant with the public good (10:126).[28]

An added benefit to representation in the extended republic is that the broader constituency would tend to encourage a broader outlook in the candidate.[29] Representatives are thus seen to possess at least some degree of virtue greater than representatives in smaller republics; they are not the impassioned defenders of self-interest upon which some pluralist interpretations are built. This would, of course, be especially true of the presidency as it would be filled by the only representative with a completely national origin who would be the sole representative chosen from such an extended and diverse territory and population.

Distance

There is a second result of the extended republic that directly affects our inquiry into the presidency and Publius' thought on representation. By extending the territory over which the government rules without a corresponding increase in the number of representatives in government, each office holder will be charged with representing a larger area containing more constituents and hence more diversity. The inferred result is that representatives will be somewhat removed from the temporary passions that may from time to time sweep their constituencies.

The logic of this point seems to have been on Madison's mind at the Constitutional Convention when he argued against a large number of Senators because, "The more the representatives of the people [are] multiplied, the more they [partake] of the infirmities of their constituents, the more liable they [become] to be divided among themselves either from their own indiscretions or the artifices of the opposite factions, and of course the less capable of fulfilling their trust."[30] In such an extended republic, the people will have to entrust power to a few representatives who are not as "representative" as they would be in a small republic or with more numerous representatives. Office holders, representing large and diverse populations, will be less open to specific instructions from their constituents and will thus, of necessity, largely rely on their own best judgments. Such a result is especially true in the case of the president—the only nationally elected officer.

The Deliberative Republic

Even if they are virtuous and distant, are Publius' representatives able to apply their reasoned judgment toward the goal of making policy in the public interest? Most contemporary interpretations, drawing on the work of pluralist theorists who in many cases trace their genealogy to *The Federalist*,[31] argue that they cannot. To put it very briefly (perhaps unfairly briefly), Dahl and others hold the governmental realm to be an arena for the competition of self-interests and the government's role to be simply that of a "neutral mediator" between these competing groups.

The problem inherent in the pluralist view is that it is based on a misunderstanding of the nature of political representatives, and so it arrives at an erroneous conclusion as to their work in government.[32] What we need instead is an interpretation of the function of government and representatives that accounts for the elements we have examined so far. Such a function or process of government can be found in a "discussion model" or "deliberative" view of governmental action and affords us a more complete understanding of Publius' thought.[33]

Rather than seeing government as a "synthesizer" of, or "neutral mediator" between, rival and competing parochial interests, a model of government as a deliberative unit(s) holds its primary function to be one of engaging in a conversation on the means and ends of public action and then carrying through the policies arrived at through this conversation. Government as such a deliberative system can account for the characteristics of representatives, and the quality of policy outcome, we saw above. Virtuous representatives are to deliberate among themselves on the proper means toward the end of government—justice and the promotion of the common good. Reason and not passion should hold sway in such a deliberation between men making up a "chosen body of citizens." It is not a mere reflection of local interests or majority will that is to govern, nor is it the product of the competition of self-interested actors. Rather, "The republican principle demands that the deliberate sense of the community should govern. . . . " (71:409). It is the case that "the people commonly *intend* the PUBLIC GOOD. . . . But their good sense would despise the adulator who should pretend that they always *reason right* about the *means* of promoting it" (71:410—emphasis in original). The right reasoning is to be supplied by the representatives of the people combined in institutions designed to facilitate the emergence of the *deliberate* sense of what is in the public interest. As Kenneth Grasso has pointed out, "All of Publius' efforts are designed to assure that the place of reason is not usurped by mere desire or self-interest. He thus seeks to establish a decision-making process that will act as a barrier to factious majorities by filtering out proposals originating in either interest or passion."[34] That decision-making process involves deliberation by representatives elevated for the virtues they possess and toward the ends of justice and the common good.

As we have noted, the extension of the sphere over which the government is to operate played a central role in the acquisition of upright representatives who could act independently. But what of the "pluralist" implications of number 10?

> Extend the sphere and you take in a greater variety of parties and interests; you
> make it less probable that a majority of the whole will have a common motive

to invade the rights of other citizens; or if such a common motive exists, it will be more difficult for all who feel it to discover their own strength and to act in unison with each other (10:127).

This principle of a multiplicity of interests in the larger republic has mistakenly been raised to nearly biblical status by many of the contemporary interpreters who wish to claim it as all-encompassing of Publius' republican theory.

At most, Publius' pluralism provides for a half solution to the problem of factions and tyrannical majorities (which is to say it offers no *solution* at all).[35] The pluralism of the extended republic *facilitates* government action and promotes the common good rather than creating a "deadlock." As Paul Eidelberg has suggested, the plethora of interests in the extended republic was consistent with the principle of *divide et impera*, to facilitate the rule of just majorities by checking (and hence emasculating) parochial self-interest against parochial self-interest.[36] On this point Kenneth Grasso has noted that "given a profusion of factions Publius believed that interest would check interest, and thus secure the capacity of the government to act purposively for the common good."[37]

Pluralism thus serves to secure the government's independence from any single interest and the independence of representatives in the deliberative process. This diversity also has the effect of slowing the decision-making process, thereby improving deliberation by securing the ascendence of reason over temporary passions. A more complete reading of Publius' design for the American Republic must take into account the elements of representation and public policy that we have seen above, along with the pluralistic elements that so many read as Publius' whole project. Publius' pluralism is at most a modified one and is designed to encourage the independence of representatives from partial and temporary interests.

Institutional Separation:
Toward a Compound Theory of Representation

Traditionally it was generally held that the members of the legislative branch of government were the only officials capable of being political representatives. In particular, some Antifederalists maintained that no body could be representative unless it was numerous and close to the people. To some, in fact, even the Senate was not considered to be a representative institution. Rather, as one Antifederalist put it, "This body [the House] is the true representative of the democratic part of the system; the shield and defence of the people."[38] But even the House wasn't representative enough for some Antifederalists. Richard Henry Lee, for instance, maintained that: "The only check to be found in favor of the democratic principle in this system is, the house of representatives; which I believe may justly be called a mere shred or rag of representation."[39]

Such sentiment, however, is derived from a view of the role of representatives as instructed delegates or "mirrors" of their constituencies—a view Publius did not share. Publius' general theory of representation needn't be limited to the House of Representatives or even the legislature as a whole. Rather, all branches of government were to be representative in the American system of free government. As he writes, in the Constitution "the whole power . . . is lodged in the hands of the people, or their representatives and delegates" (8:115). Publius defines republic in *Federalist* 10 as "a government in which the scheme of representation takes place " (10:126), and in number 39 he defines republic as "a government which derives all its powers directly or indirectly from the great body of the people, and is administered by persons holding their offices during pleasure for a limited period, or during good behavior" (39:255). Because all powers were derived from, and were to be exercised according to, the dictates of republicanism, each institution of the new government was to be considered a place of political representation.

Conceiving each political institution under the Constitution as one of representation was based on a certain view of representation and republican government that I have explored above. Before delving further into each branch in particular, however, it may be useful to more explicitly outline Publius' thought on the requirements of political representation.

First, we must be sure of what is clearly not necessary for representation to exist. The representative needn't in any way be "representative" in the sense of being an average citizen who could simply reflect his constituent's opinions and beliefs in government. Neither was it necessary that the representative be beholden to the mandates of his fellow citizens. Indeed, Publius is concerned that these not be the characteristics of representatives. As I have argued, Publius was concerned with establishing a constitutional distance between the government and the citizenry—a distance that would allow the representatives the freedom and independence necessary for the deliberative process. Such a constitutional space was made possible primarily by the extended republic, indirect elections for senators and the president, and relatively lengthy terms with reeligibility.

But would such independence from the people render the new government by definition unrepublican and dangerous to liberty as the Constitution's opponents claimed? Publius believed it would not because the scheme of representation established also provided for the needs of republican safety. Such needs were met at the most basic level by the fundamental fact that all governmental power was recognized as originating from the people themselves. Such power was delegated through the Constitution to those temporarily empowered within the institutional scheme which itself provided for the system of checks and balances outlined in *Federalist* 51. Further safeguards to republican liberty were found in the fact that each member of the House and Senate, along with the president, was to be elected by the people or the people's servants for limited terms and, should it prove necessary, was subject to a process of removal from office.

Perhaps most fundamental to Publius' concept of representation is the distinction that is found between responsiveness and responsibility. While some opponents of the Constitution argued that a representative must be kept responsive to the public's wishes, Publius held responsibility to be the more necessary element. The former would require compliant delegates who would act according to the people's wishes, the latter that the representative be returned periodically to stand the judgment of the people or their servants. It was retroactively the people's voice that was to be heard the loudest and most unfiltered. They were to render judgments on the *effects* of governmental actions, not on the appropriateness or inappropriateness of the proposed measures themselves. Representatives would be held responsible to the people through the electoral process—an element found in each of the institutions.[40] Indeed, as I will show below, on this essential point Publius argued that the unitary office of the presidency was actually more representative than the other institutions as it offered a more intense focus of responsibility on one man than was possible in a numerous body.

The Senate and the presidency as well as the House of Representatives were designed to be representative institutions. They were not, however, designed to be uniformly representative or to bring the same basic elements to government. As Publius tells us, "the several members of government [stand] on as different foundation as republican principles will well admit" (55:339).[41] With our understanding of Publius' concept of representation we can see in *The Federalist* "levels" or "tiers" of representation that correspond to these constitutional institutions. Each of these levels, including the presidency, uniquely contribute to the deliberative republic. Before exploring the representational aspects of the presidency, it is necessary to briefly explore the other major institutions of the deliberative republic, as is required by Publius's own logic of a deliberative republic comprised of separate and equally legitimate representative institutions.

The House of Representatives

Clearly, the institution established by the Constitution of 1787 that was to be closest to the people themselves was the House of Representatives. The members of the House were to be the only members of the new government to be elected directly by the people and the members would be elected from the smallest constituency and for the shortest term of any member of the federal government. They are "the immediate representatives of the people" (58:350). But, what does Publius have in mind by the phrase "immediate representatives"?

In refuting charges by the Antifederalists that the Constitution would serve "the elevation of the few on the ruins of the many," Publius returns to his argument in essay 10 when he assures us that to extend the size of the constituency of each representative is to help insure the requisite "fit characters." "Reason assures us that as in so great a number a fit representative would be most likely to be found" (57:343). And why will the man of fit character be elected by the people? Because the "object of popular choice" will be "every citizen whose merit may recommend him to the esteem and confidence of his country" (57:344). Publius appeals to his understanding of human nature and experience to refute the Antifederalist position "that a diffusive mode of choosing representatives of the people tends to elevate traitors and to undermine public liberty" (57:347). Contrary to those who find in *The Federalist* an uncompromisingly Hobbesian view of man, the public is seen here to have at least some degree of virtue that enables it to see and elect men of upright character and to render mature judgments on the effects of governmental actions.[42]

Composed of members directly elected by the people who have to return for their vote every two years, the structure of the House provided most directly for the expression of republican jealousy. The people have direct control of the House—at least they control the makeup of the House and can change that composition biennially. But, as we have seen, the extended republic helps distance the members from their constituents' opinions and interests and limits the people's control of the operations of the House. Such independence is essential to the deliberative process.

While not beholden to constituency opinion, the special contribution of the House does involve parochial interests.[43] Representatives are not only to bring their uncommon virtue and good judgment to the deliberative process but are also to bring a knowledge of the conditions and interests of their local constituency. Publius tells us that the "representative ought to be acquainted with the interests and circumstances of his constituents" (56:339). Such knowledge brought to the deliberative process and reported to the other representatives enhances the quality of the discussion and the legislative product that is the result.[44] The outcome is that, through the deliberative process, the members collectively "will provide a picture of the whole so that, unlike an ordinary constituent, the representative can weigh and measure with greater knowledge and certainty the impact of particular policies upon the whole country, not just one section or district."[45]

The Senate

Further insulated from the passions that may from time to time sweep through the people, the Senate stands as a stabilizing force against legislation emanating from passions and temporary interests. Any popular influence on the Senate must first pass through the state legislatures, themselves a chosen body of citizens. The mode of election for senators also contributes to the upright character of its occupants. Election by the state legislatures rather than the people at large would favor a deliberate choice encouraging "a select appointment" (62:364).

As Publius argues about the electoral college method of electing the president, the state legislatures "will in general be composed of the most enlightened and respectable body of citizens" who will turn their attention and their votes "to men only who have become the most distinguished by their abilities and virtue, and in whom the people perceive just grounds of confidence" (64:376). The result would be the election of men who "will always be of the number of those who best understand our national interests, whether considered in relation to the several states or to foreign nations, who are best able to promote those interests, and whose reputations for integrity inspires and merits confidence" (64:376).

The Senate will provide a "due sense of national character" to the system that will help protect the Republic from "unenlightened and variable policy" (63:369). Essentially, the senators bring three primary elements to the policy-making process: their enlightened characters, the knowledge of national and international affairs that is derived from combining their enlightened character and their extended time in office, and stability. These elements are beneficial because there are times when the people "may call for measures which they themselves will afterwards be the most ready to lament and condemn" (63:371). In such times when the public is "stimulated by some irregular passion," Publius tells us of the Senate, "such an institution may be sometimes necessary as a defense to the people against their own temporary errors and delusions" (63:370-371).

The Senate's special sense of national character is a stabilizing element in government that provides a check on the mutable and sometimes unenlightened legislation that may from time to time emanate from the lower house. Publius concedes that on occasion those representatives closest to the people could bow to their temporary delusions, mislead them through demagogic appeals, or sacrifice the public interest to more parochial ones. Exercising their independent reason through deliberation, the Senate is here to step in and delay the progress of such legislation until time allows the cool and deliberate sense of the community to return to the public councils. All legislation, after all, must be considered by the institution embodying this "national character" before becoming law. The Senate houses representatives, drawn from the individual states, of order and stability, rather than immediate popular majorities.

The Presidency

In explaining and defending the aspects of the Constitution relating to the presidency, Publius realized his chief task would be to undermine that type of republican jealousy that had manifested itself in the criticisms that found in the office an embryonic monarchy. To that end he dedicates *Federalist* 69 in particular. The thread that runs through this essay is the concern to develop an understanding that there can be a middle ground between a monarchical institution, on the one hand, and a completely weak, compliant, and perhaps even fragmented executive authority, on the other.

That middle ground he shows to be occupied by the American presidency through a comparison of the characteristics and powers of Great Britain's monarchy, New York's own governor, and the presidency. That is to say, Publius here lays the foundation for the concept of a representative executive authority.

The officer most removed from the people themselves was to be the chief magistrate of the Republic. Governing over one extended land and elected by electors drawn from every state, he alone among elected officials would have an entirely national origin. Despite his distance from the people and what critics termed a despotic nature, the president, nonetheless, was considered a representative according to Publius' republicanism. As with the House, but to a greater extent, the elements of the extended republic would tend to distance the president from parochial interests and the diversity of interests within the Union would encourage his independence from any one or combination of them. He would occupy different constitutional and political ground from that of both houses of the legislature, which may afford a different perspective on governmental measures and the needs of the nation. Despite the differences with the legislative bodies, however, the president's origin, powers, and the nature of his responsibilities make him a central representative in the American political system.

The mode of electing the president was particularly capable of producing the choice of an enlightened and upright citizen possessing those virtues and qualities with which we have seen Publius so concerned. Though the sense of the people is desirable in the choice of the president, they were not to make the final decision themselves. Here again we see Publius' distinction between the voice of the people themselves and the voice as it is expressed by a chosen body of citizens.

> It was . . . desirable that the immediate election should be made by men most capable of analyzing the qualities adapted to the station and acting under circumstances favorable to deliberation, and to a judicious combination of all the reasons and inducements which were proper to govern their choice. A small number of persons, selected by their fellow-citizens from the general mass, will be most likely to possess the information and discernment requisite to so complicated an investigation (68:393).

This indirect mode of election, like that for the Senate, does not make the presidency less of a republican institution or its holder less of a political representative. In such an electoral situation it would still be true that "the sense of the people [would] operate in the choice of the person to whom so important a trust was to be confided" (68:393).

One dominant interpretation of the electoral college has been that it was designed from the beginning to fail, to permit the legislature to choose the president and vice president. This interpretation finds no support in *The Federalist* and, indeed, it is completely incompatible both with Publius' checks and balances scheme of *Federalist* 51 and with what he says explicitly about the electoral college in Number 68. Rather, the proper functioning of the electoral college can be seen as a microcosm of the proper functioning of the government as a whole. There is no word of the electors being instructed delegates, but they were to exercise their independent judgment to "vote for some fit person for president" (68:394). Neither would the electors meet in a pluralistic free-for-all of passions and interests. A fit character would emerge in the same way as fit legislation would emerge from government—through "men most capable" meeting "under circumstances favorable to deliberation" (68:393).

Being a temporary body established solely for the purpose of electing the president, the electoral college's transient nature further encourages the president's ability to be an independent trustee. He is neither to be dependent upon some permanent independent body nor the House of Representatives for reelection to his post. Either situation would lessen the president's ability to act firmly and with independence, and would undermine the system of checks and balances as well as the president's important role in the deliberative process of government. Here we also might note the length of the president's term—twice that of the House—and the "space" that it creates to encourage independence of judgment and action in the executive.

From such a deliberative body, the choice for president might well be men of the highest character and virtue. In fact, Publius tells us that the process provides a "moral certainty" that the chosen president will seldom be endowed with anything less than the "requisite qualifications"(68:394-395). The electoral method has been so well contrived that it is no exaggeration for Publius to contend "that there will be a constant probability of seeing the station filled by characters pre-eminent for ability and virtue" (68:395). The chief magistracy of the nation was intended to be filled by men of unrepresentative virtue and talents who could make use of them in the process of representative government.

Besides the personal characteristics that the president was to bring to government, what else was he to bring to the representative process?

Perhaps the most important contribution of the president to Publius' republicanism was his energizing of the political system. Publius acknowledges the traditional belief which held "that a vigorous executive is inconsistent with the genius of republican government," but he goes on to argue that in actuality such an institution was absolutely essential to the survival and flourishing of that same republican form of government (70:402).

Publius tells us "Energy in the executive is a leading character in the definition of good government" (70:402). The legislature represents the people and their collective good through "the jarring of parties" that often promotes "deliberation and circumspection," while the executive represents the capacity of the people to act with firmness and vigor when such is necessitated by the changing tides of human affairs (70:405). Such times would obviously include times of war when an energetic executive would be needed to protect the community from foreign powers. An energetic executive also would be necessary as a representative of the nation in dealing with other nations, including negotiating treaties. Justice may also demand an energetic executive who would invoke his authority "to grant reprieves and pardons" both when "good policy" as well as "humanity" would dictate such actions. Here the president as the "dispenser of mercy" acts as the representative of the people's sense that there exists a higher justice than the written laws of the country could fully contain.

Such energy and dispatch would also be essential to "the steady administration of the laws" (70:402). Indeed it is in this capacity of the president as administrative head of the government that Publius specifically seems to attack the "theory" that an energetic executive is inconsistent with representative government. "A feeble executive implies a feeble execution of the government. A feeble execution is but another phrase for a bad execution; and a government ill executed, *whatever it may be in theory, must be, in practice, a bad government"* (70:402—emphasis added).

Not only was this characteristic of the presidency necessary for the execution of the laws and its holder's responsibility as commander in chief, but energy also contributes to the deliberative process of government. An energetic executive is needed as a protection against "irregular and high-handed combinations" that would act unjustly and "to the security of liberty against the enterprises and assaults of ambition, of faction and of anarchy"(70:402). Though the Congress particularly is formed so as to encourage deliberation, the president occupies a central place in the deliberative republic—that of checking, or at least slowing, the progress of legislation not containing the requisite character. It is most important to note on this front that the president's energy is designed to allow him to act with dispatch and quickness when times demand it, but it is also this same characteristic that allows the president to slow the government, cool the passions, and improve the deliberative process.

The legislative power delegated from the people to their representatives is complex and fragmented in American constitutional democracy. The presidency was not meant to be an office simply for administration and the neutral execution of the laws. Rather, the president was given an important role to play in the tricameral division of legislative powers that placed in that office the responsibility of being an institution of legislative representation. As a general rule, the House, the Senate, and the president all must agree in order to pass legislation. If they do not agree amongst themselves, they at least must interact and thereby likely influence one another before changes can occur in law.

The president combines his energy and his independence with legislative powers in the veto and becomes part of the deliberative process for the promotion of the common good. He is given a qualified negative, not an absolute one, that serves both to keep his power within republican limits as well as to put the presidency at the heart of a legislative process designed always to foster circumspection and debate rather than either to facilitate immediate action or to check activity completely. For example, if the president was given no veto power at all, improper legislation could more easily navigate the process and become law. Or, if given an absolute veto, the president would have the power to completely hinder any legislative activity with which he would disagree. As it is, the qualified presidential power of "returning all bills *with objections*" forces the legislature to further deliberate in light of those objections and thus to reconsider what they might have failed to adequately consider the first time around. As Publius notes, "The oftener the measure is brought under examination, the greater the diversity in the situation of those who are to examine it, the less must be the danger of those errors which flow from want of due deliberation, or of those missteps which proceed from the contagion of some common passion or interest" (73:419).

Publius understands that the legislature, although designed to ensure the enactment of proper legistation, cannot always be counted on to act wisely or from the right motives. The qualified veto "establishes a salutary check upon the legislative body, calculated to guard the community against the effects of faction, precipitancy, or of any impulse unfriendly to the public good, which may happen to influence a majority of that body" (73:418). To properly wield his veto, the president is to act energetically and with independence from both the legislature and any popular majority existing at the moment. But what of the challenge that such a power invested in the president may work to "clog" the system and inhibit the passage of needed legislation? Publius' natural conservatism makes him unconcerned about such dispatch in the proliferation of legislation. According to Publius, those who see the danger of mutability in legislation will be able to understand that

> every institution calculated to restrain the excess of lawmaking, and to keep things in the same state in which they happen to be at any given period as much more likely to do good than harm; because it is favorable to greater stability in the system of legislation. The injury which may possibly be done by defeating a few good laws will be amply compensated by the advantage of preventing a number of bad ones (73:419).

Clearly, Publius assumes that the slowing and perhaps even inhibiting of the passage of new laws is as much in the public good as the passage of laws themselves. But, more specifically, to what end is the president to firmly enact this important representative role? Publius is clear on this front and outlines two interrelated representational functions of the president's veto power.

First, consistent with the more limited and democratic interpretation of the checks and balances system, he is to wield the veto in self-defense against a legislature, backed or not by a popular majority, bent on intruding upon the rights of the other constitutional officers and absorbing their powers. In this respect the president is to function as the representative of the people of the Constitution. That constitutional people agreed to constrain and limit their own sovereign power and that of their most popular branch and to subject them both to the needs of a constitutional republic. Publius understood with Tocqueville that a democratic people often fail to understand the necessity of political forms and thereby will readily and imprudently attempt to rid themselves of such constraints.[46] The president was intended to defend the *forms* of constitutional government through his use of the qualified veto.[47] In this respect he was to be a representative not of any current majority but of a transcendent people with a constant interest in the maintenance of constitutionally limited democracy.

Publius makes it clear, however, that the use of the veto was not to be limited to the self-protection of the presidency and the defense of the integrity of the constitutional forms. Rather, Publius writes that a further use of the veto is to furnish "an additional security against the inaction of improper laws" (73:418). Here, as I have alluded to above, the president serves as the representative of the national good, a more long-term and reasonable public than might seem to be represented from time to time in the legislature. In this representative function, the president's most important role is to stave off legislation that might be improved or put aside upon more mature and sedate reflection. He thereby not only encourages further deliberation by the legislature, but may even qualitatively improve the deliberations due to the change in the situation engendered by his veto action and the objections to the legislation he communicated to Congress. In this way, the president as representative is an *ameliorator* of the product of government as well as an executor.

Understanding the special talents and character that the president was to have due to the electoral system from which he would be chosen, along with the energy and firmness with which he was to act, representation still necessitates some degree of safety. This being said, did Publius solely depend on the incumbent's personal traits of character to render the office safe for the maintenance of free government? Though these may provide a degree of safety, Publius is too realistic to rely simply on such a convergence of virtue and power. Rather, he turns the Constitution's opponent's arguments on their heads by contending that it is particularly the elements that they most feared in the presidency that uniquely contribute to its unthreatening nature.

What is needed for the republican safety of the office are "a due dependence on the people, and a due responsibility" (70:403). These two elements of dependence and responsibility are institutionalized in the office so as to render their services, regardless who may occupy that constitutional place. The chief magistrate being "indirectly derived from the choice of the people" (39:255), he was dependent on the people for his election to the post and will be dependent on them to return him.

Responsibility is particularly important to Publius' thought on representative government. *Responsibility* replaces the *responsiveness* of some previous thinkers on representation as the essential nature of the linkage between those represented and the political representative in *The Federalist*. The president, intentionally insulated from popular opinion, was to be responsible for the proper execution of his duties but was not to be responsive to popular majorities. The public would hold the executive in check by engaging in retroactive voting—rendering decisions on the effects of measures already taken by the holder of this public trust. Due responsibility would also be found in the provisions for removal of the president from office through the impeachment proceedings and through the punishment of the individual for misconduct that the rule of law makes available.

The paradox here is that contrary to "that maxim of republican jealousy which considered power as safer in the hands of a number of men than a single man" (70:407), Publius contends that the single executive authority would be more consistent with the needs of representative government than would be a more numerous executive body. To wit, a non-unitary executive would deprive the people of "the two greatest securities they can have for the faithful exercise of any delegated power":

> *first*, the restraints of public opinion, which lose their efficacy, as well on account of the division of the censure attendant on bad measures among a number as on account of the uncertainty on whom it ought to fall; and, *second*, the opportunity of discovering with facility and clearness the misconduct of the persons they trust, in order either to their removal from office or to their actual punishment in cases which admit of it" (70:406-407—emphasis in original).

Along with its unitary nature, the duration of the presidential term and the officer's reeligibility are both essential to the functioning of such a safety mechanism—both also having been contrary to a considerable sentiment concerning the needs of representative government. An adequate duration is needed both as it would tend to encourage the officer to "act his part well" and be necessary to give the people the time needed to adequately judge the actions of the incumbent. That is to say, "a duration of considerable extent" was necessary to give the community "time and leisure to observe the tendency of his measures, and thence to form an *experimental estimate* of their merits" (72:413—emphasis added). Reeligibility to continue in office was necessary to give the officeholder the incentive to right conduct and "is necessary to enable the people, when they see reason to approve of his conduct, to continue him in the station in order to prolong the utility of his talents and virtues, and to secure to the government the advantage of permanency in a wise system of administration" (72:413).

It is a mainstay of contemporary politics that presidents routinely attempt, with validity or not, to claim "mandates" from the people following electoral victories. Is there room in Publius' representative democracy for any such popular mandate? Publius does seem to acknowledge the potential existence of some level of popular mandate for the executive, albeit a limited one. The popular mandate acknowledged in *The Federalist* is essentially negative— one rendered in response to the current situation and past actions, rather than a forward looking one of a more positive nature. In discussing administrative changes that occur after a change of personnel at the top, Publius writes, "where the alteration has been the result of public choice [elections], the person substituted is warranted in supposing that the dismission of his predecessor has proceeded from a dislike to his measures; and that the less he resembles him, the more he will recommend himself to the favor of his constituents" (72:413).

But, as should be clear from what we have seen, *popular* mandates are not the only ones available to the chief executive in the American Republic. Nor would they be the most important. As a representative of the transcendent people of our fundamental compact, the president also has a *constitutional* mandate to defend the forms of our fundamental law and to do his part to insure that good law emerges from the legislative process. To these we can add the more specific mandates that are attached to his particular constitutional powers. If he is to properly live up to these mandates, *The Federalist* realized there would be times when he cannot also represent the existing popular majority. Publius' representational morality affords the necessary room in which constitutional officers may represent without being responsive. The president is a central player in the compound system of representation outlined in the Constitution, and being such, his method of representation is no more, and certainly no less, legitimate than that seen in Congress. Both are essential to the maintenance of the constitutional system and to the responsible reflection of the reasoned will of the public.

Conclusion

Publius was concerned with acquiring *virtuous* representatives who would come to the halls of government and *deliberate* on the means to the promotion of the common good of society. Such representatives necessitate a high degree of independence from their respective constituencies and parochial interests. Though each institution of government is to be made up of independent trustees elevated from the great body of the people, the members of the various institutions are not unidimensionally independent. The public good is promoted not just because the representatives are more virtuous, experienced, and knowledgeable than the people at large, but also because "they operate in an environment that fosters collective reasoning about common concerns."[48] The diversity of the institutions is an essential ingredient to the existence of this environment.[49]

The degrees of independence in each institution contribute to the ability of the deliberative process to formulate just laws and the promotion of the commonweal. But, as Willmoore Kendall has reminded us, there is room in such a system for at least one essential mandate, to "produce *just* policy decisions in a certain manner. . . ."[50] That certain manner is the constitutional system of deliberation I have outlined. A presidency consistent with the needs of representative government is particularly important to this deliberative process.

The office is so established as to encourage independent judgment in the executive—his virtue and knowledge making it likely that he will recognize legislation not in the public interest, and his energy and constitutional powers will allow him to act upon his judgment to slow and improve the deliberative process. For, "servile pliancy of the executive to a prevailing current, either in the community or in the legislature" is a crude and ignorant notion "of the true means by which the public happiness may be promoted" (71:409). The president as representative is an *ameliorator* of the product of government as well as an executor. The president is representative of, and not merely responsive to, popular will. Acting as the representative of the people of the Constitution he also is to act in defense of the *forms* of the Constitution, which properly limit the people's power to immediately enact their will. He is a guardian of the process of free government as well as an active ameliorator of its product.

The president, then, as a single constitutional officer is every bit as legitimate a representative as those in the legislative body, due to the necessary ingredients he brings to the process of government, his share in the legislative powers delegated by the people, and the republican safety institutionalized in the office. Indeed, one of the great accomplishments of *The Federalist* and the Constitution, which it explained, was to show that an energetic executive was necessary to free government and that such a traditionally non-republican institution could be made consistent with the jealousies and needs of representation.

Notes

1. *The Federalist Papers* were written by Alexander Hamilton, James Madison, and John Jay under the pseudonym of "Publius." I adopt their pseudonym here as they intended as I find there to be no essential differences between the authors on the central questions of our concern. For a solid and critical consideration of Publius' supposed "Split Personality," see George W. Carey, *In Defense of the Constitution,* Revised and Expanded Edition (Indianapolis: Liberty Fund, 1995).

2. For another contemporary call to take such a "systematic perspective" on such issues, see Jeffrey K. Tulis, *The Rhetorical Presidency* (Princeton, N.J.: Princeton University Press, 1987).

3. All subsequent quotations from *The Federalist* are from *The Federalist Papers*, Isaac Kramnick, ed. (England: Penguin Books, 1987).

4. Hanna F. Pitkin, *The Concept of Representation* (Berkeley: University of California Press, 1967), 145.

5. It may be argued here that in the Tenth *Federalist* Publius is not making a distinction between types of representative styles but rather is simply contrasting democracy with republican (representative) government. Though this is true, it seems obvious that the distinction is not being made simply between a pure democracy and *any* governmental structure based on *any* conception of representation. Rather, the distinction Publius makes is between a pure democracy and the type of representative government intended for the American republic—i.e., Publius' conception of representatives which is our focus here.

6. It is true Publius recognizes the possibility that enlightened men would not always be at the helm of government but, as I've noted below, the extension of the sphere makes it more likely that they will, in fact, hold power.

7. See the discussion of Burke's views on representation in the previous chapter. I do not intend to infer any direct or indirect influence of Burke on the Founding Fathers. For a recent consideration of Burke's influence see Russell Kirk, *The Conservative Constitution* (Washington, D.C.: Regnery Gateway, 1990).

8. See *Federalist* 49, 50, 55, 58, 62, 63, and 71.

9. Edmund Burke, "A Letter to John Farr and John Harris, Esqrs. -Sherrifs of the City of Bristol on the Affairs of America," in Peter J. Stanlis, ed., *Edmund Burke: Selected Writings and Speeches* (Chicago: Regnery Gateway, 1963), 187.

10. Burke, 1963, 187.

11. Martin Diamond, "Democracy and *The Federalist*: A Reconsideration of the Framer's Intent," *American Political Science Review* (March 1959), 52-68.

12. Harvey C. Mansfield Jr., "Constitutional Government: The Soul of Modern

Democracy," *The Public Interest* (Winter 1982), 57.

13. Robert A. Dahl, *A Preface to Democratic Theory* (Chicago: University of Chicago Press, 1956).

14. Dahl, 1956, 10.

15. Pitkin, 1967, 190.

16. Pitkin, 1967, 190-191.

17. Pitkin, 1967, 197.

18. Pitkin, 1967, 197.

19. Pitkin, 1967, 196.

20. For two of the few scholars who have emphasized the importance of this point see David F. Epstein, *The Political Theory of* The Federalist (Chicago: University of Chicago Press, 1984); and Larry Arnhart, "The Deliberative Rhetoric of *The Federalist*," *Political Science Reviewer* (Spring 1990), 49-86.

21. For a consideration of the Twentieth Century revisionism of the Founding Fathers, see the Introduction in George W. Carey, *In Defense of the Constitution,* Revised and Expanded Edition (Indianapolis: Liberty Fund, 1995), 3-17.

22. See also, *Federalist* 22, 37, 45, 51, 57.

23. On the ends of government in *The Federalist*, see Thomas G. West, "The Rule of Law in *The Federalist*," in *Saving the Revolution: The Federalist Papers and the American Founding*, Charles R. Kesler, ed. (New York: The Free Press, 1987), 163-167.

24. Diamond, 1959, 68.

25. Diamond, 1959, 68.

26. A similar argument is also made in the third paper in which Publius states, "more general and extensive reputations for talents and other qualifications will be necessary to recommend men to office under the national government"; the result would be "that the administration, the political councils, and the judicial decisions of the national government would be more wise, systematic, and judicious than those of individual states"(3:95). See also (27:201-202).

27. On a similar point see Charles R. Kesler, "*Federalist* 10 and American Republicanism," in Kesler, 1987, 35-39.

28. See George W. Carey, *The Federalist: Design for a Constitutional Republic* (Urbana & Chicago: University of Illinois Press, 1989). Carey would seem to dissent from my contention of the importance of the individual virtue of representatives to Publius. He contends that there will be unattached or "mediating groups" of legislators on a given issue who, though being "not enlightened statesmen, are in a position to act as if they were" (40). This view, though an important step away from the pluralist interpretation, does not offer a satisfactory accounting for Publius' admonishing of virtue in the representatives. Under Carey's reading, it would seem that on any issue that all the representatives would have an interest in, there would be no one to even "act as if" they were enlightened

statesmen.

29. Neal Riemer, "James Madison's Theory of the Self-Destructive Features of Republican Government," *Ethics* (October 1954), 38.

30. Max Farrand, ed., *The Records of the Federal Convention of 1787* (New Haven: Yale University Press, 1937), Vol I, 152.

31. See, for example, Dahl, 1956, and David B. Truman, *The Governmental Process* (New York: Knopf, 1951).

32. It is well beyond the scope of this chapter to embark on a full expounding and analysis of the pluralist interpretation of *The Federalist*. However, those elements that directly relate to my topic are considered here and elsewhere in the chapter. For a solid rejection of this approach, see Kenneth L. Grasso, "Pluralism, The Public Good and the Problem of Self-Government in *The Federalist*," *Interpretation* (May/September, 1987), 323-345. Besides those I take up directly in the text, for contemporary pluralist interpretations see Steven Kelman, *Making Public Policy: A Hopeful View of American Government* (New York: Basic Books, 1987); George F. Will, *Statecraft as Soulcraft* (New York: Simon & Schuster, 1983); Irving Kristol, *On the Democratic Idea in America* (New York: Harper & Row, 1972).

33. I owe the genesis of my idea here to Arthur Maass, *Congress and the Common Good* (New York: Basic Books, 1983).

34. Grasso, 1987, 333.

35. See Paul Eidelberg, *A Discourse on Statesmanship* (Urbana, Ill.: University of Illinois Press, 1974), 214-215. Here Eidelberg delineates the other half of the solution and finds it to be an educative function for virtuous representatives. "The other half required the education of public-spirited men who would in turn cultivate among the people 'those national feelings, those liberal sentiments, and those congenial manners'—in short, those ingredients of friendship so difficult to achieve in any society, let alone one so large and diverse as that which Madison sought to unify."

36. See Eidelberg, 1984, 179.

37. Grasso, 1987, 338.

38. Cincinnatus IV (Arthur Lee), "To James Wilson, Esquire, New York Journal, 22 November 1787," reprinted in John P. Kaminski and Richard Leffler, *Federalist and Anti-Federalist: The Debate over the Ratification of the Constitution*, Vol. I (Madison, Wis.: Madison House, 1989), 72.

39. Richard Henry Lee, "To Governor Edmund Randolph, 16 October 1787, New York." Reprinted in Kaminski and Leffler, 154.

40. On the electoral process becoming "the foundation and measure of representation," see Gordon S. Wood, *The Creation of the American Republic, 1776-1787* (New York: W.W. Norton, 1972), 447.

41. On all three branches of the government being representative, see Gordon S. Wood, *Representation in the American Revolution*, Jamestown Essays on

Representation (Charlottesville, Va.: University of Virginia Press. 1969). "Indeed since all governmental power in a republic, whatever its nature or function, was something of a delegation by the people, all parts of a republican system now seemed representative, essentially indistinguishable in their character"(53). See also Wood, 1972, 447-448.

42. On Publius' *realistic* view of human nature, see James P. Scanlan, "*The Federalist* and Human Nature," *The Review of Politics* (October 1959), 657-677.

43. There seems to be a convincing argument that the arena of government in which parochial interests were to be actively voiced and promoted were the state legislatures. The federal structure serves as a "double representation" of the people dividing the functions of representatives between those in the state and those in the national government. See Robert J. Morgan, "Madison's Theory of Representation in the Tenth *Federalist*," *The Journal of Politics* 37 (1974), 860-861; and William Kristol, "The Problem of the Separation of Powers *Federalist* 47-51," in Charles R. Kesler, 126-127.

44. On the representatives "reporting" the particular interests see Epstein, 1984, 155.

45. Carey, 1989, 42.

46. See Alexis de Tocqueville, *Democracy in America* (New York: Vintage Books, 1990), Volume II, Book IV, Chapter VII, 325-326. For an important contemporary consideration of the importance of constitutional forms, see Harvey C. Mansfield, Jr., *America's Constitutional Soul* (Baltimore: The Johns Hopkins University Press, 1991).

47. On this point see Harvey C. Mansfield, Jr., *Taming the Prince: The Ambivalence of Modern Executive Power* (New York: The Free Press, 1989), 279-291.

48. Joseph Bessette, "Deliberative Democracy: The Majority Principle in Republican Government," in *How Democratic is the Constitution?*, Robert Goldwin and William A. Schrambra, eds. (Washington, D.C.: American Enterprise Institute, 1980), 105.

49. Samuel H. Beer makes a similar point in *To Make A Nation: The Rediscovery of American Federalism* (Cambridge, Mass.: Harvard University Press, 1993). "For a government which attempts to coordinate the interests of the many, a separation of powers, each of which represents the same social body, the people at large of the nation, heightens the probability that discussion and decision will realize the economies of generalization by focusing on common interests requiring similar treatment" (287).

50. Willmoore Kendall, "The Two Majorities in American Politics," reprinted in Kendall, *The Conservative Affirmation in America* (Chicago: Gateway Editions, 1985), 42.

3

Whiggism and Presidentialism in U.S. History

The Founding Fathers had established a "system" of representation rather than centering it in one institution or branch of government. The separation of powers scheme created a complex republic in which public officials in each branch of government would play important representative functions—would be legitimate and independent servants of the people. But this conception of representative government was not the traditional one that preceded the Constitution's writing either in practice or in theory. Neither was it the one that has at all times dominated the American experience under the Constitution. Indeed, with regard to the presidency, ours is a history of ambivalence toward executive power—both loved and hated, trusted and feared.[1] This chapter explores the two positions at either extreme from the balanced and compound understanding of representation found in the Constitution as explicated in *The Federalist*.

On one extreme is the traditional whig mistrust of executive power. To such an understanding, representation is only possible in a numerous and locally elected legislative body. At the other extreme is the doctrine that finds the people's will best expressed in the unitary and nationally elected executive authority. Such a presidocentric conception underlies the writings of Woodrow Wilson on the presidency, the practice of the modern plebiscitary presidency, and the "cult of the presidency" literature best expressed in Richard Neustadt's 1961 classic *Presidential Power*.

This chapter explores some of the historic manifestations of these two positions on presidential power and representation in America, and particularly focuses on the development of the political theory that underlies each of these positions. To a great extent, the presidency has been the office the people have wanted it to be. As Barbara Hinckley has demonstrated, the presidency's "open" character makes it uniquely susceptible to becoming what people expect. This symbolic circle is closed with the realization that presidents and other political leaders, teachers, and writers all affect our expectations of the presidency and its incumbents. As Hinckley puts it, "By degrees almost imperceptible, as one kind of symbol replaces another, the office is transformed."[2] It is with this realization that we must be concerned with the symbolic representation of the office given by presidents, academics, and popular culture through American history. It is not "mere theory" we are exploring but the actual and fundamental limits and possibilities of our political institutions.

Beginning with the controversy over the Second Bank of the United States during Andrew Jackson's presidency, this chapter explores some of the most important conceptions of the office and the values and ideas that underlie them. I begin with the Jackson presidency because it marked a real crisis point in our history under representative government. In the President's arguments and those of his Senate critics, we are starkly confronted with examples of both understandings. I move from there to considering the underlying whiggism found in the various proposals that had been forwarded for a plural executive authority. On the other hand, the presidocentric conception of representation that has informed much of the theory and practice of twentieth century American governance can be traced particularly to the writings and practice of Woodrow Wilson. It is to the twenty-eighth President's thought that I then turn. The "cult of the presidency" literature of mid-century also has greatly contributed to the underlying theory of the contemporary plebiscitary presidency, and I explicate the writings of Richard Neustadt as particularly important on that front. The chapter ends with a discussion of two important manifestations of the whig conception of representation during the twentieth century.

Jackson vs. Congress and the Crisis of Representation

The clash between these two opposing views on the place of representation in the government can be seen in its most acute form in the early years of the fourth decade under the Constitution. The 1830s, and especially the election of 1832, were marked by an enthusiasm for democracy and the rule of the people that had not previously been seen in America. In the election of 1832 both major parties for the first time adopted the more democratic convention system for choosing presidential candidates and further encouraged the participation of the masses in politics. The Democrats and the National Republicans lavished wild praise upon the people for their wisdom and virtue. All had come to accept the notion that the masses should rule—an acceptance that did much to encourage the further democratization of American politics in the years to come.[3]

It is no accident that such a clash between Congress and the presidency would coincide with the great democratization of the American political ethos that occurred in the 1830s. Such a new revolutionary celebration of the mass electorate and their right to rule more directly would almost surely necessitate a rethinking of the institutions of popular control and their relationship to one another. The great clash would come when more than one institution would claim completely to represent the people—thereby claiming to be the guardian of their interests and the holder of their newly legitimized power.

Andrew Jackson's election in 1828 arguably made him the first popularly elected president in U.S. history—a fact that strengthened his conviction that as president he bore a direct mandate fresh from the source of all political sovereignty.[4] Indeed, in his "First Annual Message," Jackson urged amending the Constitution to further reduce the space between the president and the public by allowing them to directly choose their chief magistrate.[5] In office, Jackson's assertion as the people's representative came to a head in his conflict with Congress over the Second Bank of the United States. Robert Remini has called Jackson's veto of the bank bill on July 10, 1832, "the most important veto ever issued by a president."[6] Before Jackson, presidents generally held to a very narrow interpretation of the veto power—it was to be employed only when the president believed a piece of legislation to be unconstitutional. To the contrary, Jackson held the president to be empowered to reject any bill he felt would not be in the nation's interest, and, in his eight years in the presidency, he vetoed more bills than had been vetoed in the forty previous years combined.[7]

Jackson's conflict would not come with the House, as the Democrats held a substantial majority in that body. Rather, the Senate, where the Whigs led by Clay and Webster were stronger and formed an alliance with southern Democrats like John C. Calhoun, would offer the strongest resistance to the expansive view of presidential power that was based on Jackson's conception of representation. The hostilities between the Senate and the president that followed Jackson's veto of the bank bill, his subsequent dismissal of the Secretary of the Treasury, and his removal of public funds from the Bank of the United States without congressional approval, provide an enlightening case study that illuminates the intellectual foundations of these two basic theses on representation and executive power.

After months of consideration, on March 28, 1834 the Senate passed a resolution chastising the president for actions that they found unconstitutional and despotic. They resolved that "the President, in the late Executive proceedings in relation to the public revenue, has assumed upon himself authority and power not conferred by the constitution and laws, but in derogation of both." President Jackson responded to the Senate on April 15 with a long and detailed protest of that body's actions that he "respectfully requested" be placed in its Journals (it was read to the Senate on the seventeenth of that month.) The themes and doctrines found in Jackson's message of protest and the heated responses from the Senate floor provide extraordinarily rich representations of the two polar predilections under discussion here.[8]

Jackson argued that he was duty-bound to make such a protest because of the oath he had taken to "preserve, protect, and defend the constitution of the United States" and because it was particularly the place of his office to defend the fundamental law. Though couching his arguments in language maintaining the traditional balance between the institutions of government, all of which are "the servants of the American people" with a "common superior," Jackson's language and doctrines are really more radical for the time than he let on.[9] What he actually articulates is an understanding of the presidency that places the president as the undisputed sovereign in the executive aspects of government, while at the same time forging a powerful link between the officeholder and the American people. Each of these ideas made the congressional whigs cringe with a fear of monarchical despotism.

Jackson writes that the "executive power is vested exclusively in the President, except that in the conclusion of treaties and in certain appointments to office, he is to act with the advice and consent of the Senate."[10] But what role would the Senate here play in wielding these limited executive powers? At least in the realm of appointments—of most concern in the controversy— the Senate was to be "*merely* a check upon the Executive power of appointment."[11] And not enough of a check as to infringe on the president's "right to employ agents of his own choice to aid him in the performance of his duties, and to discharge them when he is no longer willing to be responsible for their acts."[12] Jackson hereby considerably lowers the role of Congress in the actual governance of the country's business by directly limiting the Senate's place in the choice of governmental officials and by placing all *responsibility* for the executive branch upon himself as president. More to the point, with responsibility follows representation.

Jackson makes it clear that the secretaries in the executive branch are not representatives of the people but are responsible only to the president. The president, himself being responsible to the people, is thereby the only representative figure in the executive branch of the national government. This seemingly limited assertion would not be a terribly revolutionary idea. If there was a representative in the executive branch, who would deny it would be the president? But Jackson does not so limit his claims. Indeed, he seems deliberate in his omission of the qualifier "in the executive branch" in his claim that, "The President is the direct representative of the American people."[13]

In fact, while Jackson carefully builds a case for his responsibility directly to the people and thereby his title of their representative, he also endeavors to undermine any claim the Senate and its members might have to that most noble title in a democratic republic. While the president has been chosen by the people and is responsible to them, Jackson finds the Senate to be chosen by electors other than the people and elected for extended terms—making them not directly responsible to and not representative of the people.

If the censures of the Senate be submitted to by the President, the confidence of the people in his ability and virtue, and the character and usefulness of his administration will soon be at an end, and the real power of the Government will fall into the hands of a body holding their offices for long terms, not elected by the people, and not to them directly responsible.[14]

The members of the Senate "represent, not the people, but the States," and their extended tenure, Jackson argues, leaves them but remotely responsible even in that capacity.[15]

But Jackson goes even further to outrage the whigs and to offend their sentiments on the representational morality of free government. The president employs his theoretical understanding of his place to maneuver himself closer to the people themselves by going over Congress' head directly to them. In claiming the support of the public, the president claimed an electoral mandate stemming from the last election and "the solemn decision of the American people."[16] He also quoted at length from state resolutions urging their officials in Washington to work against the rechartering of the Bank—thereby castigating those Senators who did not act "in accordance with the sentiments of the legislatures."[17] Indeed, it was immediately understood in Congress that this "protest" was primarily meant for public consumption, to garner public support and sympathy for Jackson against Congress. Immediately upon the protest having been read, Senator Poindexter rose to his feet to condemn the president's imprudent appeal to the public.

> This effort to denounce and overawe the deliberations of the Senate may properly be regarded as capping the climax of that systematic plan of operations which for several years past has been in progress, designed to bring this body into disrepute among the people, and thereby remove the only existing barrier to the arbitrary encroachments and usurpations of executive power.[18]

The Whigs Respond

The whigs in the Senate wasted no time and spared no words in responding to Jackson's message of protest. Henry Clay, Daniel Webster, and the other opponents of the president saw in his actions no less than a declaration of war against the Senate and the constitutional system of representative government itself. Senator Preston told his colleagues on May 6, 1834: "This protest of the poor old man, is, throughout, war to the knife, and the knife to the hilt, against the Senate."[19] In their speeches can be found many of the most important doctrines and values that underlie the whigs' understanding of congressionally-centered representation and their consummate fear of the ambitious executive.

To the whigs in the Senate, the current battle with Jackson was but one in the age-old contest "to rescue liberty from the grasp of Executive power."[20] Daniel Webster told the Senate on May 7 that "On the long list of the champions of human freedom, there is not one name dimmed by the reproach of advocating the extension of Executive authority; on the contrary," he went on, "the uniform and steady purpose of all such champions has been to limit and restrain it."[21] The danger was clear and present. Jackson's quest for power and his claim to be *the* representative of the people might well lead, it was feared, to an American president's repeating Napoleon's repetition of the declaration of Louis XIV: "I am the state!"[22] A new dictator was making his move with appeals to being *the* legitimate expression of the nation's will.

In the conflict between the Senate whigs and President Jackson, we can note several important differences that animated their various stands on the issues of power and representation in the American regime. They, in one way or another, and to one degree or another, have remained important elements in related debates up to the current century.

First, and perhaps most importantly at the time, Jackson and his opponents in Congress held to vastly different fundamental views on the nature of representation. The first essential question of representation must always be: who is it that is to be represented? On this count, the two sides disagreed widely. To Jackson, "the people" were to be represented; a "people" of the United States of America who were scattered over an extended republic and yet were more than capable of possessing a single mind—an interest that transcended the various boundaries within the nation. Jackson, as the single head of government, fashioned himself the direct representative of this people—in his unity was embodied the essential unity of the nation.

To one degree or another, Jackson's opponents held to a different understanding of the entity worthy of representation in a free government. There was more than a mass national populace to be represented, if that was even possible at all. While the membership of the House represented the people in their local communities, "The members of the Senate are representatives of the States" said Daniel Webster, "and it is in the Senate alone that the four-and-twenty States, as political bodies, have a direct influence in the Legislative and Executive powers of this Government."[23] South Carolina's John C. Calhoun made the case for the representation of the people of the individual states even more clearly in his challenge to the Jacksonian doctrine.

> He [Jackson] tells us again and again, with the greatest emphasis, that he is the immediate representative of the American people. He the immediate representative of the American people! I thought the President professed to be a State rights man . . . that he believed that the people of these States were united in a constitutional compact, as forming distinct and sovereign

communities; and that no such community or people, as the American people, taken in the aggregate existed. I had supposed . . . that the American people are not represented in a single department of the Government; no, not even in the other House, which represents the people of the several States, as distinct from the people in the aggregate . . . yet he claims to be not only the representative, but the immediate representative of the American people. What effrontery! What boldness of assertion![24]

The American people are not just some undifferentiated mass, Jackson's opponents argued. Rather, the American nation is comprised of variety that equally deserved representation. Besides, Calhoun argued, the president, despite his claim to be close to the people, was not elected directly by them. The legislatures that elected him and the rest of the Senate, he further reasoned, are actually more representative of the people than is the electoral college, the logic of which would put the people closer to the Senate than to the president.

Along with variety and complexity within the body to be represented in government, Webster and the others also argued for complexity within government as opposed to what they perceived to be Jackson's quest for simplicity and concentration. Here the whig opponents of Jackson were reiterating Publius' doctrine that tyranny was the accumulation of all powers in the same hands, regardless by what methods those hands came to their position of authority.[25] They believed they were fighting to defend the constitutional system that had established a system of separated powers and checks and balances to limit the ability of any one aspect of government to make encroachments upon the public liberty.[26] "Nothing is more deceptive or more dangerous," spoke Daniel Webster, "than the pretense of a desire to simplify government." "The simplest governments are despotisms;" he went on, "the next simplest, limited monarchies; but all republics, all governments of law, must impose numerous limitations and qualifications of authority, and give many positive and many qualified rights."[27] On the contrary, the spirit of presidentially-centered representation that Webster saw as Jackson's agenda, and that would later guide the thought of those like Woodrow Wilson and Richard Neustadt, is against the complexity, fortifications, and limitations that the spirit of liberty seemed to demand. The emphasis is rather upon overcoming these barriers in the name of presidential representation of "the people as a whole." To the whigs, simplicity in government was the doorway to despotism, to the Jacksons and the Wilsons it was the pathway to an invigorated democracy.

Two other closely related themes were articulated by the opponents of presidential power and representation. First, they made a direct challenge to the president's claim to be "responsible" to the people—on the basis of which he could claim his special representational role. And second, they made a direct and unambiguous challenge to the president's attempt to forge a special relationship with the American people. They realized these two elements of the president's program would, if successfully developed into accepted constitutional morality, undermine Congress' place in government and legitimacy with the American people and lead to the simplification of the complex republic into government by executive.

In his protest, Jackson as president claimed to occupy the sole place of responsibility in the executive branch of government. But to whom is the president responsible? The president is, Jackson argued, "elected by the people and responsible to them," not only for his own actions, but for the activities of the other executive officers as well.[28] To this claim the president's opponents raised a number of objections. Calhoun objected that the president's responsibility is not limited to the people, but extends to the legislature as well. That is, where the legislative department's mission was a deliberative one that would end with the passage of legislation, the president's was limited to ascertaining what that law was and then carrying it into effect. In this capacity, Calhoun argued, the president is to be responsible to Congress as much as to those who indirectly participated in his election. Here Calhoun has articulated the basic assumption of those who have historically taken the congressionally-centered view of representative government.[29]

Daniel Webster rose to his feet on May 7, 1834, to lay down a direct challenge to the underlying premises of Jackson's doctrine of responsibility—a doctrine that encapsulates the foundation of the modern conception of the plebiscitary presidency. What does the president mean that he is "responsible," Webster asked rhetorically. He then noted two possible types of responsibility. First, the president could mean legal responsibility. But clearly this is not the doctrine of his protest, for the president is not saying that he is impeachable or otherwise punishable for the actions of others in the executive branch. On such a basis then, the president could not claim that all are his personal agents.

The avenue of responsibility that Jackson does assert is the one running directly between himself as president and the American people. As Webster puts it, the president's claim is no more than "merely responsibility to public opinion."[30] In explaining Jackson's thoughts, Webster also describes with amazing accuracy the conception of responsibility that has guided the presidency in our own day. "It is a liability to be blamed; it is the chance of becoming unpopular, the danger of losing a re-election. Nothing else is meant in the world. It is the hazard of failing in any attempt or enterprise of ambition."[31] To whig thought, such "responsibility" is no real responsibility at all. Indeed, such weak and ineffectual chains have historically been broken by ambitious executives and even turned into weapons to be used against popular legislatures. In a spirit that would be rekindled by critics of the "imperial presidency" in the current century, Webster reminds his colleagues and the nation of the dangers to free government from a popular executive who believes his mandate superior to the restraints of the Constitution and the rule of law.

> It is precisely the responsibility under which Cromwell acted, when he dispersed Parliament, telling its members, not in so many words, indeed, that they disobeyed the will of their constituents, but telling them that the people were sick of them, and that he drove them out "for the glory of God, and the good of the nation." It is precisely the responsibility upon which Bonaparte broke up the popular assembly of France. I do not mean, sir, certainly, by these illustrations, to insinuate designs of violent usurpations against the President; far from it; but I do mean to maintain that such responsibility as that with which the protest clothes him, is no legal responsibility, no constitutional responsibility, no republican responsibility; but mere liability to loss of office, loss of character, and loss of fame, if he shall choose to violate the laws and overturn the liberties of the country. It is such a responsibility as leaves every thing in his discretion, and his pleasure.[32]

One might also note the grounds here for another challenge to the plebiscitary presidency of the twentieth century. Though no president has had "designs of violent usurpations," one might find a systematic design for the peaceful usurpation of the legislature's role in the deliberative process of government involved in the presidential strategy of "going public" to pressure Congress to do the president's will.

This indeed is an important aspect of the Senate's whiggish attack on the president's protest. They believed it to be a "breach of privilege" that the president would venture to interfere in the relationship between the Senate and their constituents by charging them "with acting contrary to the will of those constituents."[33] Though appeals of this sort have become routine in the modern presidency, Webster declared with outrage at the time that not even an English sovereign "since Cromwell's time, dared to send such a message. "[34]

But why Jackson's attempt to wedge himself between the people and their elected representatives in Congress? The president's opponents well understood that in a democratic republic popularity and claims of representation mean power. What they saw Jackson attempting is what since Woodrow Wilson has been the standard presidential tactic in modern America—the attempt to "excite the sympathy of the people, whom he seeks to make his allies in the contest."[35] Calhoun saw a particularly ominous sign in the president's strategy.

> But why all this solicitude on the part of the President to place himself near to the people, and to push us off to the greatest distance? Why this solicitude to make himself their sole representative, their only guardian and protector, their only friend and supporter? The object cannot be mistaken. It is prepatory to farther hostilities—to an appeal to the people; and is intended to to [sic] prepare the way in order to transmit to them his declaration of war against the Senate, with a view to enlist them as his allies in the war which he contemplates waging against this branch of the Government.[36]

This conflict between President Jackson and the Senate was not simply for power over governmental actions concerning the Bank and the public revenues. It was more widely a fight over the rights and duties accorded to representatives in the American Republic. It was about the place of the various branches of the national government and the place of the American people in the governing of the nation. The Jacksonian presidency affected those that would follow to the point that though the Whigs elected presidents dedicated to congressional supremacy in the years that followed, even they would not completely live up to the whig doctrines.[37] The case of Jackson's protest and the Senate's subsequent response provides a crucible for understanding the basis for these two basic conceptions of representation in a system of separated powers. It is particularly Jackson's conception of the presidency that would come to dominate the literature and the practice of the office in the twentieth century and the whiggish defense of the traditional constitutional order that would inspire many of its critics.

Whiggism and the Idea of a Plural Executive

One recurrent manifestation of the old whig distrust of executive power was the call for the division of executive authority among several officers. The New Jersey plan at the Constitutional Convention provided for a plural executive with more than one in every four delegates supporting some such division of executive power.[38] It also was a proposal forwarded by a number of the Constitution's opponents during the ratification process, and it was an idea that some have recently revisited.[39] The question of a single versus a plural executive goes directly to the heart of our concern as those who have made such proposals have, directly or indirectly, raised questions about the representative nature of any executive power vested in a single officer such as the U.S. President.

Those who have forwarded such proposals have made several relevant arguments in its favor. Connecticut's Roger Sherman, for one, made the argument that the executive authority was nothing more than the servant of the people's representatives in the legislature where "the supreme will of Society" was held.[40] As such, the executive authority, however it be constituted, is to be beholden to the legislative authority. As the mere servant of the legislature, that branch should be free to decide the number of hands into which the executive power should be placed, Sherman maintained. As merely a practical matter, several hands would be better for this task than one, he further argued at the Constitutional Convention. Such an argument leaves little room for an executive officer to be a representative of the public in his own right.

A more common argument in favor of the division of executive power was one based on the perceived needs of republican safety. The historic whig mistrust of centralized authority and leadership and the dislike of the British monarchy combined against a unitary executive. A unity in the executive was seen to contain, in Edmund Randolph's phrase, "the foetus of monarchy."[41] George Mason argued at the Convention that "If strong and extensive powers are vested in the Executive, and that executive consists only of one person, the government will of course degenerate . . . into a monarchy."[42] Because of their understanding of the frailties of human nature, the Framers perceived power to be safer in several hands than in one. As we have seen in the previous chapter, this is an assertion Publius particularly tries to undermine in *The Federalist.*

The far more interesting, and from our perspective the most important, argument that has been forwarded in favor of a plural executive is one that directly challenges the representative possibilities of a unitary presidency. The argument, a variation of which we saw above in some of the senatorial responses to Jackson, is that a single officer would be incapable of representing an extended republic in any meaningful way. These arguments all directly undermine a central basis of the plebiscitary presidency that would develop in the twentieth century. That is, such a thesis denies the very existence of any national majority worthy of representation. Rather, these arguments find their basis in the conception of the nation as one comprised of a number of distinct and unmergeable interests—the representation of any one of which might well prohibit the representation of the others.

At the Constitutional Convention, North Carolina's Hugh Williamson argued against a unitary executive by noting the difference between the English situation and the one prevailing in America. While the former was more capable of having a single executive because "there is a sameness of interest throughout the Kingdom," in the latter "there is an essential difference of interests between the [northern and southern] States," which meant that, "the power will be dangerous, if the Executive is to be taken from part of the Union, to the part from which he is not taken."[43] George Mason asked his fellow delegates on the fourth of June, 1787, "Have not the different parts of this extensive government, the several States of which it is composed a right to expect an equal participation in the Executive, as the best means of securing an equal attention to their interests?" To make the executive magistracy more representative, Mason proposed a three-man executive, each chosen from a different region, who would "bring with them, into office, a more perfect and extensive knowledge of the real interests of this great Union."[44] There being no real single national interest, a single man would necessarily be incapable of rendering representation to each part of the Republic. Numerous Antifederalists offered similar critiques of the presidency, but such a representational argument against the office was most systematically developed by the ex-Vice President, U.S. Senator from South Carolina, and seminal political thinker John C. Calhoun.

Foreseeing the great constitutional crisis that was fast coming to a boil in the mid-nineteenth century, Calhoun proposed the division of the executive power among two officers as one potential remedy to the crisis. Calhoun's proposal ultimately finds its theoretical justification in his understanding that there are majorities that deserve representation and power other than the one simple national numeric majority of many democratic theories.[45] Practically, Calhoun's concern was to redress the political balance that he saw tipped in favor of the northern section of the country, which he perceived to be a threat to the interests and way of life of the South. His concern was that the North had become so large that it had effectively attained a monopoly on representation in the national government.

To redress such an imbalance would necessitate an organic change—"a change which shall so modify the Constitution as to give to the weaker section, in some one form or another, a negative on the action of the government."[46] What was needed was the creation of an institution in which the two major sections of the country could both find permanent representation in the national government. Calhoun reminds those who would object to such a "radical" alteration that it was just such a concern that led to the creation of the Senate where the small states would be guaranteed equal representation with the larger states. The founders erred only in misreading the nature of societal conflict, it being not primarily between the larger and smaller states but between the two great geographic sections of the nation—north and south.

What Calhoun proposed was the reorganization of the executive department, "so that its powers, instead of being vested, as they are, in a single officer, should be vested in two; to be so elected as that the two should be constituted the special organs and *representatives of the respective sections* in the executive department of government . . . ."[47] And what would the powers and responsibilities of these two officers be? Each individually would be responsible for either domestic or international affairs, which one during a given time to be decided by lot. They would act separately in their administrative duties, but would be forced to concur on legislation passed by Congress—both having to agree to legislation that would give each section a veto over national policy.

Calhoun, in an ominous foretelling of the great crisis that would mature with the ascension of Abraham Lincoln to the presidency just eight years later, goes on to argue that such a proposal for separately elected executives would contribute to the stability and permanence of the Union. One man cannot represent a diverse nation of conflicting interests, he argued. Only when each section felt itself represented in the executive department would "harmony and concord" be restored to the country.

It would make the Union a union in truth—a bond of mutual affection and brotherhood—and not a mere connection used by the stronger as the instrument of dominion and aggrandizement, and submitted to by the weaker only from the lingering remains of former attachment and the fading hope of being able to restore the government to what it was originally intended to be, a blessing to all.[48]

We can see in the historic manifestations of the plural executive argument not only the traditional whig reservations about the concentration of power, especially executive power—but also note a vastly different conception of national representation than the one that would later come to support the aggrandizement of presidential power in the name of democracy in the twentieth century. To Calhoun and those who proposed the plural executive at the founding, there was no monolithic national majority to be represented in government.[49] Rather, a nation of diverse interests requires diversity in its representatives. According to such an understanding, it is easy to comprehend the challenge to the power of a unitary (and, by definition, unrepresentative) chief executive. The plural executive was one important manifestation of a whiggish understanding of American government.

What has come to be called the "traditional presidency" of the nineteenth century was essentially based on this whig conception of the correct balance of power and the position of Congress as the place of representation in the American regime. As Ryan Barilleaux has put it, "Before the rise of the modern presidency, the Chief Executive was not expected always to be the driving force in the government."[50] Indeed, neither was the presidency institutionalized for activism nor was the doctrine of presidential leadership firmly established as democratically and constitutionally legitimate. The extremely limited staff support also left the presidency without the resources that would be needed by a chief executive bent on taking leadership back from the legislature.[51] As for the nineteenth century doctrinal limits on the president's relationship to the people, Andrew Johnson, who delivered about seventy policy declarations on the stump, was the subject of an attempted impeachment, in part because of his rhetorical appeals to the people over the heads of Congress.[52] There was no consistent and accepted theory for the close relationship between the public and their chief executive. This would all change with the radical alterations that came in the twentieth century.

We can summarize some of the basic assumptions underlying the whig sentiment on presidential representation in a few, perhaps overly simplified, observations. First, republican self-government demanded the central place of governmental power and leadership reside in the popular legislature. Congress was the first branch of government. Second, the emphasis is placed on representation through deliberation, which is the role of the legislature, rather than through action and activity, which is more available to the executive magistrate. Third, the entity to be represented is a diverse and varied people with similarly different interests and opinions. Only a locally elected legislature, elected from either districts or states, can possibly represent such a public—the unitary executive can represent only the ephemerally existent mass national public. Fourth, the dedication is to complex government and divided powers rather than to simplicity as the best guarantor of public liberty and good government. Such a dedication was particularly manifest in a deep-seated historical mistrust of executive power, whether found in an hereditary monarch or an elected president.

The Plebiscitary Presidency[53]

The doctrine of presidentially-centered representation certainly has its antecedents before the current century. Besides the presidency of Andrew Jackson, one might, for instance, point to Lincoln's centralization of authority and power in the presidency during the Civil War. As a congressman, Lincoln had denounced the vigorous use of executive power. "Were I President," he had said, "I should desire the legislation of the country to rest with Congress, uninfluenced by the executive in its origin or progress, and undisturbed by the veto unless in very special and clear cases."[54] His actions as president, however, including the suspension of *habeas corpus*, the expansion of the military without consent of Congress, and the spending of millions of dollars of the public money without congressional appropriation, have led some to characterize him as a dictator.[55] In his actions the president seemed to be exercising a type of emergency representation of the people of the Union and perhaps even a higher people than found in the Constitution.[56] As Richard Loss has put it, "He temporarily made the presidency dominant over Congress and the Supreme Court, overrode individual rights and set a precedent for the future."[57]

But the precedent Lincoln set, it must be kept in mind, needn't have extended beyond emergency times of considerable threat to the constitutional order. As president during the greatest crisis in the history of the Republic, Lincoln took all representation unto himself in the name of preserving republican government itself—a temporary secession of the deliberative republic, not its complete abandonment. During such extraordinary times, as Lincoln believed, it may very well be that one institution is the more legitimate holder of the people's will and power—"often a limb must be amputated to save a life; but a life is never wisely given to save a limb."[58] It was his belief that the oath he took to protect the Constitution, as he put it, "imposed upon me the duty of preserving, by every indispensable means, that government—that nation—of which that constitution was organic law."

Woodrow Wilson and the American Presidency

What would develop decades after Lincoln would be the application of this same spirit to the regime during non-crisis times—amputation of the constitutional system of representation in the name of ordinary public policy, not national survival.[59] It is probably no accident that the foremost expositor of this representational role of the presidency lived both in the world of academia and in the White House as president himself. Woodrow Wilson, political scientist and twenty-eighth President of the United States, elaborated a theory of the presidency and its role in American politics that was systematic and revolutionary. He, above all others, systematized and developed the view of the president as *the* center of representation in the American political system. While Lincoln's actions were taken in a time of extraordinary national emergency, Wilson would articulate a doctrine of government that prescribed the centralization of representation and power in the presidency during the everyday course of public policy.

Wilson's early views of American government were set forth in his important work *Congressional Government*, which first appeared in 1885. In it he outlined a picture of our constitutional system, under which Congress necessarily predominated and the presidency was a clearly subordinate and ineffectual office.[60] Nowhere do his views change more starkly than from his early conceptions of representation and the place of the executive in politics. In fact, the most important shift in Wilson's conception of the political system, for our inquiry here, is the replacement by the executive of the representational duties of Congress.

In *Congressional Government*, Wilson delineates four duties of an "effective representative body." First, it ought to *"speak the will of the nation."* Because the people as a whole are scattered and unorganized in society, Congress functions as the "corporate people, the mouthpiece of its will."[61] That is, the representative body of the nation provides a voice for the unorganized voices of mass society; it creates organized meaning out of a collective babble. What Congress did not do so well, however, was to "lead it [the nation] to its conclusions," "utter the voice of its [nation's] opinions," and "to serve as its [the nation's] eyes in superintending all matters of government."[62]

Wilson's second function of leadership is most important because we can see a clear shift of this function from Congress to the president in Wilson's later work. Wilson conceives of the representative body's function of *teaching* or *instructing* the people. In fact, in a fascinating passage, he seems to elevate this instructional representation above the traditional representational role of developing laws and of giving the national sanction to them. "The informing function of Congress," he writes, "should be preferred even to its legislative function."[63] This representative body, functioning as a teacher, is to debate and discuss proposed legislation in a manner that proves interesting and instructive to the people. What he saw in Congress, however, was just the opposite tendency given its lack of a coherent discussion on a unified program. Here Wilson's preference for a parliamentary style of representative government comes strikingly to the fore and, along with it, his denunciation of the Founder's system of the separation of powers. This teaching responsibility of "the assembly which represents the nation" extends also to its supervision of, and discussion concerning, the administration. Wilson writes, "the conscience of every member of the representative body is at the service of the nation. All that he feels bound to know he can find out; and what he finds out *goes to the ears of the country.*"[64] Note here the separation of function Wilson seems to be pointing to between representation and governing.[65] According to Wilson: "It is the proper duty of a representative body to look diligently into every affair of government and *to talk* much about what it sees. It is meant to be the *eyes and the voice*, and to *embody the wisdom and will of its constituents.*"[66]

What is important to see here in Wilson's early view is that he clearly shows Congress to be *the* representative body of the nation (though it may not function in that capacity to his satisfaction), and he differentiates it from executive functions. He also expresses the view that a representative has a pedagogical duty to enlighten the people on the affairs of government—not simply to "re-present" their views or interests. We are concerned with his early views because in their transformation to his presidocentric later conception we find many elements of both dominant views of the president as representative—the whiggish favor for Congress and the presidocentric outlook—that Wilson championed so completely in his later life.

The change in Wilson's thought is readily apparent even upon first glance at his two volumes. Representing his new thinking on the presidency, the executive moves from the back of his first volume to the first institution considered in the second. This change seems important beyond merely the ordering of the chapters. To wit, the logic of *Congressional Government* follows that of the Constitution itself—the House being the first institution, then the Senate and finally the executive office; while the ordering of *Constitutional Government* follows Wilson's new logic of the system with the presidency predominant and the "center" of national leadership and representation.[67] In this change in the form of his writings on American government, we can also see the result of Wilson's theory of constitutionalism. To Wilson, the Constitution was not a document of constant or stable meaning. Neither did it establish a stable and constant political order consistent with the doctrine of checks and balances (though such a "mechanical theory" was the understanding of the Founders, Wilson concedes). Instead, Wilson puts together a conception of the constitutional order that rejects the Founders' intentions and even the very idea of an established constitutional order. By rejecting the "literary theory" of the Constitution, Wilson stitches together a "living Constitution" that is based on the idea of constant adaptation and change by the system to the needs of its environment. The constitutional institutions and the constitutional order that regulates them are subject to fundamental change and growth to "express the changing temper and purposes of the American people from age to age."[68]

But Wilson, who would become the first president to criticize the Constitution, goes even further toward withdrawing from the constitutionalism of the Founders.[69] Not only does the government change with the evolution in the American people and the political needs of the nation, thereby naturally changing from its original principles established in a different time,[70] but he also finds the very ideas and intent of the

Framers to have been fundamentally flawed and untenable from the beginning. The Founders attempted to establish the unestablishable, to found a government on the Newtonianism of the whig theory of politics with separate institutions operating "upon a theory of checks and balances which was meant to limit the operation of each part and allow to no single part or organ of it a dominating force."[71] To Wilson, active political leadership was essential to any government and it must be lodged somewhere so as to bring all the organs of government into concert. Montesquieu's "gravitational theory" of politics, upon which the American Founders based their Constitution, must be doomed because, "No living thing can have its organs offset against each other as checks, and live."[72] To Wilson, Darwin must replace Newton as the basis of politics because,

> Government is not a body of blind forces; it is a body of men, . . . with a common task and purpose. Their cooperation is indispensable, their warfare fatal. There can be no successful government without leadership or without the intimate, almost instinctive, coordination of the organs of life and action. This is not theory, but fact, and displays its force as fact, whatever theories may be thrown across its track.[73]

The politics of the Founders, the constitutionalism embodied in *The Federalist*, was just such a theory thrown across the track of Wilson's political reality. The Constitution is to have no meaning and hence no protections but "the spirit of the age."[74]

The importance for the American presidency is that, following the logic of such a "living constitution," the office has "been one thing at one time, another at another."[75] To Wilson, the Founders might have intended the president to be "only the legal executive," with a veto that "was only his 'check' on Congress," without the function of promoting good law, as it was only "empowered to prevent bad laws."[76] And yet, these constitutional chains were unable to prevent the president from largely escaping (or at least greatly expanding) the tethers of "theory" that bound him. They could not prevent his becoming the "unifying force," the "guide of the nation," and its chief political representative. The Darwinian forces of changing circumstances shaping the Constitution, with the responses of individual officeholders, have made the president more of a political leader and less of an executive officer.[77] As "No one else represents the people as a whole," the president has become the center of representation in the American system; a position that gives him the ability, if power is wielded skillfully and if he rightly interprets the national thought, to become irresistible. Regardless of any constitutional grant of authority, it is the president's direct relation with public opinion that empowers him as the center of government. The *zeitgeist* has replaced the Constitution as the source of institutional position, power, and influence.[78] The constitutional *forms* of representation, according to Wilson, have been rightfully outgrown and replaced by the fluctuating nexus between mass opinion and the sitting president.

Central, then, to the president's position as *the* national representative is his place in speaking for and to the nation. Where we saw the assembly to have a teaching function in Wilson's earlier thought, this responsibility is now transferred to the executive.

> The nation as a whole has chosen him, and is conscious that it has no other political spokesman. His is the only national voice in affairs . . . . His position takes the imagination of the country . . . . When he speaks in his true character, he speaks for no special interest. If he rightly interpret the national thought and boldly insist upon it, he is irresistible.[79]

As a rhetorical teacher, the president is not only the mouthpiece for the opinion of the people but, a "President whom it trusts can not only lead it, but form it to his own views."[80] Here the result also is the undermining of the constitutional (and representational) authority of the other branches of government. If the president can win the public to his view, he writes, "the leadership is his whether the houses [of congress] relish it or not. They are at a disadvantage and will probably have to yield."[81]

Wilson's own position on presidential power comes even more clearly into relief as he writes of the president "at liberty, both in law and conscience, to be as big a man as he can."[82] The Constitution will not set the limit to presidential power, but the only limit will be the officeholders' own capacity; "and if Congress be overborne by him, it will be no fault of the makers of the constitution, —it will be from no lack of constitutional powers on its part, but only because the President has the nation behind him, and Congress has not." The presidency is essentially formless, holding the position that facilitates leadership but nearly completely dependent upon the ambitions and talents of the occupant. "His office," writes Wilson, "is anything he has the sagacity and force to make it."[83] Wilson's is not an "empty" theory of the presidential vessel, however. The outcome he wants is clearly to have an active president leading the nation and "whipping" the individual organs of government into a "vital synthesis" that would negate the Founder's system of checks and balances and the spirit of the separation of powers.[84] He criticizes those "Presidents [who] have deliberately held themselves off from using the full power they might legitimately have used" for failing in just such an endeavor.

In sum, with Wilson we have the establishment of a new doctrine of presidential representation, a doctrine that would have fundamental importance for the political regime in the twentieth century. Wilson elevates the presidency to the center of political leadership and representation in the American system. To do so, he rejects any type of "fixed" meaning for the Constitution and specifically undermines the "original intent" of the Founders. In so doing, Wilson also marks the end of the constitutional people, the constitutional majority seen in *The Federalist*. The public are reduced to being merely the transient majority of a given moment in history—the only people to be given representation in the Wilsonian system are the temporarily empowered numbers. For instance, consider the following statement from Wilson's 1912 presidential campaign on his relationship to the people.

> I have often thought that the only strength of a public man consisted in the number of persons who agreed with him; and that the only strength that any man can boast of and be proud of is that great bodies of his fellow citizens trust him and are ready to follow him. For the business of every leader of government is to hear what the nation is saying and to know what the nation is enduring. It is not his business to judge *for* the nation, but to judge *through* the nation as its spokesman and voice.[85]

With a direct link to this public opinion that the other institutions of government lack, the presidency is able to dominate the government in the name of the "nation as a whole," and toward the end of the efficient synthesis of the political institutions and powers that the original "theory" of the Constitution made separate. By so elevating the presidency, he correspondingly reduces the legitimacy of the other representative institutions. There is room in Wilson's thought for but one expression of popular self-governance, one locus of representation. This same conception of the president's necessary centrality in giving representation to the people is found also in the thought of Wilson's predecessor in the White House, Theodore Roosevelt. "In theory, the executive has nothing to do with legislation. In practice, as things are now, the executive is or ought to be peculiarly representative of the people as a whole. As often as not the actions of the executive offers the only means by which the people can get the legislation they demand and ought to have."[86]

Closely connected with this conception of the office as the focus of representation in the American political system has been the expansive view of presidential power that also is found in Wilson and that was brought into political reality in the presidency of Franklin D. Roosevelt. These two views seem to merge into one in most thinking, as is dictated by their logic. The conception of the presidency as *the* legitimate representative of the people provides ideological cover for the expansion of presidential power and influence in a democracy. And, conversely, in a democracy the center of power and influence should logically be occupied by *the* representative of the people. In Wilson we can see the basic elements found in the thinking of most of the later exponents of the president as the center of representation and leadership in the American polity.

Though risking hyperbole, it might not be terribly far from the mark to liken Wilson's doctrine of presidential government to the reversal of the whig revolution of 1689. Here parliamentary supremacy was recognized over the King. The more numerous legislative body elected by the people alone could represent them, it was believed. In Wilson the tide is turned with the people's direct and exclusive link to the single man in the White House as their only national representative. Wilson's was not a constitutional revolution in the strictest sense; it was a revolution in the understanding of the idea of representative government. It was not based in a formal transference of power, but one that found its support in a skillful and ambitious incumbent in league with the people.

Jeffrey Tulis and others who have written critically about Wilson's rhetorical revolution in the presidency have done valuable work in pointing us to the changing doctrines of presidential speech.[87] These scholars, however, seem to miss the most profound aspect of the post-Wilsonian presidency. Rhetoric is but one central aspect of a new and more important conception of the office. Rather than launching just a "rhetorical presidency," Wilson inaugurated a new representational presidency with rhetoric standing as the primary representational link between the people and their governors. Indeed we might say that Wilson's great contribution was to "raise into consciousness" the doctrine of presidocentric representation—to have made it popularly and ideologically legitimate.[88]

Richard Neustadt and the Political Science Presidency

This view of presidentially-centered representation was systematically legitimated first by Woodrow Wilson and, as is discussed in the chapters that follow, was subsequently institutionalized with the depression- and war-era presidency of FDR. Such is not the whole story, however. Wilson's doctrine of presidocentric representation also became the dominant symbolic representation of the office in the scholarly and popular literature on the modern presidency, thereby reinforcing the doctrine in the popular mind as well as legitimating it for incumbents. Though such a view can be seen at least tangentially in the near gushing praise of the office from scholars like Clinton Rossiter,[89] it was the publication of Richard Neustadt's *Presidential Power*[90] in 1960 which especially saw such a view come to dominate the literature and thereby shape our expectations for the office and its incumbents.

In Neustadt's pathbreaking study we see the general doctrine of presidential representation found in Wilson further developed with practical advice to the would-be power wielder in the White House. Neustadt demonstrates a Wilsonian dedication to the centralization of leadership and power in an activist presidency whose powers are completely dependent upon the relationship between the individual incumbent and the public. The Constitution, we are told, offers the president merely the "vantage points" from which he can attempt to cultivate power. Indeed, in passages rich with symbolism for the presidentially-centered theory of representation, Neustadt reduces all other public actors to the status of presidential "constituencies." The public, his partisans, foreign peoples, let alone Congress and executive officials are not independent and coequal entities. Rather, they are all, the legislature included, dependent upon the president as the represented are dependent upon their empowered representative.[91]

In this system of "separated institutions *sharing* powers," it is particularly the president's responsibility to unite the fragments of power that the Constitution partially distributed.[92] Like Wilson, Neustadt seems to reject both the Framers' understanding that there exists different kinds of power as well as their dedication to the necessity of maintaining at least a significant degree of independent distribution between the branches.[93] Seeing governmental power as an "undifferentiated mass,"[94] Neustadt's prescription is for the active presidential channeling of that power into the president's own hands. The presidency is to become the home of representation as the president ambitiously builds and guards his power and influence over the rest of the government.

But does presidential power necessarily equal presidential representation? Neustadt's logic seems to point to just such a conclusion. The "pursuit of presidential power," Neustadt writes, "is good for the country as well as for him."[95] Elected "by the nation" the president is unmatched by any other officer for judging potential public measures. "Our system affords nobody a better source of clues," Neustadt writes, and he adds, "In the sphere of validity [of public policy] our system can supply no better expert than a President intent on husbanding his influence."[96] Will all such presidents represent wisely? Neustadt writes that "because the President's own frame of reference is at once so all-encompassing and so political, what he sees as a balance for himself is likely to be close to what is viable in terms of public policy." The president is the central legitimate representative authority, Neustadt teaches in the end, because the public good and the good of the individual incumbent are inescapably linked in a unison of mutual needs and aspirations. "What is good for the country is good for the President, and vice versa."[97] In such striking clarity, we see the delegitimization of the other representative branches that is an inescapable part of a presidentially-centered system of representative government.

And how is the president to whip the government into a unified actor for progress and policy? Though on the surface Neustadt seems not to stray far from the presidential role in Publius' deliberative republic, a closer look shows Neustadt's rejection of any such role on behalf of reason. Though the central lesson of his volume is that presidential power is "the power to persuade," Neustadt explicitly rejects a reliance on reasoned argumentation. Rather, to persuade Congress and other actors to do his will, a president must rely on "the coin of self interest."[98] through the exploitation of "needs and fears."[99] Presidential persuasion is not about the merits of public policy reasonably discussed in the legislature and among the branches. Rather, the president's object should be, "to induce as much uncertainty as possible about the consequences of ignoring what he wants. If he cannot make men think him bound to win, his need is to keep them from thinking they can cross him without risk, or that they can be sure what risks they run."[100] In the quest for presidentially-centered government, Neustadt does away with the deliberative republic in any meaningful sense. The complex representation of the Constitution is reduced to representation by one man in the name of the public interest and the public's other bodies are reduced to the status of hurdles the president must seek to overcome.

Neustadt's work also demonstrates that a Wilsonian presidocentric scheme of representation was not completely dependent upon presidential mass rhetoric. In fact, Neustadt nearly completely ignores (at least in his original formulation) the role of presidential rhetoric.[101] And yet he still maintains Wilson's close interaction between the officeholder and his constituents, though he ascribes to the people perhaps less influence than did Wilson. In Neustadt's formulation, the relation between the public and the president seems twofold. First, as we have seen, the public good is nearly indistinguishable from the good of the president, hence their interests completely merge to the point where his quest for personal power is the highest form of representation of the national interest. Second, the president's personal power is to some degree affected by his prestige with the public because the other players in Washington are concerned with public opinion. Here we see the rational defense of the same basic formulation of presidential plebiscitary representation that inspired Wilson and that was carried to its practical height by FDR.

Neustadt's prescriptive formulations have inspired other students of the office, presidential aides, and presidents themselves since 1960.[102] Indeed, this Neustadt-Wilsonian view of the presidency is the one that came to dominate most public and academic circles from the 1950s at least until Vietnam and Watergate, and it is a view that is still prevalent in various forms today. This cult of the presidency, or as Tom Cronin called it the "textbook presidency," was based on the premise that the individual in the presidency was the only officer who could save the nation from the changing fortunes of modern life and whose character was unsoiled by the flaws of the rest of humanity.[103] As Cronin has put it, this textbook presidency "describes and extols a chief executive who is generally benevolent, omnipotent, omniscient, and highly moral."[104] For our purposes we can note five major ingredients in the conception of plebiscitary presidential representation that can be found particularly in the thought of Woodrow Wilson and Richard Neustadt.

1. There is a need to rectify the errors of the checks and balances and separation of powers system established by the Founders. The "deadlock" and "checking" must be overcome in favor of unity and a "vital synthesis" in government. An energetic presidency is the only office capable of overcoming this flawed or anachronistic "theory" of the Constitution.

2. Action is clearly favored over deliberation. Here Wilson and Neustadt reject Publius' deliberative republic in favor of governmental activism under presidential direction. The energetic executive is not needed

to facilitate the deliberative process of representation; rather, he is needed to make his will the government's and thereby to unite the parts of the government in a holy synthesis for progress. Moreover, this progress is implicitly defined in terms of an egalitarian and statist agenda.

3. The Madisonian majority of locally elected officials meeting in the seat of government to come to policy choices should be superseded by "the voice of the people as a whole," a truly national majority that the president alone adequately represents. The president is formulator of national policy and he must mold the pluralistic legislature to a more homogeneous view of the common good and national purpose. Democracy comes to be viewed here in terms of a plebiscitary choice by a national majority between two competing programs forwarded by presidential candidates—"the people," the national majority less inhibited by "lesser representatives" should get their wishes.

4. A great emphasis is placed on the presidential role of providing representation by being the nation's "teacher." Through mass or popular rhetoric the president is to influence and/or shape and express public opinion; thereby "activating" that public opinion to pressure Congress (overcoming the separation of powers "problem"), while he also uses the office as a place for FDR's "moral leadership." As Thomas Cronin has shown, this view of the office as one of "instructing the nation as a national teacher and guiding the nation as national preacher," became a central part of the elite orthodoxy of the 1950s and 1960s.[105] Beyond his doctrinal contribution to the rhetorical presidency, Wilson brought mass speech to the forefront of our politics by reviving the century-long dead practice of delivering the state of the union address to Congress in person and in his speaking tour on behalf of the League of Nations.[106]

5. Presidential power is conceived in "realistic" terms rather than in formal or constitutional terms. That is to say, the "theoretical" limits to the office found in the text of the Constitution and the intent of the people who ratified it are less important (perhaps of no consequence at all) than the "real life" experience of that office and the expanded power that has come with that experience. Closely connected here is the emphasis on the characteristics, style, and leadership ability of the individual president as determinant, rather than the constitutional characteristics of the office. In essence, the constitutional institution of the presidency (and, necessarily the other institutions as well) is essentially formless; primarily it is the occupant's talents that set the boundaries to presidential power, boundaries that should be cast wide to allow for the needed activism of the office.

Whiggism in the 20th Century

Several forces at work in the current century have contributed to the institutionalization of the presidentially-centered model of representation both in practice as well as in the century's guiding ideas—its *zeitgeist*. The growth of the United States as a world leader, the revolution that came with nuclear weapons and the threat of instant Armageddon, the growth in government power and activism, and the centralizing force of national radio and television all contributed in important ways to the rise of the modern presidency. Also important, however, were the ideological underpinnings of this new presidency.

As seen in Wilson and Neustadt, the strong presidency model of the twentieth century was undergirded by the ideological demands of liberalism. From the activist presidency of Franklin Roosevelt on through the presidency of John F. Kennedy and into that of Lyndon Johnson, liberal politicians and opinion leaders were the primary torch bearers in the "cult of the presidency." Here they found both the means to support their dedication to direct democracy as well as the most effective instrument for achieving their policy goals.[107] "Influenced in large part by world events," says Thomas Cronin of these liberal pundits, "they supported a strong presidency because they believed that a strong presidency would best serve their values."[108] William G. Andrews has aptly summarized this twentieth century tendency and captures the important implications for representation found in this understanding of the American political system.

[They] allowed for no other national political or governmental leadership than the President's. He was called upon to be absolutely Number 1 in each area of activity of the national government . . . . So far as Congress entered the picture at all, it followed the President. The President was alone in the driver's seat. At best, Congress was a loyal helpmate, encouraging, offering support, obeying; at worst, it was an aggressive backseat driver, grabbing at the steering wheel, fighting to put on the brakes, threatening to overturn and destroy the whole vehicle.[109]

Though such a tendency to invest in the office of the presidency great power and leadership capacities has been the ruling representational paradigm of this century, the old whiggism has not completely resigned itself to the tomb of lost causes. Rather, we have seen two distinct and important periods of critical reconsideration of the governing understanding of the representational aspects of the presidency and Congress during the century. Both were, to varying degrees, inspired by a fear of what was perceived to be the dangerous path the nation had embarked upon, as well as by a genuine theoretical rethinking of the needs of democratic government. The first is found in the whiggish intellectual and popular writings of the conservative movement at mid-century; the other with the liberal reaction to the "imperial" presidencies of Johnson and Nixon in the early 1970s.

Whiggish Conservatism at Mid-Century

Conservatives have traditionally maintained a healthy distrust of concentrated governmental power.[110] During the middle decades of the current century two major phenomena especially raised the ire of the right on this score—the decline of traditional federalism and the growth in the presidency that came with the New Deal and the Second World War. In the flow of power from the state capitals to Washington, the right saw the end of local differences and cultures, and the seeds of tyranny. The further concentration of the expanded power of the federal government into the president's hands caused conservatives additional concern.[111]

Starting with a reaction to the presidency of the New Deal, conservative opinion leaders and politicians embraced congressional power as the authoritative representative body and as the only check on the modern presidency, which they conceived to be a dangerous tool of the big government left (both of the liberal and the socialist variety). Conservatives of the period running roughly from the 1930s into the 1960s put forth several important arguments against the presidentially-centered governmental system that seemed triumphant in America. Many of these arguments are the same as were put forth a century earlier by the whig critics of "King Jackson."

First, at perhaps the most fundamental level, conservatives expressed a vigorous jealousy of concentrated power and simplicity in government. Whereas many liberals saw a concentration of power and leadership as the best means toward the achievement of an activist political agenda, conservatives saw the beginnings of tyranny and the end of justice. As Russell Kirk put it in 1954,

Intelligent conservatives, from Burke to Adams to our time, have looked upon power as a most dangerous thing; for though unchecked power means complete freedom for the powerful man, it means abject servitude for his neighbors
. . . . Thus the conservative, reading the lessons of history, has sought to hedge about power with strong restrictions, and to divide authority among groups and institutions, that concentrated power may reside nowhere.[112]

Second, conservatives at mid-century tended to conceive of representation in a way more similar to the old whiggism of Webster and Calhoun than to the liberal appeals to the representation of "the nation as a whole." Indeed, some of their writings at times seem lifted straight from that older understanding of America and representative government. James Burnham, in his 1959 classic *Congress and the American Tradition*, provides a perfect example of this mode of thought. Contrasting the "loosely set gelatin" of "the masses" with the "varied unity of a living organism" that is "the people," Burnham argues that only the former can be represented in the presidency.

The people cannot be represented by or embodied in a single leader precisely because of the people's diversity. Their representation, if it is to be more than a masquerade, must have some sort of correspondence to their diversity. The political will of the people must therefore be projected through a multiplicity of representatives and representative institutions, both formal and informal. Only in this way can the irreducible variety of the people's interests, activities and aspirations find political expression.[113]

A legislature comprised of numerous and diverse individuals could alone adequately represent the people of the United States.

Third, conservatives made an argument that went directly to the heart of the plebiscitary model of democracy that had supported the expansion of executive power in the twentieth century. Against the "democratization" of American politics and the national idea-system, and the plebiscitary nature of presidential representation that accompanied it, conservatives tended to support the much-maligned "Madisonian" majorities found in the legislature.[114] The best expression of this conception of representative government was put forward by Willmoore Kendall in his famous "Two Majorities" essay in which he argued in favor of the inherent soundness of the Madisonian majority that was intended to govern under the Constitution.[115] Conservatives emphasized deliberation and discussion in government rather than action and efficiency.

Conservatives of this period also tended to prefer the rule of constitutional and statutory law to what they saw as arbitrary and potentially tyrannical rule by executive decree.[116] And their jealousy of executive power often was closely wrapped up with what amounted to an isolationist foreign policy among many conservatives.[117] For much of the political right at the time, an interventionist foreign policy was closely connected to the rise of the strong, dominant presidency and the expansion of government at home.[118]

For these reasons conservatives following the presidency of FDR came to a whiggish embrace of congressional representation. Only in the legislature could there be found adequate representation of the people, they argued. Centering power and leadership in the presidency was a dangerous step toward "caesarism" and the demise of the traditional liberties that the original model of the separation of powers made possible. They embraced Congress as the first branch of government much as had the whigs of the nineteenth century.

Such an intellectual embrace of the legislative body also became manifest in reform efforts forwarded by conservative and moderate Republicans of this period. Two of the most important were proposed constitutional amendments designed to prevent the presidency from growing out of republican bounds. On August 5, 1954, conservative Senator John Bricker (R-Ohio) proposed the so-called "Bricker Amendment" that would have restricted the president's ability to enter into executive agreements and treaties with foreign powers. An even more overtly whiggish reform came with the passage of the twenty-second Amendment to the Constitution in 1951. The limiting of presidential terms in the amendment had roots in whiggish thought as old as the Constitution itself, it being an important argument made by many Antifederalists.

The 1970s—Liberalism at a Crossroads

As we have seen, the general trend in liberal power prescriptions during this century has been to embrace centralization of power and leadership in the institution of the presidency. In part at least this tendency was fueled by the dedication of many on the left to "democratization" of American life. They assumed that the president, as the only nationally elected official, was the only one truly capable of representing the people of the United States.

In part this tendency also was due to the perceived need to centralize governmental authority to overcome paralysis and deadlock, which was considered the result of the traditional separation of powers system. Associated with this tendency was the institutional partisanship that stemmed from having liberal Democrats in the White House exercising leadership on behalf of a progressive agenda.

Much of the "cult of the presidency" came to an end in the early 1970s. In the aftermath of Vietnam and Watergate a reevaluation of liberal power prescriptions occurred. In its wake, many who had formerly embraced the presidency of Neustadt and Wilson turned against a strong chief executive and reembraced a resurgent Congress. The national legislature was again looked upon as a legitimately representative institution rather than one that simply functioned as a reactionary hurdle in the way of progressive presidents. The attack leveled against the presidency during the 1970s was another manifestation of the whig theory of representative government that has periodically waxed and waned as an important force in American political history.[119]

The very language of the politicians, pundits, and scholars who brought the attack on the office is reminiscent of earlier whig rhetoric. Particularly important was the challenge to the presidency's republican character. The unitary and independent nature of the American presidency has always made it susceptible to critics who would liken it to monarchy and kingship. This indeed has been the tactic of whiggish partisans of the legislature since the earliest days of the Republic. The most famous anti-strong presidency book of this period was Arthur Schlesinger's *The Imperial Presidency* with all its allusions to a monarchical office.[120] Another example of this literary attack is George Reedy's *The Twilight of the Presidency* in which he paints a picture of the White House as a royal court that waits upon and insulates "the American monarchy" from national reality.[121] Other writers called the office a "Frankenstein monster."[122]

Similar to the response of the conservatives in the middle part of the century, much of the whiggish attack on the presidency in the 1970s centered on what was seen as the abuse of foreign policy powers by recent incumbents. As Schlesinger put it, the view was that "the American President had become on issues of war and peace the most absolute monarch (with the possible exception of Mao Tse-tung of China) among the great powers of the world."[123] Saul K. Padover said the president had, for all practical purposes, become "a dictator in international affairs."[124] Such whiggish opinion and scholarship has, according to James Ceaser, led to many in Congress acting "as if that institution performs its proper duty in a separation-of-powers system when it ties the executive's hands and attempts to guide much of the nation's foreign policy through the instrument of law."[125]

Such congressional responses to presidential power were manifest in several important pieces of legislation passed during the 1970s. The Congressional Budget Act of 1974 was an attempt to give Congress a larger role in the budgetary process. In response to Nixon's massive impoundments of funds, Congress also passed legislation in 1974 to curb the president's power in this area. Perhaps most importantly, in 1973 Congress passed the War Powers Resolution in an attempt to limit presidential control over military operations and to place Congress back at the center of the national security process.

Certain tendencies with regard to representative government underlay the anti-presidency writings of the 1970s, much like the writings of their whiggish predecessors. This can easily be seen in the cries of "imperialism," "monarchy," and "creeping caesarism." As *The New Republic* opined, the assumption was that the presidency had assumed so much power as to contradict "the principles of democratic government..." as the presidency, "is not as compared with Congress, an institution of participatory democracy."[126] The fact should not be lost, however, that much of this literature was inspired, at least in part, by less lofty principles.

The origin of the presidocentered understanding of representative government in America was inspired at least in part by liberal presidents pursuing an activist and progressive political agenda, and the reaction against the presidency during the 1970s was led by liberals unhappy about the foreign policy of Lyndon Johnson and the foreign and domestic activities of his Republican successor Richard Nixon. This type of "institutional opportunism," it should be noted, has not been a malady limited only to liberal Democrats. Starting with the Nixon presidency, some conservatives began to embrace presidential power in domestic politics as well as in the struggle against imperial communism.[127] Conservative Dartmouth Professor Jeffrey Hart in 1974 argued in *National Review* that it was time for conservatives to embrace executive hegemony while a conservative Republican was in the White House and perhaps in a position to undue some of the liberal sins of his predecessors.[128] This trend accelerated significantly during the presidency of Ronald Reagan with many conservatives becoming nearly gleeful at the self-destruction of Congress and exceedingly jealous of presidential prerogatives.[129]

Conclusion

The whiggish distrust of executive power, especially unified executive power, led to an understanding of representation that basically excluded the presidency from any share in it. Such a tendency has been the dominant one in nearly all serious considerations of the concept of representation. Indeed, the dynamics of political representation in America have been nearly exclusively the bastion of students of Congress and legislative politics. But, more than that, the whiggish doctrine of representation leads to a power prescription weighted heavily in favor of Congress and to the delegitimization of any energetic and independent executive. As the authors of *The Federalist* knew well, such a power imbalance would seriously threaten free government in the United States.

The modern model of representation (Wilson's and Neustadt's) rejects government as deliberation in favor of governmental activism. To this end an energetic presidency is needed, not to facilitate the deliberative process of representation as was the case in *The Federalist*, but to make his will the government's and thereby to unite the separate institutions of government in a vigorous activism in the name of the public good. Under such a model, the other elected representatives of the people, combined in the two houses of Congress at the other end of the avenue, are reduced at best to the handmaids of the president and at worst to outright obstacles in the way of progress and the march of the people's will through their government. The complex representation of the deliberative republic is replaced by the unitary representation of presidential leadership with the other institutions loosing legitimacy and their constitutional prerogatives subverted in the name of majority rule.

The two understandings represent dangerous ends of the spectrum of representative government. Their coming to the fore at one time or another in American history has led to our unhealthy tendency to swing from prescriptions for presidential power to calls for congressional supremacy and back again. The swing during the 1960s and 1970s from the "cult of the presidency" to the fear of "the imperial presidency" represents one recent example of the dangerous instability with which these two theses leave us.

A particular problem with both these positions is that they lend themselves so easily to institutional opportunism and partisanship. As we have seen, these two understandings of representative government offer deliciously inviting fruits to those bent on implementing certain policy goals and values. Our history of fluctuation between these two understandings has made it even easier to embrace one institution over the other in the name of policy, efficiency, or democratic rule. Politics is about the struggle over means and ends of public policy, and it is on this level that ideological struggles are meant to take place. The problem arises when these struggles ascend to the realm of constitutionalism and the institutional system established in our fundamental law.

Arguments on behalf of congressional representation and a legislatively-centered federal system have led to corresponding arguments in favor of a resurgent presidency to "whip" Congress into line in the name of the people. This is the pulse of our understanding of representation in America. Originating in the centuries-old philosophical and practical debates on representative government and fueled by the immediate policy goals of our politicians, pundits, and scholars. These two arguments have periodically pulled America toward one extreme or the other. A more stable understanding of political representation and representative institutions in place of this pulse would render better service to the American republic.

Notes

1. On our ambivalence, see Harvey C. Mansfield, Jr., *Taming the Prince: The Ambivalence of Modern Executive Power* (New York: The Free Press, 1989); and Richard M. Pious, *The American Presidency* (New York: Basic Books, 1979).

2. Barbara Hinckley, *The Symbolic Presidency: How Presidents Portray Themselves* (New York: Routledge, 1990), 9.

3. As Robert Remini has put it, "Both parties accepted the principle that the great masses of plain people throughout the United States should rule. Whereas, thirty years earlier, Alexander Hamilton had called the people a 'beast' and John Adams and other Founding Fathers expressed fears that anarchy was the natural consequence of democracy, in the Age of Jackson these fears evaporated in a celebration of the mass electorate." *The Revolutionary Age of Andrew Jackson* (New York: Harper & Row, 1976), 147.

4. Wilfred E. Binkley, *The Powers of the President: Problems of American Democracy* (Garden City, N.Y.: Doubleday, Doran, 1937), 68.

5. "To the people belongs the right of electing their Chief Magistrate. . . . Experience proves that in proportion as agents to execute the will of the people are multiplied there is danger of their wishes being frustrated. Some may be unfaithful; all are liable to err. So far, therefore, as the people can with convenience speak, it

is safer for them to express their own will." Indeed it is most interesting here to note that Jackson makes his assumptions explicit—that even in the popularly elected House of Representatives, "the will of the people is still constantly liable to be misrepresented." Andrew Jackson, "First Annual Message," in *Messages and Papers of the Presidents Vol. II,* James D. Richardson, ed. (Bureau of National Literature and Art, 1903), 447-448.

6. Roger Remini, *Andrew Jackson and the Course of American Freedom, 1822-1832* (New York: Harper & Row, 1981), 369.

7. Jackson vetoed twelve bills during his administration while all previous presidents had only vetoed nine acts of Congress. Jackson also put the "pocket veto" into use for the first time. Sidney M. Milkis and Michael Nelson, *The American Presidency: Origins and Development, 1776-1990* (Washington, D.C.: CQ Press, 1990), 122.

8. Here I give but a sampling of the arguments and sentiments on either side. This is not the forum for a more detailed exegesis of this important historical moment.

9. All further citations from Jackson's "Protest" and the Senatorial responses are from *Register of Debates in Congress*, 1st Session of 23rd Congress, 1833-1834, Part 2 (Washington, D.C.: Gales and Seaton, 1834), 1318.

10. Jackson, April 17th, 1834, 1318.

11. Jackson, 1324.

12. Jackson, 1325.

13. Jackson, 1333.

14. Jackson, 1334.

15. Jackson, 1322.

16. Jackson, 1329.

17. Jackson, 1333.

18. Poindexter, April 17th, 1834, 1336.

19. Preston, May 6th, 1834, p. 1658. On that same date John C. Calhoun called Jackson's protest "the war message," 1645. Henry Clay put it like this on April 30: "Already has the President singled out and designated, in the Senate of the United States, the new object of his hostile pursuit; and the protest, which I am now to consider, is his declaration of war," 1564.

20. Daniel Webster, May 7th, 1834, p. 1681.

21. Webster, 1681.

22. Webster, 1685.

23. Webster, 1672.

24. Calhoun, 1645-1646.

25. See James Madison, Alexander Hamilton, and John Jay, *The Federalist Papers*, Isaac Kramnick, ed. (England: Penguin Books, 1987), Paper Number 47: 303.

26. See for instance, Calhoun's discussion of the solely legislative nature of all "implied" powers in the Constitution and the need to preserve the balance between the institutions of government, in Calhoun, 1642.

27. Webster, 1674.

28. Jackson, 1333.

29. Calhoun, 1648.

30. Webster, 1684.

31. Webster, 1684.

32. Webster, 1684.

33. Webster, 1677.

34. Webster, 1677.

35. Calhoun, 1645.

36. Calhoun, 1646.

37. See Wilfred E. Binkley, "The Jacksonian View of the Presidency Prevails," chapter 5 in *President and Congress*, 3rd Edition (New York: Vintage Books, 1962), 105-132.

38. Forrest McDonald, *Novus Ordo Seclorum: The Intellectual Origins of the Constitution* (Lawrence, Kans.: University Press of Kansas, 1985), 240.

39. See Gary W. King and Lyn Ragsdale, *The Elusive Executive* (Washington, D.C.: Congressional Quarterly Press, 1988). It was, we should recall, common before the Reagan Presidency to ask whether the office had not become "too big for one man."

40. Max Farrand, ed., *The Records of the Federal Convention of 1787* (New Haven: Yale University Press, 1966), I, 65.

41. Farrand, 1966, I, 66.

42. Farrand, 1966, I, 113.

43. Farrand, 1966, II, 100-101.

44. Farrand, 1966, I, 113.

45. For Calhoun's conception of the "concurrent majority," see "Disquisition on Government," in *Union and Liberty: The Political Philosophy of John C. Calhoun*, Donald S. Lutz, ed. (Indianapolis, Ind.: Liberty Press, 1992). For a lucid recent commentary, see Marshall L. DeRosa, *The Confederate Constitution of 1861: An Inquiry into American Constitutionalism* (Columbia, Mo.: University of Missouri Press, 1991), 25-37.

46. John C. Calhoun, *A Disquisition on Government and Selections from the Discourse*, C. Gordon Post, ed. (New York: Macmillan, 1953), 101. This work was originally published in 1853.

47. Calhoun, 1953, 101-10 (emphasis added).

48. Calhoun, 1953, 104.

49. Russell Kirk has perceptively summarized Calhoun's thoughts on this subject. "Calhoun has rejected with scorn the demagogue's abstraction called 'the

people.' No 'people' exists as a body with identical, homogeneous interests: this is a fantasy of metaphysicians; in reality, there are only individuals and groups." *The Conservative Mind*, Seventh Revised Edition (Chicago: Regnery Books, 1986), 176.

50. Ryan J. Barilleaux, *The Post-Modern Presidency: The Office after Ronald Reagan* (New York: Praeger, 1988), 44.

51. On the history of presidential staff, see John Hart, *The Presidential Branch* (New York: Pergamon Press, 1987).

52. The tenth Article of impeachment said; "That said Andrew Johnson, President of the United States, unmindful of the high duties of his office and the dignity and propriety thereof . . . did . . . make and deliver with a loud voice certain intemperate, inflammatory, and scandalous harangues, and did therein utter loud threats and bitter menaces as well against Congress as the laws of the United States. . . . Which said utterances, declarations, threats, and harrangues, highly censurable in any, are peculiarly indecent and unbecoming in the Chief Magistrate of the United States, by means whereof . . . Andrew Johnson has brought the high office of the President of the United States into contempt, ridicule, and disgrace, to the great scandal of all good citizens." Quoted in Jeffrey K. Tulis, *The Rhetorical Presidency* (Princeton, N.J.: Princeton University Press, 1987), 91. The number of Johnson's speeches is in Tulis, 81.

53. The term "plebiscitary presidency," was originally used by Theodore J. Lowi in his *The Personal Presidency: Power Invested Promise Unfulfilled* (Ithaca, N.Y.: Cornell University Press, 1985). I use the term here, not because I mean to endorse his thesis in any way, but because the term really best captures the spirit of the presidency that followed Wilson's example and writings.

54. Quoted in James MacGregor Burns, *Presidential Government: The Crucible of Leadership* (New York: Avon Books, 1965), 50.

55. For an examination of this charge against Lincoln's presidency, see Herman Belz, *Lincoln and the Constitution: The Dictatorship Question Reconsidered* (Fort Wayne, Ind.: Louis A. Warren Lincoln Library and Museum, 1984).

56. For instance, Lincoln in his speech at Gettysburg appeals not to the Constitution as the founding document of a transcendent people but to the Declaration of Independence. He seems to give representation to that constituting people that he imagined to be "conceived in Liberty, and dedicated to the proposition that all men are created equal." This is the people of 1776, not 1787. On Lincoln's constitutionally revolutionary rhetoric at Gettysburg, see Gary Wills, *Lincoln at Gettysburg: The Words that Remade America* (New York: Simon & Schuster, 1992); and Willmoore Kendall, "Equality: Commitment or Ideal?" in *The Intercollegiate Review* (Spring, 1989), 25-33.

57. Richard Loss, *The Modern Theory of Presidential Power: Alexander Hamilton and the Corwin Thesis* (New York: Greenwood Press, 1990), 89.

58. Abraham Lincoln, *Speeches and Writings* (New York: The Library of America, 1989), Vol. II, 585.

59. Lincoln, 1989, 585. Indeed, Lincoln here makes it absolutely clear that the president is so empowered only when the constitutional order is seriously threatened and not merely when his "abstract judgement" might dictate that he act. Less so, even, it would seem, on the grounds of ordinary public policy.

60. Woodrow Wilson, *Congressional Government* (New York: The World Publishing Co., 1967—originally published in 1885).

61. Wilson, 1967, 197.

62. This list was developed from Wilson, 1967, 181.

63. Wilson, 1967, 198.

64. Wilson, 1967, 197 (emphasis added).

65. This distinction seems very close to the one made by John Stuart Mill as in the assembly's role in "talking." See *Considerations on Representative Government*, H.B. Acton, ed. (London: J.M. Dent & Sons, Ltd., 1988).

66. Wilson, 1967, 198 (emphasis added).

67. All subsequent quotations of *Constitutional Government* are from *The Papers of Woodrow Wilson*, Vol 18. Arthur Link, ed. (Princeton, N.J.: Princeton University Press, 1974).

68. Wilson, 1974, 107.

69. Harvey C. Mansfield, Jr., *America's Constitutional Soul* (Baltimore: The Johns Hopkins University Press, 1991), 5.

70. Wilson, in fact, acknowledges that all governments, not just the American system of government, are ruled by the evolutionary process and change with the ages. See, 1974, 104-105.

71. Wilson, 1974, 105.

72. Wilson, 1974, 106.

73. Wilson, 1974, 106.

74. Wilson, 1974, 115.

75. Wilson, 1974, 107.

76. Wilson, 1974, 108.

77. Wilson, 1974, 113.

78. See Wilson, 1974, 141.

79. Wilson, 1974, 114.

80. Wilson, 1974, 114.

81. Wilson, 1974, 141.

82. Wilson, 1974, 116.

83. Wilson, 1974, 115.

84. Wilson, 1974, 141.

85. Quoted in Charles R. Kesler, "Woodrow Wilson and the statesmanship of Progress," in *Natural Right and Political Right*, Thomas R. Silver and Peter W.

Schramm, eds. (Durham, N.C.: Carolina Academic Press, 1984), 123.

86. Quoted in Alfred De Grazia, *Public and Republic: Political Representation in America* (New York: Alfred A. Knopf, 1951), 181.

87. See James W. Ceasar, Glen E. Thurow, Jeffrey K. Tulis, and Joseph M. Bessette, "The Rise of the Rhetorical Presidency," *Presidential Studies Quarterly* (Spring, 1981), 158-171; and Jeffrey K. Tulis, *The Rhetorical Presidency* (Princeton, N.J.: Princeton University Press, 1987).

88. I borrow the phrase "raise into consciousness" from Jacques Maritain who argued that the contribution of Machiavelli was to have raised into consciousness the idea that leaders must at times use evil means toward the ends that they would pursue. That is, he wiped away their bad consciences that once held their ruthlessness to some degree in check. See Jacques Maritain, "The End of Machiavellianism," reprinted in Joseph W. Evans and Leo R. Ward, eds., *The Social and Political Philosophy of Jacques Maritain* (New York: Charles Scribner's Sons, 1955), 292-325.

89. Clinton Rossiter, *The American Presidency*, Revised Edition (New York: Mentor, 1960), first published in 1956.

90. Richard E. Neustadt, *Presidential Power and the Modern Presidents* (New York: The Free Press, 1990), originally published in 1960.

91. Neustadt nowhere makes his understanding of presidential representation explicit. Nevertheless, it is my contention that his presidocentric understanding of the system is built around the implicit assumption that the presidency is the one legitimate representative in the American political system. Hence, as he believes, the public good can be equated with that of the presidency. There being no presidency that can be differentiated from the individual incumbent, what is good for the individual power seeker is good for the public. Presidential representation could hardly be expressed in a clearer relationship.

92. Neustadt, 1990, 29.

93. Terry Eastland, *Energy in the Executive: The Case for the Strong Presidency* (New York: The Free Press, 1992), 8.

94. Joseph Bessette quoted in Eastland, 1992, 8.

95. Neustadt, 1990, xix.

96. Neustadt, 1990, 155.

97. Neustadt, 1990, 156.

98. Neustadt, 1990, 40.

99. Neustadt, 1990, 32.

100. Neustadt, 1990, 55.

101. I contend that Neustadt's lack of concern with presidential rhetoric is not simply a misunderstanding on his part. Rather, it demonstrates that the Wilsonian revolution in the presidency had much wider consequences than simply the legitimation of a "rhetorical presidency"—though this was a crucial change. A

presidentially-centered plebiscitary system of representation is what links the modern presidency to Wilson, Neustadt, and others who have praised active presidential government over the past few decades.

102. See, for instance, Neustadt, 1990, xvi; Garry Wills, *The Kennedy Imprisonment: A Meditation on Power* (New York: Pocket Books, 1981), 182-194.

103. As William Andrews put it, "In summary then, the 1960 writers glorified the presidency, especially in foreign and defense affairs. That institution incarnated governmental virtue. If only it could be made virtually omnipotent through institutional reforms and by electing men with enough will power and skill, the presidency could solve as many of our problems as is humanly possible." William G. Andrews, "The Presidency, Congress, and Constitutional Theory," in *Perspectives on the Presidency*, Aaron Wildavsky, ed. (Boston: Little, Brown, and Company, 1975), 27.

104. Thomas E. Cronin, "The Textbook and Prime-Time Presidency," in *The State of the Presidency*, 2nd Edition (Boston: Little, Brown and Company, 1980), 76.

105. Cronin, 1980, 78.

106. See Ceaser, et al., 1981, and Tulis, 1987.

107. On the liberal political agenda's importance to the modern presidency see Barilleaux, 1988, 61-64.

108. Cronin, 1980, 88.

109. Andrews, 1975, 26.

110. I use the word "conservative" as a generic term for those of the right who were intellectually and politically active during the middle decades of the twentieth century. I include under the term "conservative" both the traditional/cultural conservatives of the "Old Right" as well as their libertarian cousins. Though they differed fundamentally on key values and ideas, on their opposition to presidential power they were soulmates. For a good sampling of the intellectual disagreements between these two groups, see George W. Carey, ed., *Freedom and Virtue: The Conservative/Libertarian Debate* (Lanham, Md.: University Press of America and The Intercollegiate Studies Institute, 1984).

111. For an example of how these two phenomena were connected in the minds of conservatives, see Barry Goldwater, *Where I Stand* (New York: McGraw-Hill, 1964), 88-93.

112. Russell Kirk, *A Program for Conservatives* (Chicago: Henry Regnery Company, 1954), 251.

113. James Burnham, *Congress and the American Tradition* (Chicago: Henry Regnery Company, 1965), 321.

114. See, for instance, Alfred de Grazia, *Republic in Crisis* (New York: Federal Legal Publications, 1965); James Burnham, 1965; Russell Kirk, 1954, 263.

115. Willmoore Kendall, "The Two Majorities in American Politics," chapter 2 in *The Conservative Affirmation in America* (Chicago: Gateway Editions, 1985). This essay was originally published in *Midwest Journal of Political Science* (November 1960), 317-345.

116. On this point see, J. Richard Piper, "Presidential-Congressional Power Prescriptions in Conservative Political Thought Since 1933," *Presidential Studies Quarterly*, Vol. XXI, Number 1 (Winter 1991), 35-54.

117. On the change in conservative foreign policy prescriptions from isolationism to interventionist anti-communism during the 1950s and 1960s see chapter 4 in George H. Nash, *The Conservative Intellectual Movement in America Since 1945* (New York: Basic Books, 1976), 84-130.

118. Capturing this sentiment concerning the relationship between foreign policy adventures, increasing democratization, and the concentration of power in the executive was the conservative Frenchman Amaury de Riencourt in his *The Coming Caesars* (New York: Coward-McCann, 1957). "Our Western world, America and Europe, is threatened with Caesarism on a scale unknown since the dawn of the Roman Empire. . . . [E]xpanding democracy leads unintentionally to imperialism and that imperialism inevitably ends in destroying the republican institutions of earlier days; further, . . . the greater the social equality, the dimmer the prospects of liberty, and . . . as society becomes more equalitarian, it tends increasingly to concentrate absolute power in the hands of one single man," 5.

119. For a critical rendition of this history of changing liberal power prescriptions during the 1960s and 1970s, see M. Stanton Evans, *Clear and Present Dangers: A Conservative View of America's Government* (New York: Harcourt Brace Jovanovich, 1975).

120. Arthur M. Schlesinger, Jr., *The Imperial Presidency* (New York: Popular Library, 1974).

121. George E. Reedy, *The Twilight of the Presidency* (New York: Mentor, 1970).

122. Marcus Cunliffe, "A Defective Institution?" *Commentary* (February 1968), 28.

123. Schlesinger, 1974, 11.

124. Saul K. Padover, "The Power of the President," *Commonweal* (August 9, 1968), 575.

125. James W. Ceaser, *Liberal Democracy & Political Science* (Baltimore: Johns Hopkins University Press, 1990), 210.

126. "Swing of the Pendulum," *The New Republic* (March 27, 1971).

127. For a solid evaluation of the recent "institutional partisanship" of both conservatives and liberals, see Ryan J. Barilleaux, "Liberals, Conservatives, and the Presidency," *Congress & The Presidency* 20, Number 1 (Spring 1993), 75-82.

128. Jeffrey Hart, "The Presidency: Shifting Conservative Perspectives," *National Review* (November 22, 1974), 1351-1355.

129. See Gordon S. Jones and John A. Marini, eds., *The Imperial Congress: Crisis in the Separation of Powers* (New York: Pharos Books, 1988); L. Gordon Crovitz and Jeremy A. Rabkin, eds., *The Fettered Presidency: Legal Constraints on the Executive Branch* (Washington, D.C.: American Enterprise Institute Press, 1989); Terry Eastland, *Energy in the Executive: The Case for the Strong Presidency* (New York: The Free Press, 1992). Some conservatives did maintain a more traditional caution against such a one-sided institutional embrace. See Samuel Francis, "Imperial Conservatives?" *National Review* (August 4, 1989), 37-38; Mickey Edwards, "Of Conservatives and Kings," *Policy Review* 48 (Spring 1989); William F. Buckley, Jr., "Agenda for the Nineties," *National Review* (February 19, 1990), 39-40.

4

The Public Presidency

Conceiving the American presidency as an institution of political representation inevitably draws us to two general sets of interrelated questions. The first we may term the "external" question of the president's relationship to the American public. The second we can conceive of as the "internal" question of presidential representation, or the nature of the president's relationship to the rest of the national government.

On both these fronts, the American political system has undergone revolutionary change during the twentieth century. Since Franklin Roosevelt's first inauguration in 1933, the presidency's place in the regime and the place of individual presidents in the American political culture have seen a fundamental transformation. In this chapter I consider the "external" question of the modern presidency's relationship to the public; the question of the contemporary presidency's place in the regime is discussed in the chapter that follows.

The Traditional Presidency
and Its Transformation

The presidential office of the traditional era (roughly 1791-1933) was a limited one, with limited responsibilities and equally limited resources. The structure and nature of the regime during most of this period was very much in keeping with the whig understanding of congressionally-centered and limited national government. In most every conceivable way Congress was the first branch of government and an activist presidency was more the exception than the rule.

In relation to the American public, traditional presidents for the most part did not forge strong direct links to the electorate. With the possible exception of Andrew Jackson, presidents during the traditional period tended to stand as constitutional officers at a considerable distance from the general public rather than intimately connected to them. The situation remained much as Madison had written in *Federalist* 49—in a battle for the hearts and minds of the public, members of the legislature held the distinct advantage over the distant executive officer. As Jeffrey Tulis has shown, norms regarding presidential rhetoric also kept popular speech by presidents to a minimum during the nineteenth century, thus keeping the presidents at a distance from the public.[1]

During the traditional period, the federal government's role in the economic and social spheres of the nation was limited as was the place of the presidency within the government itself. As Theodore J. Lowi has put it, "the nineteenth century was the golden age of the legislature."[2] This was an era of congressional government, of a dominant legislature and a passive chief executive. Presidents had no organized legislative program and were not actively engaged in lobbying the legislature for the passage of one. During this period, presidents were guided by a "rule of restraint"[3] that prohibited them from acting unilaterally except in certain extraordinary instances that necessitated more forceful executive action, such as was the case with Lincoln and the Civil War.

Politically, members of Congress functioned as the central representatives in the land. Presidents remained primarily in their role as the representative of the constitutional people and the constitutional morality that informed the regime. According to the standards of the nineteenth century, presidents restrained their activity within what was considered to be the bounds of respect for a republican chief of state. Thus, as I have noted, presidents spoke far less often to the public in the last century than in the twentieth and hardly ever attempted to appeal to the public on policy grounds. The public speech that they did engage in, consistent with the role of the presidency as constitutional representative, was primarily one of public instruction on constitutional principles and the general direction of the government and the nation.[4]

This situation was to change dramatically in the twentieth century with the presidency coming to occupy a position much closer to the people and of vastly more power and influence over the national government than had previously been the case. As we saw in the previous chapter, the pen of Woodrow Wilson did more than any other to lay the foundation for the perceived legitimacy of such a new conception of the presidency. The presidency of Theodore Roosevelt and the "stewardship" doctrine of executive power that undergirded his administration also marked an important early moment in the evolution of the representational place of the presidency in American political life. Roosevelt recorded in his autobiography that he regarded the president as "a steward of the people bound actively and affirmatively to do all he could for the people, and not to content himself with the negative merit of keeping his talents undamaged in a napkin."[5] Roosevelt held the president to be bound only to serve the people and to do all he could in their name that wasn't explicitly prohibited to him by the Constitution.

Despite these clear precedents, it was not until TR's cousin Franklin Roosevelt came to the office that the new conception of presidential power and representative government was truly inaugurated and institutionalized as the norm for the regime. As Fred I. Greenstein has observed, "With Franklin Roosevelt's administration . . . the presidency began to undergo not a shift but rather a metamorphosis."[6] With FDR the president for the first time became intimately connected to his constituency. The presidency was transformed into an office of plebiscitary representation from its more independent predecessor. Also, the center of representation within the government itself was transferred from Congress to the presidency as that institution acquired ever more resources and responsibilities. These two transformations, it is important to note, were not distinct and independent occurrences. Rather, they worked in a synthesis: closer ties to the public feeding calls for more power centered in the White House and more power and responsibility invested leading to more public attention on and concern about the individual in the office.

The President and the Public in the Modern Era

FDR's depression- and war-era administrations marked a great turning point in the relationship between the American people and their presidents. Previously, citizens had surely held a number of their presidents in very high esteem and celebrated their virtue and accomplishments in popular culture and educational materials. FDR's revolution, forged out of the progressive's celebration of democracy and executive power, brought new and direct links between the people and their president; links that would fundamentally alter the presidencies of every chief executive who was to follow.

In 1932 Roosevelt campaigned for the presidency on a platform promising relief from the devastating ravages of the depression. His campaign gave hope to millions and the people immediately responded, not only by sweeping him and his fellow Democrats into office but also by reaching out to personally connect with their new chief executive. Before FDR's move into the executive mansion, daily mail to the White House during peak periods averaged about one thousand pieces a day. By contrast, Roosevelt's averaged 5,000 a day and his inauguration was greeted by an astounding 460,000 letters. It took a staff of fifty to handle Roosevelt's mail where Hoover had needed but one.[7] The American people were forging a bond with their president during their time of crisis and Roosevelt did what he could to encourage it, as has nearly every president since.

A central aspect of this new relationship between the president and the American people was the transformation that took place in the *filters* that traditionally had mediated the relationship between the executive and the public. During the traditional era certain institutionalized representational filters existed that worked to encourage a certain independence in the White House from the masses. Whether it was provided by the political parties, rhetorical prohibitions on demagoguery, or lack of the technological means for acquiring an instant check of the public pulse, there existed considerable constitutional *space* between the presidency and the people. In the constitutional morality of *The Federalist* this space was provided primarily by the president deriving his position directly from the Constitution itself and thereby not being dependent on either Congress or the public. This is the representational space that was greatly transformed and at least partially lost in the development of the plebiscitary presidency in the twentieth century.

The Electoral Connection:
From Indirect Control to Unmediated Plebiscites

Elections are the only relationship between representative and represented provided for explicitly in the Constitution. And even this relationship for the presidency was to be an indirect one. Direct popular election of the president was proposed at the Constitutional Convention at least twice but both times was solidly rejected by the delegates. The Founders, fearing mob rule and the tyranny of the majority, settled instead for a more indirect method of choosing our chief executive. The electoral college and, in cases where it failed, the House of Representatives were established as mediating institutions between the president and the public. Early in our national experience under the Constitution, however, the electoral college system was effectively transcended by the development of the two-party system.

The electoral college method of electing the president was designed, in part, to filter the public voice through a chosen and temporarily empowered body of citizens.[8] The independence of action that would ensure its ability to function as a mediating body, however, did not long outlast the nation's first president. By 1800 the beginnings of a national two-party system had begun to take shape and states began to make partisanship a requirement for service in the electoral college. Eventually the system would develop into a partisan-based, winner-take-all system of direct popular vote in most states.[9] With such a change, electors lost their independence and became little more than the tools of popular majorities expressing a party or candidate preference. With such a major alteration of the electoral system, presidents themselves became more dependent upon majority will expressed through the mechanisms of the two-party system.

The outlines of the electoral process have remained generally unchanged from the way they developed in the early decades of the nineteenth century. Presidential candidates compete as partisan representatives of their parties, and presidents are elected by an electoral college that serves as little more than an accounting tool for national majorities comprised of smaller state majorities.[10] It is the way the political parties have chosen the candidates they would send forward in general election contests that has changed substanially over U.S. history. These changes have had profound effects on the presidency, its relation to the American public, and the office's place in American national government.

George Washington had been elected president and John Adams vice president by the unanimous vote of the electoral college. In these first two elections, and indeed in the general theory of the Founders, there was no need for any contest or decision to be made before the electoral college met. As early as 1796 this situation had changed. The two-party system had begun to develop out of the Hamilton-Jefferson disagreements about the direction of the new nation, and both sides for the first time chose their own champion to compete with the other in the electoral college. Federalist leaders turned to John Adams and Republicans in Congress chose Jefferson as their candidate in 1796.

By 1800 the practice of the congressional party members choosing the party's presidential candidate was firmly in place for both parties. This Congressional caucus method of choosing presidential candidates offered a way to limit a direct, popular, and potentially demagogic appeal to the people that many of the early political leaders were so suspicious of, but it also violated the spirit of the Constitution by allowing Congress to effectively choose the presidential nominees.

In 1824 the caucus method met its end in the fractured election in which several states put forward their own candidates to compete with the ones chosen by the congressional parties. The electoral vote was divided and the House eventually chose John Quincy Adams as the president. "King Caucus," as it was known by its critics, was not used again after 1824 primarily due to the collapse of the Federalist party and Andrew Jackson's stern opposition to such an institution.

Individual state legislatures, conventions, and caucuses subsequently became more active in choosing presidential candidates. But such state-oriented structures tended to choose candidates representative of themselves who were not as readily able to find a national constituency. These "favorite son" candidates were too representative of their state or region and too unrepresentative of the nation as a whole. To fill this representational gap, national nominating conventions began to develop in the 1830s. These traditional conventions enabled the party elite to effectively control the nomination process and kept candidate choice out of the hands of the general public and away from candidates who might otherwise be tempted to engage in demagogic appeals and the manipulation of mass passions.

The Rise of Primary Elections

In the early twentieth century progressive reformers began to urge a more democratic way of nominating candidates. The progressives wished to break the monopoly on power that was held by the party leadership, especially state bosses and their political machines. These reformers strove to put the presidential candidates, and hence the president himself, in closer contact with the American public. More than a dozen states responded by initiating some form of presidential primary elections during the first two decades of the twentieth century. But following World War I the number of primaries began to decline, as did their importance in influencing party decisions. With the rare exception of perhaps John Kennedy's victories in the primary elections of West Virginia and Wisconsin in 1960, the primaries that did exist were not terribly influential in determining who would be a party nominee until the 1970s.

This situation changed dramatically after 1968, as did the presidential relationship with the public and the nature of election campaigns themselves. The 1968 Democratic convention sparked violence in the streets of Chicago and caused the Democrats to make radical alterations to the way the party chose its presidential candidates. The call of those who were dissatisfied with the outcome of the process was for more democracy—more power in the hands of the rank and file and less in the possession of the party "bosses." The Democratic party's commission that was formed to deal with the new demands responded, guided by the spirit that, to use their own words, "the cure for the ills of democracy is more democracy."[11]

The crisis of confidence that confronted the McGovern-Frasure Commission (1969-1972) was one fundamentally of representation.[12] The old "mixed" nomination process emphasized both pluralistic elements of interest negotiation and compromise among party and group leaders, as well some plebiscitary elements found in the existent primaries. To those dissatisfied with the product of the system, namely the nomination of Hubert Humphrey in 1968, this process did not adequately represent the Democratic party in the electorate. For many elements of the party by 1968, nothing short of the unfiltered will of the membership should control the nomination process and elect the presidential candidate who would emerge from that process.

What the reformers won was a major transformation of the system into what would amount to a state-by-state plebiscitary road to the Democratic party's nomination. The people (or at least that fraction of them that participated in the primary elections and caucuses) became the supreme force in the nomination process of both parties during the 1970s. Though originating in the Democratic party, Republicans soon followed with many similar "democratic" reforms of their nominating process. Guided by a representational theory that linked the public directly to the candidates, the reforms transformed American politics and the presidency.[13]

Primary elections proliferated after 1968 and they became decisive in determining who would be the party nominee. As a consequence, the power and influence of party elite declined, as that of ideological and other activists and rank and file participants increased. More importantly, the nature of the candidates and their search for the nomination changed profoundly.

The decentralized nature of the nomination process has made it possible for the "outsider" candidate to win the party nomination without necessarily having much support within the party organization itself. Jimmy Carter in 1976 and Ronald Reagan in 1980 ran such "outsider" campaigns, won their party nomination, and ultimately the presidency itself. In a similar way, the nomination process also has become one that rewards entrepreneurial candidates. As Ryan Barilleaux has put it, "Prospective presidential candidates self-select themselves to run for office, build their own campaign organizations, strategies, and circle of advisors, raise money for themselves, and seek nomination and then election on their own."[14]

Presidential contenders must "sell" themselves, they must forge a bond with the primary-voting electorate and caucus participants of their own party. Though candidates still make use of direct appeals delivered in person at factory gates or town hall meetings, the "selling" takes place today primarily through the intermediary force of the media. Such a situation places the established media in a filtering role like that which was once performed by the political parties, albeit in significantly different ways.[15]

Today's general election campaigns also retain this candidate centeredness, as candidates do not rely on the parties for support and strategy but keep their own organizations in place, which they have built for the primaries. Candidates maintain their own personal campaign organization, run on their own issues, and attempt to establish a direct and personal connection to the public—a connection that remains essentially unmediated by the traditional party organizations. And general election campaigns today are even more "media-intense" than are the nomination contests. Presidential campaigns at all levels have become the most plebiscitary elements of a plebiscitary presidential system.

The Decline of Political Parties

Political parties originated in English history out of a desire to limit and restrain executive power.[16] Similarly, the American version of the party system was founded on the Jeffersonian-Republican concerns regarding the dangers of centralized governmental power and executive aggrandizement. Legislative bodies, it was believed, need parties to balance executive institutions that are able to remain strong without them.[17] Originating out of the necessities of maintaining limited republican government, traditional parties functioned as a "wall of separation" between government and society.[18] The parties served representative government by mediating the linkages between officials and the public and by strengthening the legislative body.

Political party organizations, which once were so central to the electoral process and to governing, have declined significantly in importance since the reforms that followed 1968. They have lost much of their traditional place as independent political entities within the political system and have become creatures of their standard-bearer whom they had little say in selecting. But the process of party decline did not start in 1968. Rather, this transformation was the outcome of the modern presidency inaugurated in the 1930s by Franklin Roosevelt and his transformed concept of executive representation.

As Sidney Milkis has observed, "The institutional reforms carried out during the 1930s recast the relationship between political parties and the executive, thus fundamentally redefining the concept of representation in American politics."[19] FDR's New Deal revolution itself had the effect of centralizing governmental power in the federal government and within the federal government in the executive branch. It thus undercut much of the foundation that had supported the traditional decentralized, parochial parties.

But Roosevelt also deliberately sought to transform the Democratic party and make it an ideological tool in the service of his quest for power and policy success. He supplanted the traditional party-based patronage system with one primarily based on ideology that was to a degree non-partisan. He developed policy without consultation with members of his party in Congress. He altered the organization of the Democratic National Committee (DNC) to reflect the values of his New Deal program, established independent divisions for blacks, women, and labor within the party, and relied on non-partisan groups to support his reelection and the passage of his programs. In 1938 he even attempted a "purge" of the more conservative elements of the Democratic party by intervening in local and state primary elections. All was done in the attempt to create a "personal party" loyal only to the president and the president's progressive agenda. One legacy of the New Deal was weakened political parties and a strengthened administrative presidency with direct, plebiscitary connections to the American people.[20] This legacy was intensified with the nomination reforms that followed 1968.

Modern Elections and Representation

The consequences that modern political parties and elections hold for the American presidency and the political system have been profound. Modern presidential elections serve as the great democratic spectacle in American politics. They are the events around which the rest of the political world revolves. Every presidential initiative, every scandal, every policy, in one way or another is measured on the yardstick of the next election, no matter how far away that might be. Even foreign policy is not immune from such pressures.

As the great democratic spectacle, people expect policy results to follow from the choice so made. Presidential victors waste no time after the returns are tallied to claim to have received a "mandate" from the American people. Claiming such a mandate cloaks the presidents' initiatives in a veil of democratic legitimacy, thereby providing them with an air of worthiness that they might not otherwise have earned. Representatives in Congress often are well prepared to accept such a claim. David Mayhew has written, "Nothing is more important in Capitol Hill politics than the shared conviction that election returns have proven a point."[21] Presidents make great efforts to exploit such democratic sentiment in their dealings with the legislature. One of President Reagan's aides made their strategy clear in early 1981: "We are going to push the mandate as far as possible. . . . The strategy is to keep the pressure on the Democrats, to keep jolting them back to November 4, 1980."[22]

Charles O. Jones has rightly commented, "A basic assumption of any theory of representative democracy is that there is a link between elections and policy-making."[23] But it is also right to acknowledge that a basic assumption of any method of selecting representatives is that it will encourage the selection of candidates with the characteristics valued in political representatives. It follows then that our mode of electing our presidents may well encourage the selection of a certain type of representative officer.

In the contemporary electoral situation presidential candidates must be telegenic and must possess considerable rhetorical skills. They must be prepared to make explicit promises of action and policy, and they must diligently follow and respond to short-term fluctuations in public opinion. What we encourage in candidates, we receive in representatives. It is no less so with our modern president than it is with our congressmen and senators.

Without the traditional party structure, presidents now are more directly connected to their mass national constituency than ever before. Our elections put a high degree of importance on personal candidate responsibility, and this situation carries over into government where presidents are seen to be individually responsible for nearly all aspects of governance at the national level. The consummate campaign need to "manage" the news, to regularly be in front of the cameras, and to "sell" themselves and their policies have become central aspects of White House operations as well. As James Ceaser has noted, "Modern presidents now stand directly before the bar of public opinion, and one should not be surprised if they become more assertive in their claim to authority and more "popular" or demagogic in their leadership appeals."[24]

The Rhetorical Connection:
Going Public and Rhetorical Representation

To a significant degree, presidential governing has taken on the look of presidential election politics. The president personally has become the center of public focus in government. Presidents continually attempt to build popular support and watch the polls with no less vigor than they did during the campaign. Governing has become electioneering toward other ends, in this case public policy and presidential influence in government. As Godfrey Hodgson has remarked, "The distinction between being a President and being a presidential candidate has been progressively rubbed away."[25] The most important element in this mix of public relations and governing is presidential rhetoric and presidential activities that are played out before a national audience watching the spectacle unfold on television.

As was seen in the previous chapter, Woodrow Wilson was largely responsible for laying the foundation of legitimacy for a presidency based largely on rhetorical appeals to the mass public. Theodore Roosevelt as well had been active in his use of the "Bully Pulpit," most notably in promoting the Hepburn Act of 1906. But much of this rhetorical practice was lost with Taft's presidency and the Republicans who followed Wilson. It was not until FDR's administration that the rhetorical presidency became institutionalized in the operation of the office and in the public mind.

FDR was himself only partially responsible for this transformation of the office. His presidency occurred during a profound national economic crisis in which the people looked to Washington and the president not only for programs and remedies but also for hope and confidence. The people were ready for the president to speak to them and inspire in them confidence in the nation's future as well as in their own. In this way the presidency functioned as a place of moral leadership, as FDR would describe it. World War II, economic downturns, and various Cold War crises that would develop in the decades after FDR's passing also would call presidents to make similar appeals to the nation's spirit. Eisenhower took to the airwaves to speak to the nation while it was gripped by the fear engendered by the Soviet Union's launching of Sputnik. In July 1979, Jimmy Carter spoke to a nation he found to be in a spiritual malaise. Ronald Reagan endeavored to rhetorically rebuild America's sense of mission and self-confidence that many perceived to have been lost during the 1970s.

Also of great importance to the development of the rhetorical presidency were the significant advances that had been made in media technology during the twentieth century. During the previous, traditional era any president who would have chosen to flaunt convention and tradition by making direct mass appeals to the public would also have been hindered by existing media forms. Widely circulated and inexpensive newspapers were the dominant medium of the nineteenth century. Such a form of communication offered the president little chance to connect directly with a mass audience. Presidential words reaching the public often depended on the quality of the mediation provided by journalists, and newspapers simply demanded much more effort on the part of their audience than do the essentially passive mass media technology of our own day.

With the invention and wide proliferation of radio and later television, presidents gained an unmediated link between themselves and nearly every household in America. With these technological advancements, the presidency had gained the one-way communication link that would be an essential ingredient in the development of the plebiscitary presidency (the corresponding communication link running in the opposite direction from the people to the president would be provided by the proliferation of public opinion polling.) Presidents had also gained the most effective way to tap into public approval, which George Edwards has called the "greatest source of influence" for presidents.[26]

FDR made great use of radio technology to forge an undiluted and unmediated connection with the citizenry. His major tools were the "fireside chats" that he used regularly to build mass support for his programs and to encourage the public to pressure Congress. His influence on the future of presidential politics was enormous. As Mary Stuckey has put it, while previous presidents were able to choose whether or not to engage in mass rhetorical appeals, "No president after Roosevelt had such a choice: Presidential leadership became, by definition, public leadership."[27]

Though not possessing the rhetorical skills of his predecessor and although significantly less charismatic, Harry S. Truman did nothing to change the nature of the public presidency inaugurated by FDR. With Eisenhower, and later with Kennedy, the presidency moved further into the everyday lives of Americans through the emergence of television as the new dominant form of media.[28] With pictures of the president beamed daily into their living rooms, the new plebiscitary linkages between the people and their only nationally elected figure grew ever stronger. And as was demonstrated so clearly in the first Nixon-Kennedy presidential debate of 1960, the rules of plebiscitary politics were changing as well. Those listening to the debate on radio, aware only of the words uttered by the two men, felt Nixon had been the clear winner. Those watching on television saw the younger and better looking Kennedy and chose him the victor. Among other effects, television has the tendency to reduce dialogue and reasoned arguments over specific public policy to visual images and simplistic, generalized appeals that are capable of holding the public's attention and being easily understood.

Since the emergence of television to its current status as the dominant form of media in America, the rhetorical presidency has grown immensely. Presidential speeches to the nation, personal, video taped, or satellite fed appearances to smaller audiences, and official travel around the nation and around the world are the primary fibers by which the president is today connected to the American people. As Samuel Kernell has shown, since the administration of Herbert Hoover, presidents have steadily made more and more use of direct, personal appeals to the public. Though the number of direct appeals to a national audience (major addresses) has not grown significantly during that time, there has been an explosion of minor addresses, those delivered to special audiences. On average, Reagan delivered about twice as many major national addresses as did Hoover and gave six times as many minor speeches to more limited audiences each year.[29]

But it is not only presidential speeches that have grown steadily in number and importance as a major link between presidents and those they claim to represent. Rather, closely corresponding to the rise of the rhetorical presidency has been the rise of what we might call presidency by spectacle. As the rhetorical presidency proper developed primarily out of the new doctrine of leadership first legitimated on a wide scale by Woodrow Wilson and facilitated by the developments in media technology, so the importance of the presidency as a place of spectacle grew as the demands of television and of presidential cultivation of popular support became ever more central to political leadership.

Besides carefully crafted policy addresses, presidents also "go public" by presiding over various ceremonies, appearances in front of groups or in sight of television's ever watchful eye, and through political travel. Kernell has documented a significant increase both in presidential appearances as well as presidential travel, fueled at least in part by advances in transportation technology over the past several decades.[30] All of it, of course, done in the name of cultivating the public approval without which modern executives are greatly enfeebled in their constitutional office.

Bruce Miroff has defined a spectacle as "a kind of symbolic event, one in which particular details stand for broader and deeper meanings," and he has shown how manipulation of such symbolic events has become a central part of the public presidency.[31] Through the use of such spectacles presidential character can be defined in a way that the general public might find appealing. The president's character also is routinely "magnified" by those in the White House and through the media. As Miroff puts it, "The spectacle makes the president appear exceptionally decisive, tough, courageous, prescient, or prudent. Whether he is in fact all or any of these things is obscured. What matters is that he is presented as having these qualities, in magnitudes far beyond what ordinary citizens can imagine themselves to possess."[32]

For this reason, Miroff contends, many "events" are created particularly to show presidents at their best and not necessarily to produce tangible, public policy or foreign policy results. Though such use of political spectacle had roots in earlier presidencies, including the two Roosevelts, Miroff credits the presidency of John Kennedy with demonstrating the promise of such a public relations strategy as a central element in presidential leadership. From Kennedy's administration on, this aspect of the presidential relationship with the public grew to the point that under Jimmy Carter "spectacle specialists" like pollster Patrick Caddell and advertising expert Gerald Rafshoon became prominent members of the administration. From his cardigan sweater, to his walk down Pennsylvania Avenue at his inauguration, to his town meetings, Carter sought to create a spectacle of a modest, democratic presidency to contrast with the perceived "imperial" presidencies of Johnson and Nixon. But no president was more successful at such spectacles than was Ronald Reagan, a true master of wielding cultural and political symbols.

Rhetorical representation and representation through public relations has become the norm; indeed, perhaps it is the most legitimate form of representation available after the institutionalization of the plebiscitary presidency. And there is evidence that the public itself has come to accept the thesis that to be a good president one must also be a "great communicator."[33] The result is that presidents must regularly, almost constantly, be before the television cameras.

The representational link of rhetoric and public politics indeed is so fragile, it is so weak, that presidents must constantly tend to its health. They may only make a few major national policy addresses each year, but they still need to make daily appearances at ceremonies, give speeches to groups where news cameras are constantly present, or just take a few questions from reporters on the way out of the White House or during picture taking ceremonies. Presidential representation in the age of television means constantly being seen; constantly having an opinion, a program, and regularly being heard; or at least hearing of the president and his activities on nightly news described by trusted advisors and his public relations men.

Consequences of Rhetorical Representation

The rhetorical nature of much of presidential activity and the public relations aspects that are such an important part of so much of the modern presidency raises important questions for representative government. What effects has it had or is it likely to have on the complex system of representation that we have seen to be the Founders' intent? In what position of influence does rhetorical representation place other non-elected figures in American public life? What impact has the new presidential rhetoric had on deliberative democracy?

Among the most important effects of the modern presidential practice of rhetorical leadership is the effect that it has on that other important branch of political representation, Congress. Presidents have forged their linkages to the public to a considerable degree at the expense of the traditional role of the legislature in the representative process of free government. The president's is the one national political voice that almost always can command the attention of television and can draw a national audience. No other political star shines as bright, except perhaps during general election campaigns every four years when opposition party candidates are treated as a central news maker as much as the president himself. As an institution, Congress is greatly disadvantaged in our age of personalized politics.

Whereas in earlier years presidents primarily bargained with Congress and engaged legislators on their own ground, the new leadership strategy of going public subverts the role of the legislature.[34] Presidents go over the heads of Congress to persuade congressional constituents in hopes of pressuring members to vote as the president would wish.[35] Such a leadership strategy is closer to brute force than to persuasion, as presidents call upon public opinion to force Congress to bend to their will. As Samuel Kernell has noted, this type of leadership "usurps their [Congressmen's] prerogatives of office, denies their role as representatives, and questions their claim to reflect the interests of their constituents."[36]

Representation through rhetorical appeals has the effect of simplifying representative government and of further centralizing it in the presidency, the institution often said to be the one legitimate determiner of the national interest. Congress thereby is delegitimized to the same degree as the president claims primacy in providing representation. With the direct, plebiscitary link between the people and their president, a Congress bent on doing its duty in a deliberative republic comes to be perceived as only an obstacle in the way of popular measures. Their role as independent representatives is denied; they are brought within the plebiscitary nature of the president-public relationship and there the deliberative role of the legislature withers. Television and "going public" considerably upsets the balance between the executive and the legislature.[37]

Another important question dealing with the rhetorical presidency and representation involves those we may loosely term "unelected representatives." Michael J. Malbin has raised important questions about the role played by congressional staff in the decline of actual deliberation in our national legislature.[38] Similar questions might be raised about the rhetorical presidency.

Experts in advertising, spin-doctoring, and public relations have grown in importance in the modern White House. One of Lyndon Johnson's closest aides was Jack Valenti, an advertising specialist who later went into the motion picture business. Richard Nixon had several aides who came to the administration from advertising firms, including his chief of staff H.R. Haldeman. Carter moved his advertising director, Gerald Rafsoon, from his 1976 campaign into an important place on the White House staff. One of the three most important men in the Reagan White House during his first term was Michael Deaver, a longtime Reaganite and professional P.R. man from California. Deaver was primarily responsible for crafting the "visuals" intended to define the President and the administration in the eye of the public. In the age of television, these aides are afforded an important place in determining the political "reality" of Washington.

Presidential aides to deal with the press have been important at least since Franklin Roosevelt. In 1969 Richard Nixon created the White House Office of Communications to exploit the potential of media outlets by giving the White House more of a capacity to manage the news coverage. Though Gerald Ford initially attempted to govern without such an office, he soon established one of his own and the structure has since become institutionalized in the White House. By the Bush administration the Office of Communications had grown into a central player in the White House structure with its own large staff resources. With the importance of the media and "image creation" in modern politics, no president could afford not to have such an organization.

Of particular concern is the central place that has been accorded speech writers in the White House by most modern presidents. Peggy Noonan, the most celebrated wordsmith of the 1980s, captured the centrality of word-weavers in the Reagan White House, "speechwriting. . . was where the philosophical, ideological, and political tensions of the administration got worked out." She went on, "Speechwriting was where the administration got invented every day."[39] With the centrality of presidential speech comes the centrality of presidential speech writers to representative government. That is not to say the principal elected representative, the president, is no longer "in charge" or no longer responsible. Rather, it is simply to note that with the new representational linkage between the president and the public, other non-elected figures have come to occupy a central place in determining the nature and character of representation.

Alexander Solzhenitsyn observed in a 1978 speech at Harvard University that "the press has become the greatest power within the Western countries, more powerful than the legislature, the executive, and the judiciary."[40] Though perhaps Solzhenitsyn overstates his case, there is no but that the media have become one of the most important institutions in contemporary representative government. In presidential politics the broadcast media function as the conduit for communication between the president and the public. The media perform a "linkage function" between the people and their central political and symbolic representative.[41] This is a symbiotic relationship; the presidency and the media feed on each other.

> The media has found in the presidency a focal point on which to concentrate its peculiarly simplistic and dramatic interpretation of events; and the presidency has found a vehicle in the media that allows it to win public attention and with that attention the reality, but more often the pretense, of enhanced power.[42]

Members of the media operate as non-elected representatives and are particularly concerned with what they perceive to be the public's "right to know." It is through the broadcast media that the president can most directly reach the people. But the media is not merely a value-free or value-neutral vehicle for presidential communication. Rather, members of the media function as the gatekeepers of our public politics. They decide what angle of the story is told, they decide whether or not a certain presidential activity is worthy of coverage, they more than the members of any other institution are the ones who are most responsible for evaluating presidential facts and performances and provide instant analysis of presidential speeches. The media has become an ever present player in the drama of representative government in America.

Indeed, plebiscitary presidential politics places the media in such a central place that some have argued they have superseded in importance the more traditional branch of representation, the legislature. Theodore Otto Windt has argued that the importance of presidential rhetoric to modern governance and the centrality of television in American life have led to a new system of checks and balances that is far from what the Founders had envisioned. While Congress now serves primarily as a check on the presidency, the news media now has come to function as a "rhetorical check" on presidential pronouncements, Windt argues.[43] Harvey Mansfield has warned that the prevalence of the non-elected representatives of the media marks a radical departure for representative democracy in America. We are moving, he argues, to a type of "formless representation" that undermines the representative institutions established by the Constitution to promote deliberative and free government.[44]

The relationship between presidential rhetoric and its transmitters in the media also raises another problem for reasoned argument in politics and government. The media routinely reduces presidential rhetoric to the soundbites that seem almost natural in the age of television and that have come to be expected by a populace raised on the medium.[45] During the 1988 presidential campaign, Michael Dukakis's campaign chairman Paul Brountas was told by a reporter, "Goddamn it, Paul. You've got to get your candidate to stop pausing between sentences. He's taking twenty-two seconds to complete a thought."[46] Information and argument about complex budgetary, economic, and social issues are reduced to one-liners that could not possibly convey any of the nuances of the issues or arguments. What is more troubling, the already short have gotten even shorter. From 1968 to 1988 the average soundbite for presidential candidates on the evening news shrank from 42.3 seconds to just 9.8 seconds[47] and did not change appreciably in 1992.[48]

And television is not the only medium where candidates' words have shrunk. The average continuous quote or paragraph of a candidate in a front page story of the *New York Times* was fourteen lines in 1960 but had shrunk to an average of just six lines in 1992.[49] Upon such a pittance a healthy democracy could hardly be built.

Of further consequence to public policy and the health of the polity, presidential representation through rhetoric and television coverage necessitates creation of the image of the officer always "doing something."[50] To fulfill the representational duties that come with the plebiscitary presidency, there is pressure on presidents to have instant reactions to domestic and international events and to have almost instant answers to problems that arise in the course of the nation's life. There is often precious little time to deliberate, to just sit and think. As Stephen Hess has put it, "While doing something may be imperative, the pressures to act often mean the alternatives are not carefully weighed."[51] This haste, this rush to react in real time, is closely connected to the other central plebiscitary linkage between the people and their representative in the White House. Namely, it is primarily because of the rewards found in the opinion polls that presidents are driven to the necessity to act and react constantly. They are rewarded for such activity and punished for failing to so act.[52] It is public approval and what it can bring in Washington that necessitates the constant campaign centered in the White House.[53]

Taking Our Pulse:
Pollsters and the Proliferation of Opinion Polls

In 1970 George Reedy remarked, "The exercise of leadership has little or nothing to do with the personal popularity of a president. Among the responses that a president should seek to invoke from the people, liking is probably the least important."[54] Such a statement, however constructive it might be in theory, shows little understanding of the actual operations of the plebiscitary presidency of the twentieth century. Public approval has become one of the most central ingredients in presidential representation in the contemporary polity.

Republicans tried opinion polling as early as the 1896 presidential election and the magazine *Literary Digest* began conducting and publishing polls in 1916, but it was not until the 1930s that they began to be taken seriously by presidents and the Washington community. It was in 1935 that George Gallup began asking the famous "Do you approve of the president" question that has since been used in some version by nearly all polling organizations.[55]

In FDR's effort to build a mass national constituency he paid careful attention to the polls done by Gallup, Roper, and various publications and even began the presidential practice of commissioning his own opinion polls.[56] Polling and pollsters have been a central aspect of the modern presidency and American politics ever since. They now function as a near constant referendum on the individual in the office and his program.

This constant referendum has entrapped modern presidents. In Washington and in the media, poll results matter, a fact of which presidents and their aides are well aware. At least in part, this situation is one for which presidents themselves are responsible. When up in the polls and when backing legislation that has found a welcome home with the public, presidents have wielded poll results as proof that they are one with the public whose will should be enacted. Lyndon Johnson, for instance, regularly carried poll results around in his pocket and brandished them freely when they supported his position. And polls do matter in Congress. George Edwards has shown that the higher the public's level of approval of the president, the more support his program tends to receive in Congress.[57] Ronald Reagan's media expert Michael Deaver put the understanding this way: "You have to inspire support for the President if you are going to rally support for his policies. This is basic. This is the essence of good P.R. This is politics."[58] This, we might add, is presidential representation in the twentieth century.

But if presidential power thrives by the polls, it might also die by the polls. While popular presidents tend to get much of what they want and are willing to fight for, unpopular presidents are trapped and constrained by the polls. As a senior aide to President Carter mused about that president's problems with a Congress controlled by his own party, "When the President is low in public opinion polls, the members of Congress see little hazard in bucking him. . . . They read the polls and from that they feel secure in turning their backs on the President with political impunity. Unquestionably, the success of the President's policies bear a tremendous relationship to his popularity in the polls."[59] Without effective public relations, modern presidents and their programs wither on the vine of public opinion.

Two examples will serve to illuminate this connection. In 1972 President Richard Nixon won one of the largest landslides in U.S. electoral history. In addition to his own victory, Republicans gained twelve seats in the House and two in the Senate. By 1973 the Vietnam war had nearly ended and Nixon had replaced his unpopular vice president Spiro Agnew with the experienced legislative leader Gerald Ford. Despite this situation that would seem so favorable to presidential success with Congress, Nixon's support on Capitol Hill dropped dramatically in 1973 from previous years as he won just barely half of the votes on which he took a position. (His previous low, 1972, was 66 percent.) What is to explain it? "The most reasonable explanation for Richard Nixon's substantial decline in support among members of Congress in 1973," notes George Edwards, "is his equally substantial decline in public approval, primarily because of the Watergate affair."[60] Nixon's approval rating dropped thirty points in one year from 59 percent in December 1972 to 29 percent in 1973. When his popularity slipped, so did his influence in Congress.[61]

A good example of the positive influence public opinion can have on presidential power and legislative success can be found in the example of Ronald Reagan's 1981 success with Congress. Though Reagan entered office with only the modest approval rating of 51 percent, by mid-May it had exploded to 68 percent in large part due to the honorable way he handled the attempt on his life that spring. This boost in popularity was just in time for the important Congressional votes on the president's budget and tax cuts and was important in their passage. Even Democratic leaders like Speaker of the House Tip O'Neill and Senate Democratic leader Robert Byrd acknowledged the difficulty with which Democrats could oppose the popular president. In contrast, by November Reagan's approval rating had dropped 19 points with a subsequent loss of support in Congress. When the White House sent up a bill calling for additional budget cuts, it never even made it to the floor of either chamber.

This is clearly not to argue that presidential popularity is the sole, or even the most important, ingredient that goes into the congressional decision-making process. However, it is to make the argument that presidents have become trapped by their own plebiscitary linkages to the American public. They are trapped within the reinforcing spiral of public relations, polling data, public expectations, and congressional decision-making processes. At least to a degree, presidential influence and presidential power fluctuate with the rhythms of the public mind. The direct link between the president and the people that was intended to make that office the most democratically legitimate and hence most legitimately empowered political institution has in actuality weakened the office before the tide of political fortune. Where the presidency's power was originally to lay in the firm but narrow foundation of the written Constitution, the modern presidency's power and influence has been built upon the shifting sands of public opinion and political fortune.

In their efforts to cope with this situation, presidents have turned both to public relations men, as we have seen, as well as to professional pollsters. Franklin Roosevelt was the first president to retain a pollster when he tapped Hadley Cantril of the Institute for Social Research in Princeton, New Jersey to measure public attitudes before and during

America's involvement in World War II. Since the administration of John F. Kennedy all presidents have retained private polling firms and some pollsters have served as close presidential advisors. According to Lyndon Johnson's press secretary, Bill Moyers, Johnson used polls in two ways: "as a bludgeon to convince wavering and uncommitted constituents or as a feather to tickle; and secondly, as a source of intelligence to find out where he was weakest so he could shore up that area." According to Harry O'Neil and Robert Teeter, who conducted polls for him, President Nixon was particularly concerned about polls. According to Teeter, who would later do polls for presidents Ford and Bush, "Nixon had all kinds of polls all of the time; he sometimes had a couple of pollsters doing the same kind of survey at the same time. He really studied them. He wanted to find the thing that would give him an advantage."[62]

President Carter was the first to have an "in-house" pollster who also served as an important political advisor and a de facto member of the White House staff, though his salary was paid by the Democratic National Committee. According to fellow Democratic pollster Peter Hart, Patrick Caddell was more involved in the day-to-day operations of the White House than any previous pollster. Indeed, Caddell shared a home in Washington with two of Carter's top aides; Hamilton Jordan who would become Carter's chief of staff and Tim Kraft who was in charge of political affairs for the president.[63]

Even more than in the Carter White House, Reagan's chief pollster was an important player in the administration. Whereas Pat Caddell had dealt mainly with a few top aides during his time working for President Carter, Richard Wirthlin, Reagan's pollster, regularly met with the president himself and had frequent conversations with chief of staff James Baker, his deputy Michael Deaver, and counselor to the president Edwin Meese, along with a number of lesser players in the White House.[64] During the 1980 campaign, Wirthlin was heavily involved in planning and strategy and functioned in the same capacity during the transition. It also was Wirthlin who devised the plan to exploit the force of public opinion during the administration's first hundred days to keep pressure on Congressmen and overcome the opposition to the Reagan program.[65] Wirthlin, like Caddell, was paid by the party's national committee, not the White House.

"Perhaps more than any other administration," concluded presidential watcher Dom Bonafede in 1981, "the Reagan White House uses polling, public opinion analysis and media and market research as contributory elements in the decision-making process and the selling of the presidency."[66] During the Reagan administration, Wirthlin not only made wide use of traditional survey methods of polling but also made considerable use of focus groups and electronic means of measuring people's responses to individual presidential phrases during speeches. According to Bonafede, much of Wirthlin's job and that of the Planning and Evaluation Office of the Reagan White House, which was headed by one time Wirthlin consultant Richard S. Beal, was to insure that the president's policies were timed correctly so as to "fit" the political climate. Polls, however, did not drive policy in the Reagan administration, according to Wirthlin. He cited Reagan's firing of the air traffic controllers in 1981, which the polling data said would be very unpopular, as evidence of the president's ability to act independently of polling data.[67] Still, Reagan speech writer Peggy Noonan has written, "When I left the Reagan White House [1986] I felt that polls are now driving more than politics, they are driving history."[68]

In the Bush White House, the president and his first chief of staff John Sununu continued the obsession with public opinion data. Though the president himself denied on several occasions that he was concerned with polls, they played an important role in his administration. In November 1991 Bush told reporters, "I don't live and die by the polls," but went on to concede otherwise, "Thus I will refrain from pointing out that we're not doing bad in those polls."[69] Bush is said to have made use of polls in private lobbying sessions showing his position to be more popular than the opposition's, and he and Sununu frequently consulted a chart comparing his month by month approval scores with those of his predecessors. There also is evidence that concern for his scores affected Bush's approach to the office, the issues he took up, and his personnel decisions.[70] Indeed, Bush became the first president ever to make mention of his own poll ratings in his State of the Union address.[71]

The centrality of polling and the institutionalized place of presidential pollsters continue unabated, indeed they may have even intensified with the inauguration of William Jefferson Clinton in 1993.[72] In his first year in office, Clinton spent nearly two million dollars on polling, purchasing three or four polls every month and an equal amount of focus groups.[73] Clinton's pollster Stanley Greenberg personally met at least once a week with the President during that same time, which is more than twice the rate at which Reagan met with his pollster during 1981. Greenberg, though on contract with the national party and not the White House, as has been the custom with presidential pollsters, was at the White House almost daily participating in one meeting or another. According to Greenberg, Clinton was so obsessed with poll results that he could recite minute details about survey data off the top of his head. In December 1993, Greenberg went so far as to admit that the administration had made a major decision about financing its health care plan after consulting poll results showing a new tax would be unpopular.[74] Public approval rates for both presidents and individual policies have become of central importance to the media and the Washington community. Pollsters now have found a permanent home in the institutionalized White House and have become important players in the public policy process.

Representational Consequences

"In this and like communities, public sentiment is everything," said Abraham Lincoln in the first of his debates with Stephen Douglas in 1858. "With public sentiment nothing can fail;" he went on, "without it nothing can succeed."[75] Such a state of affairs has never been more the case than in American politics of the twentieth century. Advances in polling technology, a more radicalized democratic ethic, and presidential use of public approval to support programs have empowered public opinion to a degree greater than at any other time in the history of the American polity. But what of this development's impact on presidential representation and representative government more generally?

First, the prevalence of public opinion polling and the degree to which it is taken seriously by the media and political leaders raise questions about the style of representation possible to contemporary presidents. What effects do public opinion polls have on the "space" of independence that was designed to separate our representatives in the national government from the public at large and thereby facilitate the development of a deliberative public will?

Presidents regularly claim to make decisions according to what their judgment tells them is in the nation's best interest, whether those decisions are popular or unpopular. In a 1970 speech on the invasion of Cambodia, Richard Nixon said, "I would rather be a one-term president and do what I believe is right than to be a two-term president at the cost of seeing America become a second-rate power and to see this nation accept its first defeat in its proud 190-year history."[76] In 1980 former president Gerald Ford commented, "I do not think a President should run the country on the basis of the polls. The public in so many cases does not have a full comprehension of a problem. A President ought to listen to the people, but he cannot make hard decisions just by reading the polls once a week."[77]

Though presidents may claim to provide representation in the spirit of Burke, at other times they have celebrated their perfect harmony with the public. Especially when pushing programs that have found favor with the public, presidents have found it in their interest to claim to be one with the will of the people and have urged their opponents to fall in line with the people's desires. It may well be the case that the dynamics of public opinion polling and their centrality as news stories and as benchmarks in Washington, has made the independent style of representation exceedingly difficult for contemporary presidents—especially on issues in which the public has shown a particular interest or strong opinions.

An instructive example of this situation can be found in Richard Nixon's use of the rhetorical cloak of the "silent majority" with which he covered his actions and programs. When elite opinion and activists were against him, Nixon claimed to represent a truer national majority. He could have asserted that his actions accorded with his own best judgment as an elected constitutional officer that needed no other sanction. But the president seemed to understand well the importance of being perceived to be of one mind with the public in modern politics. At the very least, presidents today must rhetorically make claim to doing the public's bidding.

More than a century and a half ago, Alexis de Tocqueville worried that allowing the president to seek reelection would lead the incumbent to be concerned chiefly for his own popularity and chance for reelection. Such a situation, Tocqueville pointed out, tended to reduce the president to "an easy tool in the hands of the majority," rather than the independent force in government that the Founders intended. "He adopts its likings and its animosities, he anticipates its wishes, he forestalls its complaints, he yields to its idlest cravings, and instead of guiding it, as the legislature intended that he should do, he merely follows its bidding."[78] Though such reelection concerns can be said to be endemic to the office of the presidency, they were one of the republican safety mechanisms placed intentionally in the office by its Framers. The modern practice of polling can be seen to regularize and intensify such tendencies in the presidency.

As Paul Brace and Barbara Hinckley have noted, the time frame of democracy itself has been altered by the modern practice of polling.[79] The four year cycle of reelection has been crammed into thirty-day races to perform well in the next month's opinion polls. Regularized polling makes the pressures and concerns of public opinion more imminent—from the polls there is no respite. Presidents, like most of us, tend to want to be liked, they want to be popular. Modern presidents also are well aware that, as Lyndon Johnson put it, "Presidential popularity is a major source of strength in gaining cooperation from Congress."[80] To the extent that the polls are watched in the White House, reported in the media, and to the degree presidents perceive the success of their presidency and pet policy projects dependent on their own personal popularity and that of their policies, independence in presidential decision making is threatened. This would be especially true for issues that are of great public concern, that have been made into major stories by the media, or on which Congress would need considerable persuading. On other types of decisions, such as on issues of little public concern on which congressional action is not necessary (executive orders, vetoes, lower-level appointments), presidents would seem to be afforded freer reign to disregard what little public opinion they might perceive to exist.

The personalization of representation in the presidency as best exemplified in the importance of presidential approval surveys also holds import for the style of representation offered in Congress. Congressmen have come to take presidential approval as one of a number of cues that go into their decision-making process. To the degree that they allow such information to color their decisions, either out of a concern for their own reelection or out of a genuine belief that presidential approval represents the will of the people which should hold sway in government, Congressmen are placed in a closer and more coercive relationship with the public. The proliferation of polling has altered both the conditions and the incentives under which government decisions are made.

The almost constant presidential search for new "mandates" also may have the effect of speeding up the process of governance. The timing of presidential proposals, Congressional action, and official announcements have become dependent upon the timing and results of public opinion surveys. Popular presidents have more legislative success than less popular ones. As presidential support tends to diminish over a president's time in office, he must act quickly after his inauguration before public approval begins to decay and with it support for his program in Congress.[81] Certain unforeseen, and perhaps even uncontrollable, occurrences also may happen from time to time to extend or renew support for the president among the public and therefore on Capitol Hill, such as Reagan's reaction to the attempt on his life in 1981. And during these times as well, presidents must act quickly to make the most of the opportunity.

The classic example of this circumvention of the slow, deliberative process of government can be seen in Lyndon Johnson's "Great Society" program. Johnson himself was very perceptive of his need to strike quickly while his popularity held-up. Despite winning one of the largest landslide elections in history in 1964, Johnson already perceived his approval slipping by January 1965 and he set out to push all his goals and programs at once. He explained to his congressional liaison men, "I was just elected President by the biggest popular margin in the history of the country—16 million votes. . . . I've already lost about three of those sixteen. After a fight with Congress or something else, I'll lose another couple of million. I could be down to 8 million in a couple of months."[82]

The desire to move very quickly on a whole myriad of issues created what Doris Kearns has referred to as a politics of haste that affected both the substance and the style of the Great Society. Kearns has written, "the need for haste often resulted in a failure to define the precise nature and requirement of social objectives. Legislative solutions were often devised and rushed into law before the problems were understood."[83] For a visionary president such as Johnson, operating in the polling-intense days of the late twentieth century, such politics of haste was a great enticement. When the standards of success for the media, the public, and in Washington are measured by the number of presidential programs passed, presidents will follow the poll dynamics and their incentive will be to strike quickly and encourage equally quick disposal in Congress. To that exent the deliberative process of representative government is undermined. Deliberation is strangled by the need for haste; it can thrive only with time.[84]

In addition to adequate time, deliberative democracy requires that representatives and the represented be separated by sufficient "space" to enable the representative to freely engage others in the political realm and to be open to persuasion as facts and arguments merit. As we have already noted, the centrality of pulse-taking of the public to some degree at least undermines the integrity of this space. But there is one other way in which it has this same effect. Due largely to the intensified democratic ethos of the twentieth century and to the way polls are covered by the media, the concept of political truth itself has been altered.

Various polling organizations and media institutions take monthly opinion polls measuring the public's attitude toward the president and regularly ask the public about their opinion on specific major presidential programs and legislative initiatives. Such measures have changed the way the public and its political class think about public policy. In the age of polls, what is popular becomes what is true; what the people seem to prefer becomes the definition of good public policy. A popular president is perceived to be a successful president, and his policies are taken to be more worthy of passage than if proposed by a less popular chief executive. Popular legislation becomes, by definition, good legislation.

Conclusion

The American presidency was established originally not only as an executive institution but also as a check on the legislative branch and a facilitator of the deliberative process of government. As such, the office was designed in such a way as to insulate the officeholder from many of the temporary gusts and swells of public opinion. Toward this end, presidential power found its most solid foundation in the Constitution itself. Throughout most of the nineteenth century, the presidency essentially functioned in that way with Congress maintaining its place as the first branch of government and its closer connection to the public, albeit a public divided according to the established basis of legislative representation.

Backed by an understanding of executive power and democratic politics championed by the progressives of the early twentieth century, Franklin Delano Roosevelt and those who followed him to 1600 Pennsylvania Avenue transformed the presidency's relationship to the public. Through modern elections, direct rhetorical appeals by radio and television, and the proliferation of public opinion polls, modern presidents have become directly connected to the changing mind of the mass public.

Some presidents and commentators have considered this a liberation of the office from the narrow confines imposed on it by the formalistic power structure of the Constitution. They have argued with Wilson and Franklin Roosevelt that a strong "personal" presidency was needed to bring the government into concert in the name of democratic progressivism and/or public policy implementation. In actuality, however, this development can be understood as an enfeeblement of the representational presidency as presidential authority has become dependent on the rhetorical ability of presidents and their personal popularity.

For the good "salesman" in the office who is personally popular and forwards proposals that have met with popular favor, the developments of the twentieth century have indeed been empowering ones. But for presidents who cannot count great oratory or salesmanship among their other gifts and who would challenge the reigning public prejudices, the dynamics of the contemporary presidency function as barriers that limit and constrain presidential influence in government.

In this situation the costs of an independence style of presidential representation become exceedingly high and the incentives to be a compliant delegate of a temporary majority become very enticing indeed. In this atmosphere in which the traditional line between "popular" and "right" has been blurred, presidents and their opponents must function primarily as P.R. men for their side. "The story" centers, not on reasoned argumentation about costs and benefits, but on the "horserace" of who's up and who's down that is the way the media tends to portray so many political stories. In this situation the space between representatives and their public is reduced. Armed with the latest public opinion numbers, political figures can too often overcome the most well-reasoned arguments about the public good. The plebiscitary nature of the modern presidency leads to the atrophy of much of the "space" necessary for representatives to act in a deliberative republic. The deliberative aspects of the government decay in turn and, as we will see in the next chapter, produce what has become the presidentially-dominated administrative republic of the twentieth century.

Notes

1. Jeffrey K. Tulis, *The Rhetorical Presidency* (Princeton, N.J.: Princeton University Press, 1987).

2. Theodore J. Lowi, *The Personal President: Power Invested, Promise Unfulfilled* (Ithaca, N.Y.: Cornell University Press, 1985), 30.

3. Rexford G. Tugwell, *The Enlargement of the Presidency* (New York: Doubleday, 1960).

4. See Tulis, 1987.

5. Reprinted in Harry A. Bailey, Jr. and Jay M. Shafritz, eds., *The American Presidency: Historical and Contemporary Perspectives* (Pacific Grove, Calif.: Brooks/Cole Publishing Company, 1988), 34.

6. Fred I. Greenstein, "Change and Continuity in the Modern Presidency," in Anthony King, ed., *The New American Political System* (Washington, D.C.: American Enterprise Institute Press, 1978), 45.

7. Sidney M. Milkis and Michael Nelson, *The American Presidency: Origins and Development, 1776-1990* (Washington, D.C.: CQ Press, 1990), 264.

8. See the discussion of the electoral college in Chapters One and Two.

9. By 1832 only South Carolina retained the method of legislative selection of electors. It was the last state to make the change to popular vote and did so only after the Civil War. See Stephen J. Wayne, *The Road to the White House 1992: The Politics of Presidential Elections* (New York: St. Martin's press, 1992), 15 and 17.

10. Excepting of course the rare occurrence in which the candidate winning the most popular votes does not win the presidency, such as happened in 1824, 1876, and 1888. This is also not to deny that the electoral college still has other important benefits such as exaggerating the size of electoral victories and thereby strengthening the hand of elected presidents. See Walter Berns, ed., *After the People Vote: A Guide to the Electoral College* (Washington, D.C.: AEI Press, 1992).

11. Cited in James W. Ceaser, *Presidential Selection: Theory and Development* (Princeton, N.J.: Princeton University Press, 1979), 275.

12. See Austin Ranney, "Turnout and Representation in Presidential Primary Elections," *American Political Science Review* (March 1972), 21-37.

13. The Democrats did make other adjustments to their nomination process that also stemmed from a certain conception of representation. Namely, they instituted a quota system by which more women, blacks, and young people would attend the party convention, thus making it more "representative" of the party electorate. The Republican party has never made such a representational assumption, nor has it instituted such a quota system for delegates.

14. Ryan J. Barilleaux, *The Post-Modern Presidency: The Office After Reagan* (New York: Praeger, 1988), 70.

15. For the media's function in nomination campaigns, see Ryan J. Barilleaux and Randall E. Adkins, "The Nomination Process and Patterns," in *The Elections of 1992*, Michael Nelson, ed. (Washington, D.C.: CQ Press, 1993), 27-29.

16. See Harvey C. Mansfield, Jr., *Statesmanship and Party Government* (Chicago: University of Chicago Press, 1965).

17. See Wilson Carey McWilliams, "The Anti-Federalists, Representation and Party," *Northwestern University Law Review*, Volume 84, Number 1 (Fall, 1989), cited in Sidney M. Milkis, *The President and the Parties: The Transformation of the American Party System Since the New Deal* (New York: Oxford University Press, 1993), 5.

18. Milkis, 1993, 6.

19. Milkis, 1993, 9.

20. See Milkis, 1993.

21. David R. Mayhew, *Congress: The Electoral Connection* (New Haven: Yale University Press, 1974), 70-71.

22. Quoted in Paul C. Light, *The President's Agenda* (Baltimore: Johns Hopkins University Press, 1982), 30.

23. Charles O. Jones, "The Role of the Campaign in Congressional Politics," in *The Electoral Process*, M. Kent Jennings and L. Harmon Zeigler, eds. (Englewood Cliffs, N.J.: Prentice-Hall, 1966), 21.

24. Ceaser, 1979, 17.

25. Godfrey Hodgson, *All Things to All Men: The False Promise of the Modern Presidency* (New York: Simon and Schuster, 1980), 211.

26. George C. Edwards III, *The Public Presidency: The Pursuit of Popular Support* (New York: St. Martin's Press, 1983), 1.

27. Mary E. Stuckey, *The President as Interpreter-In-Chief* (Chatham, N.J.: Chatham House Publishers, 1991), 35.

28. Eisenhower was the first to use televised campaign commercials and he hired actor Robert Montgomery as a consultant for television appearances. And, according to Ted Sorensen, no problem of the presidency concerned John F. Kennedy more than did those of public communication. For this point on Kennedy, see Theodore C. Sorensen, *Kennedy* (New York: Bantam, 1966), 346.

29. Samuel Kernell, *Going Public: New Strategies for Presidential Leadership* (Washington, D.C.: CQ Press, 1986), 86. These figures are from the yearly average for the first three years of the first term for Hoover and Reagan. The numbers for Reagan do not include his weekly radio address to the nation, which, if calculated, would greatly inflate his figures.

30. Kernell, 1986, 93-98.

31. Bruce Miroff, "The Presidency and the Public: Leadership as Spectacle," in *The Presidency and the Political System*, 2nd edition, Michael Nelson, ed. (Washington, D.C.: CQ Press, 1988), 290.

32. Miroff, 1988, 293.

33. In a CBS News/*New York Times* Poll from February, 1984, 76 percent of respondents said that being a "great communicator" was necessary to being a good president. Cited in George C. Edwards III, *At the Margins: Presidential Leadership of Congress* (New Haven: Yale University Press, 1989), 129. Or, witness the June 1996 poll commissioned by *U.S. News and World Report* that pitted GOP presidential candidate Senator Robert Dole against President Bill Clinton. Voters were asked to imagine they were starting a business with the candidates. By a margin of 55 percent to 24 percent, voters preferred candidate Dole to keep the company's books while 73 percent to 19 percent thought Clinton would be better at *selling* the product—this at the same time that the poll reported Clinton ahead of Dole by 13 percent. Gloria Borger and Linda Kulman, "Does Character Count?" *U.S. News & World Report* (June 24, 1996), 35-41.

34. This is not to say that "elite bargaining" has been completely outlived. Rather, it is to say that "going public" has, to a significant degree, replaced it as the dominant form of presidential leadership. On issues where it is not in the president's interest to make overt public appeals, they still may choose to "stay private." See Cary R. Covington, "'Staying Private': Gaining Congressional Support for Unpublished Presidential Preferences on Roll-Call Voting," *Journal of Politics* 49 (August 1987), 737-755.

35. Of course, presidents are not always successful in such endeavors. George C. Edwards, 1983, has provided significant evidence of the forces that handicap presidential appeals over the heads of Congress to the public.

36. Kernell, 1986, 4.

37. See Robert Cirino, *Don't Blame the People* (New York: Random House, 1971); Newton N. Minnow, John Barlow Martin, and Lee M. Mitchell, *Presidential Television* (New York: Basic Books, 1973).

38. Michael J. Malbin, *Unelected Representatives: Congressional Staff and the Future of Representative Government* (New York: Basic Books, 1980).

39. Peggy Noonan, *What I Saw at the Revolution: A Political Life in the Reagan Era* (New York: Random House, 1990), 67.

40. Alexander Solzhenitsyn, "The Exhausted West," *Harvard Magazine* (July-August, 1978), 23.

41. Making a similar point see William G. Spragens, *The Presidency and the Mass Media in the Age of Television* (Washington, D.C.: University Press of America, 1978).

42. James W. Ceaser, Glen E. Thurow, Jeffrey Tulis, and Joseph M. Bessette, "The Rise of the Rhetorical Presidency," *Presidential Studies Quarterly* (Spring 1981), 165.

43. Theodore Otto Windt, Jr. "Presidential Rhetoric: Definition of a Field of Study," *Presidential Studies Quarterly* (Winter 1986), 110.

44. Harvey C. Mansfield, Jr. *America's Constitutional Soul* (Baltimore: The Johns Hopkins University Press, 1991), 163-176.

45. This is not to cast blame simply on the media, it is, of course, the very job of modern speechwriters to provide the kind of one-liners that the media then transmit to the public. There is plenty of blame to go around.

46. Reported by Paul Taylor of the *Washington Post* and quoted in James S. Fishkin, *Democracy and Deliberation: New Directions for Democratic Reform* (New Haven: Yale University Press, 1991), 63.

47. Kiku Adato, "The Incredible Shrinking Sound Bite," (Cambridge, Mass.: Joan Shorenstein Barone Center of the John F. Kennedy School of Government, Research Paper No. 2, June 1990), 4.

48. "Clinton's the One," *Media Monitor* (Washington, D.C.: Center for Media and Public Affairs, November 1992), 2.

49. Thomas E. Patterson, *Out of Order* (New York: Vintage Books, 1994), 75-76.

50. On this point see Thomas E. Cronin, *The State of the Presidency*, 2nd edition (Boston: Little, Brown and Company, 1980), 105-107.

51. Stephen Hess, quoted in Thomas E. Cronin, *The State of the Presidency*, 2nd edition (Boston: Little, Brown and Company, 1980), 106.

52. See Cronin, 1980, 105-107.

53. Particularly with the decline of the political parties, presidents have had to "go public" to achieve success in Washington. See George E. Reedy, "The Presidency in the Era of Mass Communication," in *Modern Presidents and the Presidency*, Marc Landy, ed. (Lexington, Mass.: Lexington Books, 1985), 35-41.

54. George E. Reedy, *The Twilight of the Presidency* (New York: Mentor, 1970), 56.

55. For the evolution of this question see George C. Edwards III and Alec M. Gallup, *Presidential Approval: A Sourcebook* (Baltimore: The Johns Hopkins University Press, 1990).

56. Theodore J. Lowi, *The Personal President: Power Invested, Promise Unfulfilled* (Ithaca, N.Y.: Cornell University Press, 1985), 62.

57. George C. Edwards III, *Presidential Influence in Congress* (San Francisco: Freeman, 1980), chapter 4.

58. Michael K. Deaver with Mickey Herskowitz, *Behind the Scenes* (New York: William Morrow and Company, 1987), 140.

59. Quoted in Dom Bonafede, "The Strained Relationship," *National Journal* (May 19, 1979), 830.

60. Edwards, 1989, 115.

61. Examples adopted from Edwards, 1989, 114-117.

62. This paragraph was adopted from Dom Bonafede, "How Former Presidents Have Used the Polls," *National Journal* (August 19, 1978), 1314.

63. Dom Bonafede, "Carter and the Polls—If You Live by Them, You May Die by Them," *National Journal* (August 19, 1978), 1312-1315.

64. Dom Bonafede, "As Pollster to the President, Wirthlin Is Where the Action Is," *National Journal* (December 12, 1981), 2184-2188.

65. Edwin Meese III, *With Reagan: The Inside Story* (Washington, D.C.: Regnery Gateway, 1992), 61-74.

66. Bonafede, 1981, 2184.

67. Bonafede, 1981, 2186.

68. Noonan, 1990, 249.

69. Michael Duffy and Dan Goodgame, *Marching in Place: The Status Quo Presidency of George Bush* (New York: Simon and Schuster, 1992), 75.

70. See Duffy and Goodgame, 1992, 75-77; 107; 127.

71. Brace and Hinckley, 1992, vi.

72. For the importance of public opinion surveys to the Clinton White House during the first year, see Bob Woodward, *The Agenda: Inside the Clinton White House* (New York: Simon & Schuster, 1994), 138; 226-227; 247-248; 267-269.

73. By contrast, George Bush spent about $200,000 on polls in his first year in office. James M. Perry, "Clinton Relies Heavily on White House Pollster to Take Words Right out of the Public's Mouth," *The Wall Street Journal* (March 23, 1994), A16.

74. The Clinton administration rejected a value-added tax (VAT) and instead opted for requiring employers to buy health insurance for their employees. Richard L. Berke, "Clinton Advisor Says Polls Had a Role in Health Plan," *The New York Times* (December 9, 1993), A (17 or 7).

75. Abraham Lincoln, *Speeches and Writings 1832-1858* (New York: The Library of America, 1989), 524-525.

76. Richard Nixon, "Address to the Nation on the Situation in Southeast Asia," *Public Papers of the President of the United States: Richard Nixon, 1970* (Washington, D.C.: U.S. Government Printing Office, 1971), 410.

77. Quoted in, George C. Edwards and Stephen J. Wayne, *Presidential Leadership: Politics and Policy Making* (New York: St. Martin's Press, 1985), 97.

78. Alexis de Tocqueville, *Democracy in America*, Volume I (New York: Vintage Classics, 1990), 138.

79. Paul Brace and Barbara Hinckley, *Follow the Leader: Opinion Polls and the Modern Presidency* (New York: Basic Books, 1992), 45.

80. Lyndon B. Johnson, *The Vantage Point: Perspectives of the Presidency, 1963-1969* (New York: Popular Library, 1971), 443.

81. On the decay of public approval for presidents, see Brace and Hinckley, 1992, chapter 2.

82. Quoted in Doris Kearns, *Lyndon Johnson & the American Dream* (New York: The New American Library, 1976), 226.

83. Kearns, 1976, 228.

84. Sidney Milkis has made a similar observation about the haste with which Reagan's budgetary program was pushed through the 97th Congress with little or no time for adequate public deliberation. See Milkis, 1993, 280-281. Indeed, it may be said that Congress itself has been sucked into the plebiscitary politics of haste as well. The best example of this is the congressional Republican party's 1994 "Contract with America" in which they promised to bring a myriad of legal and constitutional changes to the floor within the first 100 days if the American people would give them a majority in Congress on November 8th of that year. Nothing was said of discussion, deliberation, or the necessarily slow path of prudent legislation. All is quick, all is unmediated and unamended plebiscitary mandates. More about the 104th Congress in chapter 6.

5

The Modern Presidency
and Representative Government

Presidents in the modern era have become more closely connected to the American people than would ever have been thought possible or desirable to those who designed and established the institution more than two centuries ago. Presidential candidates make direct, unmediated appeals to the public during election campaigns, and the relationship continues with little change once in office. Modern presidents have come to rely on appeals to the public for support as a primary tool in governing. Public opinion, in turn, has become a potent force in national politics. The public and their representative in the White House have become closely linked in a plebiscitary system in which they may both at times benefit, but also may both be hindered and entrapped.

But what of that other central question that must be considered if we are to come to grips with political representation by way of executive action in America—what is the place of the modern presidency within the broader political structure of national government? We have previously suggested three general possibilities with regard to this "internal" question of representation.

In the pages of *The Federalist Papers* we have seen an approach to the question of the proper sphere of executive power that can best be categorized as one of equilibrium. Though both chambers of the legislature as well as the presidency were thought to contain different elements and tendencies, none was more necessary or more legitimate than any of the others. Among the whig theorists and congressmen, especially those of the nineteenth century, we have seen a very limited and narrow interpretation of the proper role of the executive in a democratic republic. The legislature was the institution that housed the true representatives of the people, and the institution's will should thereby be the supreme guiding force in the government, they argued. Undergirded both by a radical change in the conception of democratic legitimacy and a dedication to a more active national government, the opposite of the whig approach came to the fore in the twentieth century. In this new conception, trumpeted first by the progressive reformers of the early decades of the century, the nationally elected executive best represented the public will, and it was believed only a strong presidency could meet the needs of democratic governance in the modern world. As we will see, this presidocentric conception of representation would come to dominate the twentieth century and radically change the presidency along with representative government itself.

The Zeitgeist of the Modern Presidency

Franklin Roosevelt is widely considered to be the first of the "modern" presidents. Roosevelt came to the White House in 1933 espousing a new vision for the nation and holding a certain understanding of the place the presidency could play as midwife to the birthing of this new America. The revolution in the basic structure of the regime that came with Roosevelt's New Deal was two-fold. In accordance with FDR's vision of creating a new economic-constitutional order with the establishment of a new economic bill of rights that he outlined in his address to the Commonwealth Club in San Francisco in September 1932, the national government was to be greatly expanded. The federal government would take on more responsibilities for insuring the economic health and fairness of the nation. Likewise, the resources the national government could muster would have to be augmented to meet these new responsibilities. It was as part of this augmentation of the federal government that the expansion of the presidency and increased presidential influence in public life found their justification.

The New Deal agenda itself was highly dependent upon the personal leadership of FDR as president. Without a transformed presidency, and without a new conception of legitimate presidential influence over the political landscape, the New Deal itself could not have become a reality. The needs of establishing programmatic liberalism facilitated the creation of the modern presidency. Likewise, after becoming a reality, the legacy of the new nationalistic liberalism was the further expansion of the presidency to meet the newly created responsibilities of government. As the power of the federal government over the economic life of the nation expanded, so too did the power of the presidency. Centralization of government in Washington was equaled only by the centralization of representational responsibilities in the presidency that began with the New Deal.

Indeed, beyond the specific areas in which the modern presidency has grown in responsibilities and resources that began in earnest with the presidency of FDR, Roosevelt also set much of the tone for the modern presidency's relationship with the other players in government. That is to say, Franklin Roosevelt and his New Deal agenda not only set in motion the expansion of the federal government and the presidency's place within that government, but he also set the standard for conducting that office according to which all subsequent presidents would be judged.[1]

Roosevelt laid challenge to political convention and governmental custom from the very beginning. In the summer of 1932 he broke with the long-standing tradition that major party presidential nominees not attend their party's convention but wait to be notified of the convention's actions. On July 2nd he told the convention that he hoped his decision to personally address them would stand as a symbol that it would be "the task of our party to break foolish traditions."[2] Roosevelt did break many traditions that had been part of the presidency for decades and in so doing established new traditions, placed new expectations on the shoulders of future presidents, and altered fundamentally the workings of the American polity. All other modern presidents have lived, to use historian William Leuchtenburg's phrase, "in the shadow of FDR."[3]

As was noted in the previous chapter, Franklin Roosevelt forged a new representational relationship between himself as president and the American people during the great twin crises of the Great Depression and World War II. There has been a general intensification of that relationship over the years, with some harm suffered as a result of the public distrust engendered by Watergate and Vietnam, but the overall outlines of that relationship have not changed greatly over the past five decades. Roosevelt equally altered the place of the presidency in the national government. He was able to centralize power and influence in the White House, gain unprecedented control over the bureaucracy, greatly expand the presidency itself, and achieve unparalleled control over the national agenda.

The spirit of the modern presidency, born in the democratic ideology of the progressives and Woodrow Wilson, found a willing vessel in the person of FDR. The president as the dominant, sometimes perhaps even domineering, voice in an expanded national government was the tool FDR used to achieve his program. The president was to be master of his party, as he demonstrated in his attempt to purge conservative and moderate voices from the Democratic party in 1938. He was to control a newly expanded and empowered bureaucracy. As the most legitimate national voice, he was to enjoy a privileged place of influence with regard to the workings of the legislature. If Congress did not act as he wished, he occasionally even threatened to act unilaterally in the name of his "inescapable responsibility to the people."[4] And when a constitutional institution stood in the way of his achieving his policy objectives and a reformulation of the economic order, he attempted a hostile takeover in one of the most thinly veiled violations of the separation of powers system in American history.[5]

In sum, Roosevelt conceived of himself in office as the most legitimate of political representatives in Washington. He brought to fruition the progressives' dedication to a presidocentric system of representative government. After FDR's time in office, the American people came to look to the occupant in the White House as the embodiment of government and as the most important player in our political life. Though he may have been an extreme example in certain ways, Roosevelt nevertheless set the tone for the presidents that followed and began the institutionalization of a new presidency at the heart of a new political order.

The modern presidency inaugurated by FDR would come to occupy the central seat of representation in American politics and the modern presidents who followed him in office would not hesitate to assert their perceived new role in government. In the remainder of this chapter, I endeavor to develop a picture of the modern presidency's place among the other institutions of government and to explore some of the activities of individual modern presidents that are illustrative of the new scheme of political representation.[6]

Congress and the Presidency:
The Modern Relationship

Of particular importance when discussing political representation in America must be the relationship between the legislature and the chief executive. In the twentieth century, leadership in Congress has been fractionalized and party cohesion has been dealt a series of blows. Congress has been weakened as an institution due both to these internal developments and to a changing American conception of the scope and responsibilities of national government. Into the void has stepped the modern American presidents who has become the nation's chief legislative leaders. The center of gravity of representative government has thereby shifted away from the legislature to a similar extent.

Setting the National Agenda

"The definition of alternatives is the supreme instrument of power," wrote E. E. Schattschneider in 1960. He went on to say, "he who determines what politics is about runs the country, because the definition of alternative is the choice of conflict, and the choice of conflict allocates power."[7] Though, as John Kingdon has shown, it is often futile to attempt to trace an item on the national agenda to a single player or a single moment in time, there can be little doubt that the central player in the agenda-creation activity of modern American government is the president.[8]

This modern presidential role of agenda setting has modest constitutional origins in the recommendation clause of Article II, Section 3 which gives the president the duty from time to time to "give to the Congress information on the state of the Union, and recommend to their consideration such measures as he shall judge necessary and expedient." Upon this modest foundation has been erected a presidentially driven public policy process. Presidential elections are often considered referendums on the candidates' respective agendas. Once in office, the president's is the one truly national voice. This is especially true in regard to the annual State of the Union Address when each president outlines the public policies he wishes to see enacted by Congress. The decentralized nature of the modern Congress itself has also encouraged presidents to take an active leadership role in setting the agenda.

Forming the legislative agenda has become an important responsibility of presidents; it is one the people, the press, and the Congress have come to expect. For instance, in his first year in office, Eisenhower attempted to govern without sending a legislative program to Congress. But even this conservative Republican president soon found the expectations of the modern presidency were too ingrained to overcome. After considerable criticism, including some from Congress itself, Eisenhower sent a legislative program to Capitol Hill with his State of the Union Address of 1954.[9] Every president has done so since.

This is not to say that presidents have had absolute control over the national agenda. Clearly other players outside government, including the media, interest groups, and grass roots organizations have all been successful in getting items on the agenda that sitting presidents would have rather not seen there. Congress as well has on occasion been able to take up issues that presidents have opposed or have had little concern with. This was especially the case with the Republicans who won control of both the House and the Senate in the 1994 midterm elections. But the one dominant voice in setting the agenda for the modern American polity has been that of the chief executive.

One result of the expectations for presidents to control the national political agenda has been the creation of a leadership model that casts the president alone in the place of leadership and relegates Congress to the position of follower or inhibitor of presidential will. In this leadership model, presidential success is defined as the degree to which Congress has acceded to the president's agenda.[10]

To an extent, this bias in the standard leadership model of modern American politics is a natural result of the nature of the presidency and the needs of an activist and centralized government. Presidents occupy favorable institutional ground for establishing an agenda and for articulating it to others in government and to the American public. But to the degree that Congress has come to rely on the president to focus the nation's attention and set the agenda, Congress has relinquished a crucial representational function. All legislative proposals, all congressional votes come to be seen in light of the president's wish list for policy. The president's agenda, by design and by the acquiescence of the media and Congress, has often become the nation's agenda. Modern presidents have thereby been established as the nation's chief representatives in the legislative process.

Congressional Delegation

To John Locke, it was a maxim of good government that delegated power could not be delegated: *delegata potestas non potest delegari*. "The legislative cannot transfer the power of making laws to any other hands," he wrote in 1690, "for it being but a delegated power from the people, they who have it cannot pass it over to others."[11] Besides the near abdication to the presidency that Congress has made over the control of the national agenda, Congress has also had a long history of delegating authority over specific public policies to the executive branch. Though the federal courts have in theory generally upheld Locke's dictum that the legislature cannot delegate its lawmaking powers, in practice they have tended to allow most congressional delegations that have come before them.

From the earliest days of the Republic, Congress has found occasions to delegate certain decisions to the president. The first Congress, for instance, delegated to Washington the important decision of where the nation's permanent capital was to be built. Despite the "pro-legislature" rhetoric of the Jeffersonian-Republicans, congressional delegation to the executive branch became even more routine during Jefferson's administration.[12] Though persistent critics have worried that such delegations are unconstitutional, undemocratic, or courting administrative despotism, they have been relatively common throughout American history.[13]

Congressional delegation has been of two general sorts. First, Congress has on occasion explicitly delegated to the president or his subordinates authority to make certain decisions. For instance, the first Congress delegated to President Washington the choice of the location of the permanent seat of government. More frequently, however, Congress has delegated authority in a non-explicit, non-statutory manner. That is, Congress has had the tendency, especially during the last century, to write statutes full of vague, generalized language and non-specific mandates. Such law leaves great discretion to the administrators in the executive branch who must interpret the statutes, write implementing rules, and then execute the laws. Both types of delegation place considerable influence over the nation's public policy in the hands of the executive and his subordinates.

But why does the legislature choose to delegate some of its authority over public policy to the president, his subordinates, and independent commissions? A number of explanations have been offered. The necessity of flexibility in the laws that would allow them to be applied to future unforeseen events has been noted as one reason for the passage of vague statutes by Congress.[14] In the area of foreign affairs delegation has grown almost naturally out of the president's special responsibilities in that realm. The inherent give and take and the necessity to compromise that are part of the legislative process often leave little room to fine tune legislation. Relatedly, the representational conception of the presidency itself as the "singular representative of the American people" has been cited for congressional delegation.[15] Each explanation seems to hold a degree of truth, but none by themselves can account for the increased rate of delegation we have seen in the twentieth century.

In 1890 Congress passed a tariff act that explicitly permitted the president to suspend some of its provisions if certain conditions prevailed. In 1922 Congress empowered the president to adjust tariff rates according to his calculations of the cost of production around the world, and in 1934 it authorized him to alter set tariffs by as much as 50 percent.[16] These were important precedents, but the real revolutionary shift of power from Congress to the president came with the Great Depression and the empowerment of Franklin Roosevelt's administration to fight it. According to Theodore J. Lowi, "One administrative agency after another was given power to make important public policy decisions that had hitherto been reserved for the legislature or, in fact, not made at all."[17]

Though Congress seemed perfectly content to see their prerogatives drained into the executive structure of government, in *Schechter Poultry Corporation v. United States* the Supreme Court attempted a defense of Congress' Constitutional powers and responsibilities.[18] The Court declared the National Industrial Recovery Act (NIRA) unconstitutional, at least in part because Congress had failed to carry out its legislative responsibilities by delegating broad authority to the president and his subordinates in the executive branch, thus violating the constitutional system of separated powers. But under Roosevelt's threat to even more overtly upset the balance of power system by gutting the independence of the judiciary, the Court eventually allowed most of FDR's New Deal program and, as Lowi has noted, "the rule of the *Schechter* case was essentially extinguished by neglect."[19]

Besides the numerous examples that could be cited of times in which Congress has written vaguely defined statutes and relied on executive agencies to write the rules implementing them, we can point to several representative examples of congressionally delegated power over the last several decades. Though the stakes are often quite small, the degree to which Congress has been willing to abdicate its responsibilities as a representative institution has also been extraordinary. For instance, in the Economic Stabilization Act of 1970, Congress authorized the president "to issue such orders and regulations as he may deem appropriate to stabilize prices, rents, wages, and salaries at levels not less than those prevailing on May 25, 1970." Taking no other safeguards, the legislators had in essence handed the president near dictatorial power over a large part of the national economy. Though he did not act for some time—he was publicly opposed to wage-price controls—President Nixon eventually acted in August of 1971 to unilaterally freeze all prices, rents, wages, and salaries.[20] In essence, the Democratic Congress had passed the responsibility of representation to the president who eventually accepted the role.

A more recent example of such a delegation of power and the ultimate responsibilities of representation can be seen in Congress' extension of unemployment benefits in the summer of 1991. Citing fiscal responsibility and improving economic circumstances, President Bush threatened to veto any such measure. Congress nevertheless enacted a bill on August 2nd that included the provisions for extended benefits, but it made their disbursement completely dependent upon a presidential declaration of emergency. Bush signed the bill because it "demonstrates I am concerned," but simply refused to declare the emergency which would have triggered the statute's provisions.[21] Again, the legislature had abdicated its responsibility to make public policy and thereby delegated ultimate control to the president. On a whole host of issues, Congress has delegated similar amounts of discretion to the executive during the twentieth century.

Presidents have been more than willing to accept this situation of general congressional delegation. One way presidents have responded to this delegation is by working to strengthen their hand with the bureaucracy. In an effort to maintain maximum influence over the process of executive branch rule making, presidents have developed various bureaucratic techniques such as administrative clearance and a politicized appointment process.[22]

Representing the Nation Abroad: The President and Foreign Policy

Presidential representation could scarcely be discussed without a word about the unique place the president occupies with regard to national security and the nation's relationship with the rest of the world. By making the president the commander in chief and by placing treaty making powers partially in the office, the Constitution placed the national executive officer at the center of the foreign policy process in the United States. Though the

Constitution grants the national legislature considerable foreign policy powers, and though Congress has from time to time attempted to exercise a degree of control over foreign policy, the general trend in our national experience has been toward recognizing the president as the special representative of the nation in regard to its external relations. This has especially been the case with regard to the modern presidents of the twentieth century.

The question of the supremacy of the presidency as the representative of the nation with regard to relations with foreign powers arose early in our history. In 1798 a Philadelphia physician named George Logan, frustrated by several failures of the government diplomatically, set off for Europe to engage in his own diplomacy. That action precipitated a resolution before the House of Representatives in December 1798 intended "to punish a crime which goes to the destruction of the Executive power of government."[23] The resolution would extend punishment

> to all persons, citizens of the United States, who shall usurp the Executive authority of this Government, by commencing or carrying on any correspondence with the Government of any foreign Prince or State, relating to controversies or disputes which do or shall exist between such Prince or State and the United States.[24]

The Logan Act[25] has been successfully defied many times in American history. It has occasionally been cited by presidents and others but only one person has been indicted under the law and he was found not guilty.[26] Some have challenged the very constitutionality of the Act itself.[27] But its ultimate importance may be symbolic. It encapsulates a certain common understanding of the place of the president in foreign affairs—the president is to be the nation's voice on the world stage.

Alexander Hamilton and other friends of executive power at the founding perceived the need for a centralized, energetic, and responsible officer in charge of America's relationship with the rest of the world.[28] With the advent of modern "total" warfare, the invention and proliferation of nuclear weapons, and with an ideological enemy perceived to be bent on world domination, the need for such an officer seemed to many even more necessary in the mid-twentieth century. The risks of inaction or misaction were conceived no longer to be simple foreign affairs blunders, but the very survival of the nation itself seemed very much to be at stake. Under such an understanding, the presidency was granted even greater latitude and influence in the area of foreign affairs during and following World War II than was the case with regard to domestic public policy.

In 1966, political scientist Aaron Wildavsky published an influential essay in which he argued that America, while having only one president, in reality had two presidencies. One presidency, he argued, worked in the area of domestic policy in which the particular president was able to control the agenda and the actions of Congress only infrequently. The other presidency was the foreign policy presidency in which individual presidents were able to exercise much more control over the agenda and win the support of Congress for his actions much more frequently.[29]

Though Wildavsky's thesis has come under some criticism in the past few decades, especially due to the movement toward a more assertive Congress following Vietnam and Watergate, presidents have historically received more deference from Congress on foreign policy matters than they tend to receive on domestic policy proposals.[30] Regardless of congressional deference in matters of foreign policy, Robert Spitzer argues that the two presidencies exist also as a matter of law. The Supreme Court has regularly deferred to executive claims of authority in the area of foreign affairs, while it has not as readily done so in regard to domestic politics.[31] For instance, in *U.S. v. Curtiss-Wright Export Corp.* Justice Sutherland spoke for the Court in calling the president the "sole organ of the federal government in the field of international relations," and argued that congressional legislation "within the international field must often accord to the President a degree of discretion and freedom from statutory restriction which would not be admissible were domestic affairs alone involved."[32]

Writing for the majority in *Curtiss-Wright*, Justice Sutherland outlines a conception of executive hegemony in foreign affairs that is not found in the Constitution and is not justified by the political theory of the Founders. Indeed, there is no understanding in Sutherland's opinion of the complex representational system outlined in *The Federalist* in which each political institution is given a degree of representational responsibilities. Rather, Sutherland writes in deference to an extra-constitutional transference of the power over foreign affairs from the British Crown directly to the national government in America—a transference that owes nothing to the people's fundamental compact. He finds, "In this vast external realm, with its important, complicated, delicate and manifold problems, the President alone has the power to speak or listen as a representative of the nation."[33]

As further justification for his understanding, Sutherland cited John Marshall who said in an argument in the House of Representatives pertaining to President John Adams' extradition of a fugitive under the Jay Treaty, "The President is the *sole organ* of the nation in the external relations, and its *sole representative* with foreign nations."[34] But Sutherland pulls this phrase out of context to twist it to his meaning. A study of the debate on the floor of the House in March 1800 makes clear that Marshall was only speaking of a president's duty to *execute* existing law—he does not argue for presidential power to *make* or *formulate* foreign policy. "He is charged to execute the laws. A treaty is declared to be law. He must then execute a treaty, where he, and he alone, possesses the means of executing it."[35] In Marshall's understanding, rather than being the nation's sole voice in foreign affairs, the president is understood to be the executor of previous legislative decisions.

Like the Court, the American people seem to have come to an understanding of a special presidential role as national representative in the realm of national security and foreign relations. This is evidenced by the public's tendency to "rally" to the president in times of international crisis. Such a tendency would seem to result, at least in part, from the presidential role as symbolic representative of the nation, much like the American flag. But it also seems to be the case that the public, like the general trend in the other institutions of government, have come to recognize the presidency as the proper place to lodge foreign policy representation.

Representative of the Free World

The president has always been the chief representative of the American people and of the transcendent nation in the area of foreign affairs. This, as we have seen, became the case especially with the coming of modern warfare, the invention of nuclear weapons, and the general Cold War atmosphere that gripped the nation from the later 1940s through the late 1980s. But the Cold War and America's status as one of the two great superpowers also brought about another fundamental shift in the responsibilities and importance of the American presidency. The president became the de facto representative, not only of the American people, but of the free world itself.

With the doctrine of containment as the guiding paradigm in American foreign policy during the Cold War, presidents successively pledged

American resources and personnel to the task of containing Soviet influence around the globe. American presidents became the leaders of the free world, the defenders of the West, and the secular priests in the great moral, political, economic, and military struggle against imperial communism.

Elected by no one outside the borders of the United States and formally responsible to no one but the American people and their representatives in Congress and the judiciary, American presidents nonetheless were propelled by events into the role as the representative of an entity larger than the American nation-state. This occurred because of American power and presidential willingness to use it in defense of the national interest and those of America's allies. As the national spokesman and foreign policy leader of one of the two superpowers, the American president naturally came to occupy this place in international affairs.

Although the president's place within the international system had undergone evolutionary change for some time, it was with the collapse of the Soviet Union in 1989 that this situation began to change fundamentally. While during the Cold War the presidents were able to operate in a situation of unquestioned American military and economic might and American allies around the globe were greatly dependent upon the United States for security, now American presidents can no longer dominate the international system. This does not seem, however, to have completely negated the president's role as an international representative. Rather, it has made the presidential job more difficult because presidents now must work harder to achieve their goals internationally.[36] No longer able to command, they must cooperate, persuade, and cajole. In short, the contemporary international climate has made the president less of an absolute sovereign representative and more of a *prima inter pares* not terribly unlike the situation that has often faced presidents in the American regime itself. At least until some free-standing and self-executing international body comes into existence, it is likely American presidents will continue to function in this modified version of the role spawned by the Cold War.

Unilateral and Emergency Representation

Prerogative powers are not a new development in the history of representative government. In 1690 the English political philosopher John Locke defined prerogative as the power "to act according to discretion for public good, without the prescription of the law and sometimes even against it."³⁷ In the American context, prerogative powers are those in which the executive authority can make important national security and domestic policy decisions unilaterally. Such executive actions enjoy de facto force of law without being subject to the normal rigors of the legislative process. Through such actions, presidents assume a level of representative force unknown in any other aspect of American governance. Presidents act alone in the national interest and then may be held responsible for the consequences in Congress, in the courts, and ultimately in the court of public opinion.

Presidents, especially those we commonly refer to as "great," have seldom hesitated to invoke prerogative powers when it suited their interest or their vision of the national good. As Locke foresaw, this is especially true during times of national emergency when it may seem most prudent to allow the executive to act with dispatch and without an explicit delegation of authority from the legislature in order to save the nation, quell unrest, or prevent a wrong. The history here is telling. During the nineteenth century, Congress regularly authorized military actions taken by presidents. Both presidents and Congress seemed to understand this to be the proper constitutional process.³⁸ But in the twentieth century, presidents have routinely used military force without prior authorization from the legislature and without going to Congress after the initial action to secure their subsequent endorsement of the actions taken, as was done by Lincoln during the Civil War. Faced with this situation, Congress and the courts have tended to give the president a wide berth for action on questions of national security and foreign affairs.

During times of extraordinary emergencies, we have seen considerable centralization of representative government in the presidency. This was true during what was arguable the greatest crisis in the history of the American Republic, the Civil War. Lincoln took extraordinary prerogative action in the name of suppressing the southern states in rebellion and restoring the constitutional order. He unilaterally acted in areas such as expanding the Army, suspending *habeas corpus*, spending millions out of the public funds without congressional action, and emancipating the slaves in those states in rebellion. In effect, he had temporarily become the government; in the extraordinary emergency, Lincoln had simplified representative government to executive action.

But Lincoln also recognized that the constitutional system demanded that he seek the retroactive endorsement of his actions by the people's representatives in Congress. The President requested such an endorsement and Congress subsequently passed legislation "approving, legalizing, and making valid all the acts, proclamations, and orders of the President, etc., as if they had been issued and done under the previous express authority and direction of the Congress of the United States."[39]

But who is empowered by right to determine when such a state of emergency actually exists? According to the Lockean theory of prerogative powers and American political experience, it is the executive who in most cases holds the authority to make such a determination.[40] Congress has augmented this presidential prerogative by explicitly delegating such authority to the president in hundreds of statutes. In his first six years as president alone, Franklin Delano Roosevelt declared more than thirty-nine emergencies, leading some in Congress to accuse the president of gross abuse of power.[41] In 1976 Congress passed the National Emergencies Act in an attempt to put some constraints on the president's ability to unilaterally declare emergencies and act in the extraordinary ways such times warrant. But even this effort only put limits on the president retroactively; it did not seriously hamper presidents from declaring conditions of emergency. It simply required that Congress consider and schedule votes on the continuance of such periods after such presidential declarations. Even this requirement, however, has fallen into disuse.[42] Presidents, for all intents and purposes, retain the representational authority to determine when the nation experiences a state of emergency and when she does not.

Following the precedent set by the Civil War, presidents have been given significant powers to wage war in the twentieth century. Despite there being no direct and immediate threat to the constitutional order, as there arguably was in the Civil War, Woodrow Wilson was given expansive authority to wage World War I. FDR was then delegated even greater power to act unilaterally with regard to American economic and military life during World War II. According to the perceived necessities of modern warfare, Congress first assumed authority to regulate the lives of citizens in a score of areas that in peacetime had been left to the states or to the people themselves. Congress then delegated this authority to the president who in turn delegated it to subordinates in and out of government. In this great transference of power, the courts stood by with minimal interference.[43] The necessities of modern warfare have obliterated the line of demarcation that once existed between domestic life and the prosecution of war. The presidency in the twentieth century has gained authority in both.

In effect, Franklin Roosevelt had been delegated or simply asserted vast unilateral powers to direct explicitly military matters as well as the economic life of the nation during World War II. Roosevelt made full use of executive power during the war, pushing it beyond all previous American experience with foreign wars. For example, before Congress passed the Lend-Lease Act in 1941, FDR had unilaterally agreed to transfer aging American destroyers to Britain in exchange for the right to use bases on British islands in the Atlantic and Caribbean. The president also made defense agreements with Greenland and Iceland and months before the Japanese attack on Pearl Harbor issued a "shoot-on-sight" order to American forces in defense waters.[44] Roosevelt even went so far as to seize several defense facilities, including the North American Aviation plant in Inglewood, California.[45]

He made explicit his theory of the right of presidential action in September 1942 when he demanded Congress enact wage and price controls. "I ask Congress," said Roosevelt, "to take . . . action by the first of October. Inaction on your part by that date will leave me with an inescapable responsibility to the people of this country to see to it that the war effort is no longer imperiled by threat of economic chaos." If Congress did not take the appropriate actions, FDR warned, "I shall accept the responsibility and I will act."[46]

Franklin Roosevelt held himself as president to be *the* legitimate representative of the nation during times of crisis and was prepared to act on his vision of the public good, regardless of the will of the public's representatives in Congress or the lack of explicit authority in the Constitution. This vision also seems to have guided FDR's successor Harry Truman, who seized the nation's steel mills as a response to an industrial strike during the Korean War. Though Truman's attempt to use this particular version of the emergency prerogative ultimately was rebuffed by the Supreme Court, it is clear that twentieth-century presidents have enjoyed considerable unilateral powers during times of international crisis.[47] During such times the president becomes, at least at the outset, *the* representative of the nation, and representatives in Congress and the courts become important again only as they may respond to the executive's unilateral actions.

Initiating War and Peace

From the text of the Constitution, the power to initiate war is one that seems clearly to have been entrusted to Congress. Even Alexander Hamilton, that consummate defender of executive power, acknowledged in *Federalist* 69 that the president's commander in chief powers extend only to directing the military and not to declaring war or raising armies and navies. Congress has acted in its capacity to declare war only five times in American history.[48] But while Congress has made sparse use of its explicit powers in the field of initiating military engagements, presidents have made considerable use of what they have taken to be their implicit power in this area.

Presidents have committed American troops to combat more than two hundred times, or about forty fold as often as Congress has declared war. Though most of these instances were limited in scope and duration, some were as massive as the wars in Korea and Vietnam. Clearly the president has become the primary player in issues of war and peace. Indeed, American presidents have acquired a prerogative power to launch military actions unilaterally and have thereby come to occupy the role of national representative with regard to such issues. One of the major pillars on which this role has been built is the judicially recognized right of the president to act unilaterally to protect American citizens and property abroad.[49] This right has been a major justification for military actions from Jefferson's sending naval ships to protect American shipping against the pirate kingdoms of north Africa to Reagan's invasion of the Caribbean island nation of Grenada under the auspices of rescuing American medical students who were trapped there after the Marxist revolution in 1983.

Despite the clear legislative history behind and the explicit language of several international agreements and mutual security treaties, modern presidents have also cited such documents as granting them authority to initiate American military actions overseas. The most serious such case was Truman's citation of the American participation in the United Nations as a proper basis for his decision to unilaterally send American forces to defend South Korea in 1950. In the administration's rather curious rendering, by agreeing to the U.N. Charter, the U.S. Senate had simultaneously written both itself and the House of Representatives out of their constitutional responsibility of declaring war. The administration implied that such international agreements made the president alone responsible for war and peace in many circumstances. Citing a vague "real and present danger to the security of every nation," the North Koreans' "contempt for the United Nations," and "a clear challenge to the basic principles of the United Nations," Truman attempted to justify his actions without the constitutionally-mandated declaration of war.[50] In words the Founders would have reserved for congressional declarations alone, Truman pledged, "In accordance with the resolution of the Security Council, the United States will vigorously support the effort of the Council to terminate this serious breach of the peace."[51]

Similarly, in 1991 the Bush administration exerted considerable effort to encourage the representatives of other nations on the U.N. Security Council to authorize the use of force to expel Iraqi forces from Kuwait, but it never acknowledged the need to have the representatives of the American people assembled in Congress authorize the Gulf War.[52] Shockingly, Professor Thomas M. Franck of the New York University Law School went so far in the *New York Times* as to argue for the superiority of the representation found in the U.N. Security Council to that found in Congress. According to Franck, "[t]he new system vests that responsibility [the declaration of war] in the Security Council, a body where the most divergent interests and perspectives of humanity are represented and where five of the fifteen members have a veto power. This council is far less likely to be stampeded by combat fever than is Congress."[53] As did President Bush in 1991, President Clinton relied on U.N. actions to justify his consideration of air strikes in Bosnia in the absence of congressional authorization in 1994.[54]

After the nation's experience in Vietnam and the perceived abuse of presidential power in the area of foreign policy during the Johnson and Nixon administrations, Congress attempted to reclaim for itself a role in decisions of war and peace. First, it brought an end to the war by cutting off funds for combat activities in southeast Asia in 1973. In 1973 Congress also passed the War Powers Resolution in which they attempted to restrain a president's ability to pull the nation into war without congressional approval. Although the Act was couched in language that seemingly restricted presidential authority, in reality it made statutory what presidents had acquired through practice, namely, a sweeping prerogative to enter into military action without congressional approval or even congressional participation in the decision making process. The only serious restriction seems to be that presidents now must make decisions with the knowledge that, if the military engagement dragged on beyond sixty days, congressional approval may be needed to continue the activity.

The reassertion of congressional authority after Vietnam in the War Powers Resolution and other statutes has not proved a significant chain on presidential initiatives with American armed forces. Presidents from Ford to Clinton have not hesitated to assert a right to deploy forces in combat around the globe when they deem such action to be in the national interest. In 1975 President Ford ordered a rescue operation for the U.S. merchant ship *Mayaguez,* which had been seized by Cambodians. In 1980, Carter ordered the "Desert One" rescue effort of the hostages held in Iran. Reagan launched an invasion of the Caribbean nation of Grenada in October 1983, ordered air strikes against Lybia in 1986, and placed Kuwaiti oil tankers under the U.S. flag and protection during hostilities in the Persian Gulf in 1987. In December 1989 President Bush ordered the invasion of Panama. President Clinton ordered missile strikes against Iraq in 1993 in retaliation for an Iraqi plot to assassinate former President Bush, ordered combat operations in Somalia, was prepared to invade Haiti before the situation in that tiny island nation changed to make such an effort unnecessary, and ordered the bombing of Serbian targets in Bosnia. In each of these efforts presidents were willing to go it alone without prior authorization from Congress and without serious congressional deliberations on the merits of such military interventions.

Presidents have gained significant unilateral powers with regard to war, but they also are able to exercise significant unilateral powers with regard to making peace and to keeping it. Presidents historically have held almost complete unilateral control over how and when military engagements come to an end. Though Congress legislated the end of the Vietnam War, this has not been the usual occurrence.[55] There have been countless instances in which presidents have decided the national interest did not warrant going to war and so did not act themselves, nor did they ask Congress to act. Such decisions (or non-decisions) often have had great consequences for the nation and the world.[56]

Presidents also have been able to gain further control over the search for peace through diplomacy by means of executive agreements with other nations that do not require Senatorial approval. The government enters into more than five hundred agreements annually with other nations that do not require Senatorial consideration under the treaty provision of the Constitution.[57] Though many are made pursuant to congressional grants of authority, the important point is that they are made by the executive branch without being subject to the rigors of the deliberative process in the Senate, as the Constitution requires of all "treaties." In particular, presidents Carter and Reagan were able to gain effective unilateral control over the nation's arms control policy through the use of so-called "executive non-agreements" or parallel unilateral policy declarations (PUPD). For instance, Carter realized in 1980 that prevailing circumstances (the Soviet invasion of Afghanistan) made it impossible to gain Senate ratification of SALT II. He was able to circumvent the requirement to submit all treaties to the Senate for ratification by simply agreeing not to violate the treaty if the Soviets did likewise. Reagan also continued to abide by the unratified treaty with the Soviet Union until 1986 when he determined the Soviets were in violation and he withdrew his support.[58] Such non-agreements circumvent the role of Congress in the treaty-making process and make the president's voice the only one of significant consequence on the matter in Washington.[59]

Unilateral Domestic Powers

Presidents hold a wider authority to act on their own than simply in cases of national emergency or during times of military engagements. Though the Courts seem to be more willing to defer to presidential assertions of prerogative powers during times of war, that does not mean that presidents do not exercise certain limited prerogatives in more normal domestic policy matters as well.

The pocket veto, for instance, can be counted among the president's unilateral domestic powers as it enables the president to kill a bill passed by Congress unilaterally, without being subject to congressional attempts at an override. All the president must do is hold a bill for ten days after Congress has adjourned and the president has unilaterally scrapped a piece of legislation passed by Congress. Somewhat similarly, presidents have exerted the power to unilaterally impound funds appropriated by Congress. FDR held back funds for public works projects. Truman, Eisenhower, and Kennedy each impounded funds that Congress had added to their defense budgets and in 1966 Johnson simply reduced expenditures for certain items in an agriculture appropriations bill because he objected to Congress' addition of more than $300 million above his request. All other presidents, however, have paled in their use of impoundments in comparison with Richard Nixon's bold assertion of that authority. Casting a glow of illegitimacy on congressional appropriations which were higher than he had requested, the president simply refused to allow to be spent what he did not request. In his actions Nixon clearly implied that he and not Congress represented the national interest—at least in regard to executive branch programs and outlays. The courts in several cases undermined Nixon's position and in 1974 Congress passed the Impoundment Control Act restricting future presidential use of such a unilateral budgeting tool.[60]

Presidents also have been given prerogative declaratory powers. Such unilateral powers are of two basic types. First, presidents regularly make proclamations. Though many of these are purely symbolic, such as designating Thanksgiving Day or setting aside a week to celebrate the environment or some other special cause, others have significant substantive effects. Presidents, for example, can declare a drought-stricken part of the country a "disaster area," thus making it eligible for relief provided by Congress. Through such declaratory power, President Nixon unilaterally placed a ten percent surcharge on imported goods in 1971.[61]

Second, presidents also have issued executive orders with significant consequence. Franklin Roosevelt used executive orders in the early months of the Second World War to seize aviation plants, coal companies, shipbuilding companies, and the like. Presidents starting with FDR also used this tactic to implement antidiscrimination policies and to investigate communist activities in the United States. President Kennedy used an executive order to establish the Peace Corps in the absence of Congressional funding. The courts, however, have not given presidents a free reign in this area, as was demonstrated in 1952 when they overturned President Truman's seizure of steel mills.[62] As was noted in the discussion above, presidential rhetoric and executive branch rulemaking also provide the president with considerable power that can be used at his discretion.[63]

Like Locke's executive, the American presidency has been given significant powers to exercise unilaterally when the officeholder deems it in the best interest of the nation he represents. These unilateral powers were originally conceived for use during times in which the normal (read slow, public, and pluralistic) operation of the deliberative republic risked damage to a fundamental national interest. During times of war and other emergencies this is still the primary reasoning behind the exercise of executive prerogative. But as is also clear, presidents have gained important non-emergency prerogatives over the course of American history. When in actual use, unilateral powers give presidents a primacy in providing representation that they still lack in the normal process of public life in the United States.

Vicarious Presidential Representation[64]

Presidents not only wield political influence through their rhetoric, persuasion of Congress, unilateral actions, and the actions of their immediate underlings, but they also have been empowered by the Constitution and subsequent legislation to appoint certain important players in the drama of American governance. Namely, presidents are responsible for filling vacancies as they arise in the federal courts and in special regulatory commissions. Congress certainly does have a say in this process and occasionally rejects presidential nominees. But the institutions are not created equal in regard to the appointment process.

Presidents clearly have great influence over who sits on the federal bench and who is appointed to the regulatory commissions. All modern presidents have been able to make appointments to independent regulatory commissions. They also have all appointed numerous men and women to sit on the lower federal courts and it is only the rare president, the last being Jimmy Carter, who does not have the opportunity to appoint at least one member to the Supreme Court. This presidential role in the appointment process has become ever more important in the last few decades as the courts and the regulatory commissions have gained more and more influence over public policy. Though they often do not conduct themselves the way the presidents who appoint them expect, controlling the personnel of these institutions facilitates the president's having an impact on the political, economic, and social life of the nation—an impact that sometimes lasts for years after the president has left the White House.[65]

The federal courts, particularly the United States Supreme Court, have become much more active in the political process during the second half of the twentieth century. They have overturned congressional action, negated the action of state and local political units, and disrupted long-standing social norms and practices. Following the Warren Court revolution, many federal judges abandoned the tradition of general deference to the outcome of democratic processes. They sought to forward the needs of a new "substantive due process" that on occasion necessitated they overrule some traditional procedures of representative government along with the policy outcomes that came with them.[66]

This situation makes the president's place in the appointment process that much more important. He is the central representational link connecting an appointed, life tenured judiciary to democratic processes. The Senate is given an important role to play in confirming presidential nominees, and Congress has the power to check the judiciary through the impeachment process, by overturning Court decisions, and by restricting the jurisdiction of the Court. However, as we have seen, to the degree that Congress has become dependent upon the president to set the national agenda, Congress in essence defers leadership in these matters to the president as well.

The story is essentially the same for independent regulatory commissions. The first independent commission—the Interstate Commerce Commission—was established in 1887 and reformers during the Progressive era proposed the use of similar commissions as the principal agents of democracy and as a way of separating administration from politics. Presidents have been able to influence these commissions primarily through the appointment process, though this process places some significant hurdles in the presidents, way. The lengths of terms on these commissions range as high as fourteen years (Federal Reserve Board) and all demand a degree of bipartisanship in their makeup. These factors serve to inhibit any president's ability to influence the commissions through appointments. Presidents have also, from time to time, resorted to public or private appeals, such as so often has been the case when the Federal Reserve Board contemplates adjustments in the monetary system that the incumbent may not perceive to be in his own best political interest or that of the national economy.

Some presidents, however, have gone further in their efforts to influence these commissions. Despite some support for the conception of independent commissions among New Dealers, Franklin Roosevelt set out to seize control of them for the presidency. FDR was well aware of the revolution sweeping the political order—much of it thanks to his own efforts—that was replacing traditional politics with administration and regulation, and he aimed to gain as much control as possible over the independent commissions. In an effort to gain control over the Federal Trade Commission he endeavored to fire William Humphrey, a conservative member of the commission who had been appointed by President Hoover in 1931. In *Humphrey's Executor v. United States* (1935), the Supreme Court ruled that the president could not remove members of independent commissions for political reasons.[67] Roosevelt later proposed abolishing their independence entirely by having them placed in the traditional executive departments under the president's control, though this was never accomplished.[68]

FDR realized the frustration felt by many modern presidents at their inability to control the activities of these quasi-executive commissions. Despite not having direct control over the actions of these commissions, presidents still represent the primary democratic connection for these important policymaking institutions. And, as regulatory commissions have become more important to modern governance in America, this presidential role of appointing their membership has become one of ever more gravity.

As Congress has delegated authority and influence to independent commissions and as the courts have asserted their own independence from Congress and other elected institutions, presidents have been thrust into a central role as a representative of the American public. Just as the public elected him to represent them, so the president must appoint others whom he cannot control to represent the nation's best interest on judicial bodies and on independent commissions. Presidents offer political representation here in two ways: *directly* as they must themselves act to nominate suitable candidates, and *vicariously* as policymaking is done by presidential appointees who have been placed beyond the reach of the long arm of the White House.

Representational Resources:
The Institutionalization of the Presidency

Besides the vastly expanded representational responsibilities that have been accrued by presidents in the twentieth century, they also have achieved additional representational resources to deal with the new presidentially-centered political order. We have seen some of these resources in the previous chapter. Changes in the ethic of republican self-government and technological developments, for example, have allowed presidents to forge direct links with the public that were not possible in the eighteenth and nineteenth centuries. Modern presidents have also gained considerable representational resources in the form of a large and institutionalized executive staff structure.

In 1937 the President's Committee on Administrative Management referred to the American executive as "an instrument for carrying out the judgment and will of the people of a nation." In the spirit of the age of public administration and the developing modern conception of the representational presidency, the committee spoke of the American executive authority as the one institution that combined both "elements of popular control and the means of vigorous action and leadership—uniting stability and flexibility."[69] Presidential staff support lagged behind the expanding presidential roles and responsibilities that FDR had been primarily responsible for augmenting. The Brownlow committee found that, in their famous phrase, "The President needs help." The president particularly needed help in performing his newly gained functions as the nation's chief representative—as the agenda-setter, the chief manager, and the spokesman for the nation.

In the Brownlow committee's justification for expanding presidential staff resources we see clearly the new conception of representation that logically found its home in the presidency—a conception that combined traditional democratic legitimacy with the liberal-progressive quest for more vigorous governmental activism.

> In proceeding to the reorganization of the Government it is important to keep prominently before us the ends of reorganization. Too close a view of machinery must not cut off from sight the true purpose of reorganization. Economy is not the only objective, . . . the elimination of duplication and contradictory policies is not the only objective, . . . better business methods and fiscal controls are not the only objectives. . . . There is but one grand purpose, namely, to make democracy work today in our National Government; that is, to make our Government an up-to-date, efficient, and effective instrument for carrying out the will of the Nation.[70]

The Brownlow committee produced a blueprint for reorganizing the executive branch of government and for providing presidents with the additional staff resources they needed to perform the tasks that had recently fallen under the domain of that office. The report was everything FDR could have hoped for when he appointed the committee after his 1936 reelection. The report was so pro-executive that it went so far as to urge that even the independent commissions be placed under direct presidential control. The report caused a firestorm in Congress as opponents perceived it to be just one more element in FDR's attempt to acquire near dictatorial powers.[71] Though rejecting many of the Brownlow committee's recommendations, Congress eventually passed the Reorganization Act of 1939 that gave the president continuous reorganization authority and provided Roosevelt with six administrative assistants. Thus began the institutionalization of the presidency.

Until 1984 presidents held a considerable advantage when they wished to reorganize the Executive Office of the President (EOP). Following the passage of the Reorganization Act of 1939, presidential reorganization plans automatically took effect after sixty days *unless* Congress took specific action to disapprove the plan. In this way such presidential initiatives were often able to avoid the normal legislative process of conflict and compromise. In 1983, however, the Supreme Court declared such legislative vetoes unconstitutional in the case of *I.N.S. v. Chadha.*[72] Following the Court's decision in *Chadha*, Congress amended the procedure in 1984 so that presidential reorganization plans only go into effect if both houses pass a joint resolution approving the plan. Such congressional action must come within ninety days.[73] Though the amended process is weighted in favor of congressional power, presidents still maintain certain authority to reorganize through the use of executive orders which do not require congressional deliberation or action.[74]

From its somewhat meager origins in 1939, the Executive Office of the President has grown into one of the most important elements in the executive branch. Agencies have been added and subtracted from time to time, both from congressional action as well as from presidential reorganization efforts, but the general trend has been in the direction of expanded staff and responsibilities. From their position at the center of representative government in the United States, modern presidents have used the EOP as the primary means through which they are able to exercise control over the vast national bureaucracy and maintain a degree of control over the national agenda.

It is not easy to arrive at an accurate accounting of the size of the contemporary institutional presidency. It is difficult in part because presidents have found it in their interest to create the appearance that they have only a minimal, non-imperial, staff. This is why all modern presidents have "borrowed" staffers from other agencies who would remain on the agency's payrolls while they were "detailed" to the White House. President Clinton went even further by delegating certain responsibilities to confidants who remained in private practice outside government, many of whom were paid for their services to the president by the Democratic National Committee.[75]

But there is another problem that has also inhibited us from coming to an accurate picture of the size of the modern White House. Should we count only officials who have public policymaking responsibilities, or do we also count secretarial support, Secret Service details, White House grounds keepers, and the like?[76] Five decades after its initiation, there were in excess of 500 individuals working in the White House Office and hundreds more working elsewhere in the institutionalized presidency.[77] However the EOP is defined and counted, there is little question that it has enabled presidents to centralize executive authority and policymaking in the White House under their direct control.

The causes of the significant growth in the EOP are equally instructive for understanding the representational presidency of the modern era. Presidential scholar Thomas Cronin has noted several reasons for the "swelling" of the institution. Among the causes Cronin has cited are the additional roles that have accrued to presidents as a result of various twentieth-century crises, congressional abdication of policymaking responsibilities, and presidential distrust of the permanent bureaucracy.[78] Stephen Hess has given a similar accounting, but he adds such causal factors as the growth in the size and responsibility of the federal government and a new activist conception of the presidency.[79] What undergirds both interpretations is a general change in our understanding of the presidency and its place in national life. The growth and institutionalization of presidential staff resources was an inevitable development that followed the new understanding of the office. The representational presidency necessitated additional representational resources—resources provided by the Executive Office of the President.

The institutional presidency was conceived by FDR and the Brownlow committee as a device to help presidents meet the expanded responsibilities that had been placed in the office, and thereby better allow individual presidents to carry out their conception of the public's will. But the institutional presidency has come to operate within what might best be called a representational paradox. The "help" provided presidents has enabled them to better deal with the demands placed on them in the modern era. But it might also be argued that the growth in the size and scope of White House operations has itself contributed to the further growth of public expectations of the office—thus keeping expectations beyond the realm of presidential possibilities.[80]

Perhaps more fundamentally, as John Burke has noted, the institutional presidency forms a kind of "continuing context" within which presidents must operate.[81] With the knowledge that all presidents are not exactly alike, a problem becomes evident. Varying presidential styles create varying presidential needs from their staff resources. In this way, the institutional presidency with its own patterns and its own dynamics places certain limits on the efforts of incumbent presidents and thereby circumscribes their ability to act in different ways. The tension here is between an individual representative of the moment and an institutionalized office that transcends individual presidents.

Many scholars, particularly those trained in the tradition of public administration, have applauded this institutionalization. Presidents, however, have come to regard it as a constraint and have attempted to overcome this tension that exists between their desire for a responsive bureaucracy and the established patterns of the institutionalized presidency.[82] Ronald Reagan was particularly successful in his attempts to overcome the resistant executive bureaucracy. He established a formalistic staff structure in which the various players could be integrated and coordinated from the top, and he strove to appoint only committed conservatives to bureaucratic positions. In this way it can be said that Reagan centralized authority and politicized administration to a more significant degree than had most of his predecessors.[83]

The institutionalization of the presidency also has facilitated a certain type of political representation in the White House. Namely, the proliferation of membership in the presidential branch has vastly increased the potential for "representation as resemblance." It may no longer be completely correct to consider Congress the only branch in which the pluralism of society can be represented—though we should beware not to make too much of this observation. As Bradley Patterson has noted of the institutionalized presidency:

> These micro-offices of the executive branch are, like the Congress in its own structure, a mirror of the demographic and social microvariety of the whole country. In fact, that's how they got started. Over two centuries, needs perceived strongly enough became laws, laws authorized money, money paid for public employees, personnel were organized into bureaus and minipieces of bureaus, and the work of government proceeded, often under the attentive eye of the original advocates who publicized the need in the first place.[84]

Indeed, presidents themselves have done their share to encourage this pluralistic representation in their administrations. Harry Truman started the trend of giving presidential aides special responsibilities to be spokesmen for groups perceived to be "under represented" in the normal channels of government. By the Nixon administration, "there were White House assistants for the aged, youth, women, blacks, Jews, labor, Hispanic-Americans, the business community, Governors and Mayors, artists, and citizens of the District of Columbia, as well as such concerns as drug abuse, energy, environment, physical fitness, volunteerism, telecommunications, and national goals."[85] The Clinton administration, in its quest to have an administration that "looks like America," took this quest for the representation of diverse voices in the White House to new heights during the 1992-1993 transition and then into government.[86]

The institutional presidency has provided modern presidents with a vast political bureaucracy to help them cope with the increase in responsibilities that they have inherited in the twentieth century. While a similar expansion has occurred in the congressional staff system, it has not matched the size and scope of the changes in the presidency. The growth in the presidency that has come with the recentering of representative government has been a double-edged sword, however. While it has enabled presidents to better cope with the new representational responsibilities that come with the modern office, it has also come at some cost to presidential flexibility and some have even argued that it has had a deleterious effect on the American polity itself.[87]

Conclusion

A once weak office that was designed to provide a check on legislative abuses, to slow the process of public policy, and to provide for the energetic execution of government has been transformed into the vital center of an expanded national government and an international superpower. These changes have partially been the result of important developments in the American polity itself, including the elevation of efficiency over traditional pluralistic representation as a public good, America's place of leadership in the international community during and following World War II, and a new understanding of democracy and its needs. These changes, however, also have resulted from changes within the legislature and of direct congressional abdication to the courts, independent commissions, and presidents.

The twentieth century has been a time of executive aggrandizement in America. Presidents have been given expanded responsibilities, and public expectations of their presidents have risen to similar heights. Likewise, we have seen an increase in presidential influence in government and an augmentation of presidential resources to deal with these new responsibilities and public expectations.

Our presidents are now expected to set the national agenda. They are expected to educate the public and actively lead the nation and the

Congress. In the area of foreign policy and questions of war and peace, Congress and the Supreme Court have given presidents a wide berth in which to maneuver the ship of state. Presidents also have been empowered to act unilaterally in certain circumstances and by doing so to function as *the* representative of the nation.

The American people have invested much in the modern presidency. By placing so many responsibilities in that office and by investing so much of our hopes in incumbent presidents and presidential candidates, the American people and the nation's political class have made a pact with our presidents. We have given them vast political resources and made them central to all our politics, and, in return, we have one person in national politics who is responsible to the American people for his conduct in office and the health of the nation. Without formal constitutional amendment we have reforged the political system and have made the presidency rather than Congress the first branch of government and our primary institution of political representation in the United States today. But all may not be profit in this evolution from the understanding of representative government embodied in the Constitution of 1787 to the modern presidential republic.

Notes

1. Indeed, many of the greatest friends of the modern presidency in the scholarly community have taken FDR as their model for the proper conduct in office. See Richard E. Neustadt, *Presidential Power and the Modern Presidents* (New York: The Free Press, 1990); and James David Barber, *Presidential Character* (Englewood Cliffs, N.J.:Prentice Hall, 1972).

2. Quoted in Sidney M. Milkis, *The President and the Parties: The Transformation of the American Party System Since the New Deal* (New York: Oxford University Press, 1993), 53.

3. William E. Leuchtenburg, *In the Shadow of FDR: From Harry Truman to Ronald Reagan* (Ithaca, N.Y.: Cornell University Press, 1983).

4. This was particularly the case dealing with economic issues during World War II. In his Labor Day message of September 7, 1942, he said: "I ask Congress to take . . . action by the first of October. Inaction on your part by that date will leave me with an inescapable responsibility to the people of this country to see to it that the war effort is no longer imperiled by threat of economic chaos." Roosevelt warned, "I shall accept the responsibility and I will act." *Congressional Record*, 77th Congress, 2nd session, 1942, 7044.

5. I speak here of the "Court-packing" bill of 1937.

6. One should note that in the discussion that follows, I divide several aspects of the modern presidency for analytical clarity. Neither are they completely independent developments nor are they presented in chronological order. Development of the modern presidency was a much more complex phenomenon.

7. E.E. Schattschneider, *The Semi-Sovereign People* (New York: Holt, Rinehart, and Winston, 1960), 68.

8. See John W. Kingdon, *Agendas, Alternatives, and Public Policies* (Boston: Little, Brown and Company, 1984).

9. Sidney M. Milkis and Michael Nelson, *The American Presidency: Origins and Development, 1776-1990* (Washington, D.C.: CQ Press, 1990), p. 287. See also Richard Neustadt, "The Presidency and Legislation: Planning the President's Legislative Program," *American Political Science Review* (December 1955), 1015.

10. See for instance, *Congressional Quarterly*'s measures of presidential success. From 1954 to 1975 they tabulated a presidential box score which tracked Congressional action on each president's legislative agenda. Since 1953 they have also tabulated a presidential success rate in which they measure the degree to which Congress has voted in accordance with expressed presidential wishes. Both measures have a considerable presidentialist bent.

11. John Locke, The Second Treatise on Civil Government (New York: Prometheus Books, 1986), paragraph 141.

12. Forrest MacDonald, *The American Presidency: An Intellectual History* (Lawrence, Kans.: University Press of Kansas, 1994), 232-233, 261.

13. For one recent critic, see Theodore J. Lowi, *The End of Liberalism* (New York: Norton, 1969), 298.

14. Louis Fisher, *Constitutional Conflicts Between Congress and the President* (Lawrence, Kans.: University Press of Kansas, 1991), 96.

15. Robert J. Spitzer, *President & Congress: Executive Hegemony at the Crossroads of American Government* (New York: McGraw-Hill, 1993), 43.

16. McDonald, 1994, 293-294.

17. Theodore J. Lowi, *The Personal President: Power Invested Promise Unfulfilled* (Ithaca, N.Y.: Cornell University Press, 1985), 52.

18. *Schechter Poultry Corporation v. United States*, 295 U.S. 495 (1935).

19. Lowi, 1985, 53.

20. See Fisher, 1985, 114-115.

21. Spitzer, 1993, 45-46.

22. See William F. West and Joseph Cooper, "The Rise of Administrative Clearance," in *The Presidency and Public Policy Making*, George C. Edwards III, Steven Shull, and Norman Thomas, eds. (Pittsburgh, Pa.: University of Pittsburgh Press, 1985), 192-214; Terry M Moe, "The Politicized Presidency," in *The Managerial Presidency*, James P. Pfiffner, ed. (Pacific Grove, Calif.: Brooks/Cole

Publishers, 1991), 135-157.

23. Congressman Griswold, who introduced the resolution, *Annals*, 5th Congress, 2488.

24. *Annals*, 5th Congress, 2489.

25. 1 Stat. 613 (1799).

26. Fisher, 1991, 222-224.

27. See Kevin M. Kearney, "Private Citizens in Foreign Affairs: A Constitutional Analysis," 36 *Emory Law Journal* 285 (1987).

28. This is not meant to suggest, however, that Hamilton would have counciled the type of presidential power wielded by modern presidents over questions of foreign relations.

29. Aaron Wildavsky, "The Two Presidencies," in *Perspectives on the Presidency*, Aaron Wildavsky, ed. (Boston: Little, Brown and Company, 1975).

30. For a sampling of the literature revisiting Wildavsky's "two presidencies" thesis see Donald A. Peppers, "The Two Presidencies: Eight Years Later," in Wildavsky, 1975, 462-471; Lance T. LeLoup and Steven A. Shull, "Congress versus the Executive: The 'Two Presidencies' Reconsidered," *Social Science Quarterly* (March 1979), 704-719; Jeffrey E. Cohen, "A Historical Reassessment of Wildavsky's 'Two Presidencies' Thesis," *Social Science Quarterly* (September 1982), 549-555; Lee Sigelman, "A Reassessment of the 'Two Presidencies' Thesis," *Journal of Politics* (November 1979), 1195-1205.

31. Spitzer, 1993, 144-146.

32. 299 U.S. 304, p. 320 (1936). Similar rulings can be found in *Chicago and Southern Airlines v. Waterman Steamship Corp.* 333 U.S. 103 (1948); *Zemel v. Rusk* 381 U.S. 1 (1965).

33. *United States v. Curtiss-Wright Export Corporation* 81 L. Ed. 299 (1936) 262

34. *United States v. Curtiss-Wright*, 262.

35. John Marshall, *Annals*, 6th Congress (March 7, 1800) 613.

36. Richard Rose, *The Postmodern President: George Bush Meets the World*, 2nd ed. (Chatham, N.J.: Chatham House, 1991).

37. Locke, 1986, Paragraph 160.

38. See Louis Fisher, *Presidential War Power* (Lawrence, Kans.: University Press of Kansas, 1995).

39. 12 Stat. 326 (1861).

40. See *Martin v. Mott*, 12 Wheaton (25 U.S.) 1827.

41. Daniel P. Franklin, *Extraordinary Measures: The Exercise of Prerogative Powers in the United States* (Pittsburgh, Pa.: University of Pittsburgh Press, 1991), 55.

42. Fisher, 1991, 259-260.

43. See Edward S. Corwin, *The President: Office and Powers, 1789-1957* (New York, 1957), 234-250.

44. 10 *Public Papers and Addresses of Franklin D. Roosevelt* (1941 volume), 390-391.

45. 10 *Public Papers and Addresses of Franklin D. Roosevelt* (1941 volume), 205.

46. 11 *Public Papers and Addresses of Franklin D. Roosevelt* (1942 Volume), 364.

47. *Youngstown Sheet and Tube v. Sawyer*, 343 U.S. 579 (1952).

48. The five instances of Congressional declarations of war are: the War of 1812, the war with Mexico in 1846, the Spanish-American War in 1898, World War I in 1917, and World War II in 1941. In several of these, including the war with Mexico, WWI and WWII, it can be noted that presidents did much to lead the nation to the brink of war, which Congress then acknowledged and declared.

49. See *Durand v. Hollins*, Fed. Cas. III (No. 4186)(C.C.S.D.N.Y. 1860).

50. Harry S. Truman, *Public Papers of the Presidents* (July 19, 1950), 528.

51. Harry S. Truman, *Public Papers of the Presidents* (June 26, 1950), 491.

52. On the President's position, see *Public Papers of the Presidents*, 1991, 497 and *Public Papers of the Presidents*, 1992-93, 995.

53. Thomas M. Franck, "Declare War? Congress Can't," *New York Times* (December 11, 1990), A27.

54. 30 Weekly Comp. Pres. Doc. 219-220 (February 6, 1994).

55. See Thomas Franck and Edward Weisband, *Foreign Policy by Congress* (New York: Oxford University Press, 1979).

56. Ryan J. Barilleaux and Gary L. Gregg II, "Presidential Power After the Cold War," paper presented at the Midwest Political Science Association, Chicago, April 9-12, 1992.

56. Franklin, 1991, 58.

58. This paragraph is based on Ryan J. Barilleaux, "Executive Non-Agreements, Arms Control, and the Invitation to Struggle in Foreign Affairs," *World Affairs* 148 (Fall 1986), 217-228.

59. Starting in the 1970s, Congress has attempted to put some limits on presidential authority to act unilaterally in these situations by reporting requirements (The Case Act of 1972) and using their power of the purse. See Fisher, 1991, 241-243.

60. For a solid history of impoundments until 1975, see Louis Fisher, *Presidential Spending Power* (Princeton, N.J. Princeton University Press, 1975).

61. The courts upheld Nixon's action but a similar attempt in 1980 by President Carter to impose a fee on imported oil was struck down by a district court. See Fisher, 1991, 104-105.

62. *Youngstown Co. v. Sawyer*, 343 U.S. 579 (1952).

63. On the points in this paragraph, see Franklin, 1991, 60-67.

64. I borrow the basis for this idea from Ryan J. Barilleaux, *The Post-Modern Presidency: The Office after Reagan* (New York: Praeger, 1988), 21-24.

65. President Reagan seemed particularly intent upon ensuring the quality of his impact on the Court and that it would last for some time to come. Toward those ends, Reagan's first Attorney General established a new office in the Justice Department (the Office of Legal Policy) to organize and run the search for potential justices who adhered to a philosophy of judicial restraint and to an "original understanding" of the Constitution. But not all presidents have seemed so intent on making their mark. David O'Brien has made this observation about John Kennedy who routinely nominated lower court judges whose judicial philosophy ran against his. See David O'Brien, *Judicial Roulette: Report of the Twentieth Century Fund Task Force on Judicial Selection* (New York: Priority Press, 1988), 53.

66. Though any list of specific democratically passed policies that have been overturned by the courts since the Warren revolution would be prohibitively long to attempt, I particularly recall their overturning traditional representational procedures in the reapportionment cases of *Baker v. Carr,* 369 U.S. 186 (1962) and *Reynolds v. Sims*, 377 U.S. 533 (1964).

67. *Humphrey's Executor v. United States*, 295 U.S. 602 (1935).

68. See Franklin D. Roosevelt, *Public Papers and Addresses*, Volume V, 670-672. See also, Milkis, 1993, 115-118.

69. President's Committee on Administrative Management, *Administrative Management in the Government of the United States*, January 8, 1937 (Washington, D.C.: U.S. Government Printing Office, 1937). Excerpted in Harry A. Bailey, Jr. and Jay M. Shafritz, *The American Presidency: Historical and Contemporary Perspectives* (Pacific Grove, Calif.: Brooks/Cole Publishers, 1988), 76.

70. Excerpted in Bailey and Shafritz, 1988, 79.

71. MacDonald, 1994, 332-333.

72. *I.N.S. v. Chadha*, 103 S.Ct. 715.

73. Public Law 98-614.

74. See John Hart, *The Presidential Branch* (New York: Pergamon Press, 1987), 39-41.

75. Kenneth T. Walsh and Edward T. Pound with Gary Cohen, "Government off the Books," *U.S. News and World Report* (March 28, 1994), 28-32.

76. Pfiffner, 1994, 92.

77. Bradley H. Patterson, Jr., *The Ring of Power: The White House Staff and its Expanding Role in Government* (New York: Basic Books, 1988), 339.

78. Thomas E. Cronin, *The State of the Presidency* (Boston: Little, Brown and Company, 1975), 121-124.

79. Stephen Hess, *Organizing the Presidency* (Washington, D.C.: The Brookings Institution, 1976), 150-151.

80. More on this important point in chapter 6.

81. John P. Burke, *The Institutional Presidency* (Baltimore, Md.: The Johns Hopkins University Press, 1992).

82. See Bert A. Rockman, "The Style and Organization of the Reagan Presidency," in Charles O. Jones, ed., *The Reagan Legacy: Promise and Performance* (Chatham, N.J.: Chatham House Publishers, 1988), 3-29.

83. See Terry M. Moe, 1991.

84. Patterson, 1988, 19.

85. Hess, 1976, 9-10.

86. See Thomas R. Dye, "The Friends of Bill and Hillary," *PS: Political Science and Politics* (December 1993), 693-695.

87. See Cronin, 1975, 138-151.

6

Conclusion: Deliberative Democracy in the Presidential Republic

There is no more important concept in democratic theory than that of political representation. Although there have been those, following the spirit of Rousseau, who have urged reforms along the lines of direct democracy, such appeals were not seriously considered by the American Founders and to this point have never found a significant following. Representative government in America seems here to stay, though questions about its form and its health are ones that ought to be of the utmost concern to scholars and to the public. As George Will has written, "Today the health of the American republic requires reestablishment of contact with first principles, particularly with those pertaining to the idea of representation."[1]

Considering the centrality of the presidency to public life in contemporary America, no attempt to understand representation would be adequate without taking into account executive power, presidential responsibilities, and executive branch activities. First principles of presidential power and political representation in the American regime have been explored in the previous chapters. An effort has been made to understand the place of the presidency within the political system, as it was established by the Constitution of 1787 and as it has developed and evolved in American history.

The presidency is an office of important activity and energy, but it also is one of supreme secular symbolism. This dual nature of the institution places incumbent presidents in a universe of great tension—being responsible for policy and administration while also being recognized as a unifying symbol for a nation is not easily balanced. No president has ever mastered this tension as well as George Washington, who was both a successful administrator and the living embodiment of his young nation. He remains an important symbol in American politics even today. Although other democratic societies, such as Great Britain and Japan, have moved to separate the functions of symbolic and active representation, the American presidency maintains its dual nature.

Presidents provide active representation both as they are engaged in the legislative process and as they carry out the other responsibilities invested in the office by the Constitution, statutory provisions, and historical precedent. But in a system of separated powers, what place should the president occupy as a political representative? How much power should the executive be afforded in the political system? On these questions we have seen three general positions and three conceptions of the presidency as a representative institution.

As explicated in *The Federalist Papers*, the Constitution established a system of separated representative institutions in which each was to be a legitimate expression of the public good. Presidents were to be compliant instruments neither of the will of the public nor that of the legislature. Nor were they to dominate the political system and bend the other branches to their own will. As a representative relating to other representatives in Congress, the president's primary responsibility was to enhance the deliberative process of government and thereby to encourage reasonable public actions. As part of this responsibility, the president was to stand as a representative of a constitutional people and the structure of government they established. In *The Federalist* we see a balanced approach to the question of presidential power and institutional independence.

This balanced approach, as we have seen, has not been the only possibility put forward as the proper scope of presidential influence. Rather, Americans have tended to embrace the idea of a powerful, ambitious executive and alternately to fear executive power and to embrace the legislature as the safest and most democratic repository of their delegated power. This ambivalence toward the executive has been a consistent part of American political history, and may in fact be a more universal tendency of democratic peoples. Baron de Montesquieu in 1748 observed that in regard to legislative and executive institutions "most people. . . have more affection for one of these powers than for the other, as the multitude is ordinarily not fair or sensible enough to have equal affection for both of them."[2]

While some of this institutional favoritism stems from a genuine concern for the viability of free government, some favoritism no doubt also results from callous political calculations and ideological agendas. Whatever the motives or inspirations that have guided political thought, there have been two extreme and opposite tendencies in American history with regard to the separation of powers and political representation.

A whiggish understanding of representation has existed from the time the first free legislatures came into existence centuries ago. According to this understanding, representation can be offered only by a numerous and locally or proportionally elected legislative body. There is little place in such a view for an independent and energetic executive force. The legislature alone represents the will of the people and its will must therefore be the guide for governmental activity.

On the other hand, the modern model of representation that finds its best expression in the writings of Woodrow Wilson and Richard Neustadt is executive-centered rather than legislature-centered. According to this view, as the only nationally elected political figure, the president should possess the dominant public voice. In the name of democracy, efficiency, and governmental activism, presidents are to unite the other centers of power in government according to their own will. Accordingly, presidents alone can legitimately claim the mantle of national representative and the prestige and influence that comes with it in a representative democracy.

Although presidents have often not been able to live up to this ideal, the modern, presidentialist view of representative governance has clearly come to dominate twentieth-century American politics. Dominant conceptions of the office have celebrated presidential power and downplayed or even denigrated the role of popular legislatures in free government. Scholars, pundits, and the American people continually call on presidents to provide the leadership on which the modern American political system depends. And within the outlines of the checks and balances and separation of powers system of the Constitution, presidents have acquired considerable new resources and responsibilities in the twentieth century.

The American Founders distrusted demagoguery and aimed to establish an executive institution that would find its power in the Constitution and that would, to some degree, be insulated from the tides of the public mind. In the twentieth century, however, presidents and the American public have become linked in a direct plebiscitary political relationship. Presidents now speak directly and regularly to the people through television, and the public feeds responses back to the president and all of Washington either through letters and phone calls or, which is arguably of more import, through the medium of public opinion polls. To the degree that Washington and the media have come to rely on polling data, the constitutional "space" separating representatives and the represented is reduced or obliterated. To a considerable extent, though by no means completely, presidential power has been severed from the formalism of the Constitution and has become dependent upon an informal relationship to public opinion.

The relationship between the presidency and the rest of the national government has also shifted over the past six decades. As more and more responsibilities began to accrue to the federal government, the presidential office became the focal point of the federal leviathan. Presidents have become the chief agenda setters for the nation. Congress has delegated considerable power to the executive branch to write regulatory law and to implement vague statutes. The national legislature also has tended to more directly shift responsibility for important decisions to the executive branch. And especially in the area of foreign policy, American presidents now hold significant prerogative powers to act unilaterally. All these added responsibilities, expectations, and powers have led to an explosion in the size of the presidency itself, the staff of which now numbers in the thousands. Together these ideas and practical developments form the core of the presidential republic of the modern era.

Consequences for the American Polity

In previous chapters I have reflected upon some of the most important consequences of the changing understandings of representation and executive authority in American history. Presently I return to an understanding of deliberative democracy not terribly unlike that which is found in the pages of *The Federalist* in an effort to provide some further evaluation of the contemporary American polity and the dominant ideas regarding the presidency that have informed it.

Congress and Deliberative Democracy

An elected representative assembly is the one indispensable ingredient to any conception of deliberative self-rule. It is the walls of the legislative house that contain the primary sphere of deliberation.[3] But can we account the contemporary Congress a truly deliberative body? The answer is complex. Yes, Congress has occasionally, even in the last few decades, proceeded in a deliberative manner with free and honest discussions and reasoned argumentation on the public business. But the general tendency in the twentieth century has been toward a withering of this essential deliberative sphere, especially for more mundane legislative measures.[4] One need look no further for evidence of how far Congress has moved from the deliberative ideal than the lavish praise heaped upon the U.S. Senate for its admittedly admirable performance during consideration of the resolution authorizing President Bush to go to war in the Persian Gulf in 1991. If the "world's greatest deliberative body," as the Senate has historically been known, were really still so, such praise would have been unnecessary.[5]

Several major factors have contributed to this decline in the deliberative nature of Congress.[6] Certain major societal changes must of course be cited. Chief among these has been the invention and proliferation of television. Television is not kind to assemblies. It is a medium of individuals, in political life chiefly the president, news of whom tends to dominate national news programs. Television artificially creates boxes within which it demands all politicians be placed, whether these boxes are general ideological categories or predetermined positions on individual pieces of legislation. Television is impatient and demands instantaneous decisions from all political leaders within its view. It rewards flash, one-liners, and sentimentality rather than reasoned opinions and logical arguments. Television, therefore, does not cast a favorable light on the slow deliberative process of legislation.

This decline in deliberation also has partially been the result of more general alterations in the role of the federal government in American life. Chief among these changes has been the massive growth in the size and scope of the federal government over the last century. The national government has taken over more and more responsibilities that were once reserved to the various states or were left to the discretion of free individuals. This growth, and the corresponding growth of public demands from the federal government, has resulted in an "administrative republic" in which key decisions are made by executive branch bureaucrats and much of the activity of government takes place in regulatory agencies and not in the legislature. As George Will has noted, "it is an iron law of social life that as government grows, legislative control contracts."[7]

A related problem is that the immense growth in the power and scope of the federal government that came with the New Deal has also raised the stakes of nearly every political issue.[8] With the loss of the nineteenth-century commitment to limited government and without a similarly widespread commitment to governmental activism, nearly all issues have been elevated to conflict over first principles involving very high stakes. Such an ideologically charged situation is not readily amenable to reasoned political give and take.

The type and structure of governmental activities has also had a debilitating effect on congressional deliberations. As the federal government has pledged its responsibility for the economic health of the nation, more and more decisions have been delegated to economic "experts" to manage. Theodore J. Lowi also notes the impact of economic delegation on Congress itself. "The rise of economics as the language of the state," Lowi writes, "parallels the decline of Congress as a creative legislature."[9] Likewise, the modern tendency to cast all issues in terms of "rights" and "entitlements" has served at once to denigrate any outcome of deliberative processes by majority rule as well as to hermetically seal a whole host of issues from the effects of deliberative democracy.[10]

Such changes in the structure, scope, and responsibilities of the federal government have affected public attitudes about government and public expectations of government. Besides the general increase in the public's demand for "goods," the public has learned to expect and reward certain activities from its representatives and to similarly disapprove others. While some of the Founders may have counted it among the bulwarks of free government, "gridlock" now is nearly universally denounced by politicians, scholars, and the public alike. Relatedly, efficiency and speed are now counted among the most desirable elements in government—both of which are inimical to political deliberation. Though it is not my concern here, similarly we must note the internal reforms in Congress itself and their role in inhibiting deliberative democracy.[11]

More closely related to the current study, the decline of Congress as a deliberative body in part has resulted from fundamental alterations in the representational relationship. Despite the recent popularity of the populist argument that political leaders in Washington are too insulated from public opinion, a concern for deliberative democracy finds the opposite to be the case. Deliberative democracy necessitates the existence of a certain "space" separating political leaders from the shifts of public opinion. Democratic legitimacy unquestionably necessitates representatives be *responsible* to the public, but deliberation cannot occur if they are immediately *responsive* to mass opinion.

In modern American politics this space has suffered a considerable battering. Nearly unbounded parochialism by many members of Congress has certainly been part of the problem. In true political deliberations, parochial concerns and values certainly have their place, but a genuine concern for the national good must predominate. Congressmen also take part in what has been dubbed the "constant campaign" for reelection, and its needs tend to undermine the space that was intended to exist between election years.

Additionally, presidents have also made a significant contribution to the decay of this protective buffer in which free political argument and reasoning can take place. Indeed, it is now an established presidential strategy to intentionally undermine the integrity of this space and to exploit it for the president's own policy goals. While presidents once almost solely relied on directly engaging Congress in attempts to persuade its members of the executive's point of view, presidents now regularly go over Congress' head and make direct appeals to the public in an effort to motivate mass opinion to pressure legislators. Such a strategy undermines the role of Congress as a legitimate determiner of the national interest and denies to individual congressmen the status of independent representatives. This presidential leadership strategy of "going public" also can short circuit deliberation in the legislature as it encourages public pressure on the membership. The same results from Washington's reliance on public opinion polls for policy legitimacy.

1995 Forward—Congress Resurgent?

One thread running through these pages has been a general critique of the flow of responsibility from Congress to the executive branch that has occurred during the past several decades.[12] I have also alluded to my conclusion that proper representative government demands a more assertive legislature prepared to defend the constitutional order and act with the independence that the fundamental law assumes. At times Congress has seemed poised to recenter government once again, only to fall back into the twentieth century's reigning orthodoxy of the presidential republic.

In the 1994 off-year elections, the Republicans swept into control of both the Senate (for the first time in eight years) and the House of

Representatives (for the first time in forty years). There can be no doubt that the Republicans under the leadership of the new Speaker of the House Newt Gingrich meant to take control of the national agenda. Facing a weakened Democratic President, they did just that in 1995. In the spring of 1995 President Clinton was reduced to defending his own "relevance" and responding to the new national agenda set by the leadership of the new Congress. But do these events mark the long-term resurgence of Congress and deliberative democracy? Of course, only in retrospect will we be able to judge the lasting effects of the 104th Congress on the balance of power but we can now offer a brief reflection as to the meaning of that Congress for deliberative democracy.

To explore such a question, it is useful to separate *substance* from *process*. This, as I will make more clear below, is what is required of representative government understood as the quest for deliberative self-rule. First, just a word about the substance of the legislation forwarded by the Republican Congress. A number of their professed goals and legislation might well prove to impact deliberation in the national legislature. On the opening day of the 104th Congress they passed a series of reforms purportedly designed to make the House procedures more open. They cut committee staff, opened meetings for public and the press, put term limits on the Speaker and committee chairs, and put congressmen under the same laws as the rest of the country. And, in what was at least a great symbolic boon to the legislature as a place of reasoned discussion, they banned the use of proxy voting. Perhaps nothing more clearly symbolized the loss of the ideal of deliberation more than this practice by which a member of Congress could still cast a vote while not even present in the same city where the committee meeting was being held.

If the decline of Congress has come in part as a result of the expanded government of the twentieth century, as I opined earlier, then, if successful, the Republicans' plans to devolve government and change the nature of the entitlement programs that have largely grown beyond the control of the legislative process might contribute to the recentering of government. Only time will tell.

In the spring of 1996, the Republican Congress passed and President Clinton signed the line-item veto the Republicans had promised in their electoral platform they called "The Contract with America." Though this "enhanced rescissions" bill was a watered-down version of the line-item veto some had proposed for many years, it nonetheless holds great potential for reasoned deliberation but also considerable danger of centering even more power within the White House. For instance, a president bent on using the line-item veto simply to increase his own influence over the legislature could threaten to use or promise to withold his veto over a given legislative item in an effort to pressure its supporters into voting with him on some other item on the legislative agenda. Such an action would represent not acknowledging the reasonableness of legislation but succumbing to what can be better likened to force and manipulation.

On the other hand, a president properly motivated by the common good and a concern with deliberative processes could use the line-item veto to enhance the legislative process. For example, members of Congress have long hidden provisions in bills that could not stand the light cast by a properly discursive legislature. A properly motivated president could take it as his responsibility to ferret out these elements in legislation and return them to Congress where they would then have to stand on their own merits in the legislative arena. In this way Congress will still retain ultimate control over the fate of the provisions vetoed, but reason and the common good would be strengthened elements in that decision-making process on Capitol Hill.

Only time will tell which model of the presidency will prevail in regard to the line-item veto. What is clear is that the representational importance of the line-item veto was not lost on President Clinton..At the bill signing ceremony for the legislation, the president spoke of the "special-interest boondoggles, tax loop-holes and pure pork," found in legislation and said "[t]he line-item veto will give us a chance to change that, to permit Presidents *to better represent the public interest* by cutting waste, protecting taxpayers, and balancing the budget."[13]

But the *substance* of the 104th Congress aside, what of the more immediately important question of *process*? With the Republican campaign of 1994 and the subsequent Congress they controlled, we see clearly that a resurgent Congress is a necessary but not sufficient element in deliberative politics. The Republican Congress and the "Contract" that guided it demonstrates how far the plebiscitary politics of the twentieth century has infected American national government.

On September 27, 1994, Republican House candidates met at the Capitol for an electoral spectacle and to sign what they had come to term "The Contract with America." Written in consultation with GOP pollster Frank Luntz, the "Contract" was an attempt to nationalize the off-year elections and establish a popular mandate by outlining ten explicit policy positions to be advanced if Republicans were to take control of Congress.

No hint here of representation as a deliberative process—all becomes popular plebiscite. Like presidents who control a party platform and run on an agenda for governing, the Republicans sought to create the appearance of a popular mandate that they could ride into the process of governing.

Since Franklin Roosevelt set out to establish much of his program within the first couple of months of his term, the "first 100 days" has become a recurrent measure for new presidents. Mimicking this precedent, the "Contract" also pledged the new majority to voting on each part of the ten point document within the first one hundred days of the new Congress. Sounding much like many modern presidents and presidential watchers in the media and academics, Republican leader Newt Gingrich, when asked about this promise, thought the ambitious pace would be "reasonable since public opinion would be on our side."[14] After the elections, Republican leaders went further, promising to work "20 hours a day, seven days a week" to carry out their campaign promises.[15] Again there was no hint that time for discussion and thought could bring anything to the process of legislation. All is popular opinion; all is haste.

Though the 104th Congress has unquestionably been one dedicated to returning the national legislature to its rightful place as the first branch of government, its processes and methods are not much different from the governing paradigm of the presidential republic. An active and independent Congress, therefore, does not necessarily equal a resurgence of reasonable and meaningful discourse in the legislature.

Expectations in the Presidential Republic

Some of the same societal and governmental changes that have contributed to the decline of Congress as a deliberative body have affected the presidency. The demands and limitations of television, public opinion polls, and presidential rhetorical strategies all impact the presidency and its representational relationship with the public. Likewise, the growth in the size and scope of the federal government and the movement toward economic regulation and economic language in public life have had profound effects on the office and how presidents go about their responsibilities.

As the federal government has grown and acquired ever more responsibilities and powers, so, too, has the presidency grown. Presidents have been given great influence over the national agenda and Congress has delegated grand new responsibilities to chief executives and to the executive bureaucracy. Presidential resources in terms of money and staff have likewise grown tremendously. However, it should be noted that this has not been a "balanced" growth between presidential responsibilities/ public expectations and presidential resources to deal with them. Rather, there has been a much greater increase in the demands the system places on our presidents than there has been in regard to our presidents' ability to perform. This situation has had an important impact on the office and the American polity.

Growth in public expectations of our chief executives, fueled by near boundless campaign promises from presidential candidates and the constant credit-claiming of incumbents, has accelerated much faster than has the presidency's ability to handle them. The presidency, after all, still exists within a constitutional system that fractures power in the name of checks and balances. What we have been left with is what some scholars have called the "expectations gap" between public expectations and the ability of any president to meet them.[16] This situation, however, may more properly be referred to as a "representation gap"—the public has come to expect a certain type of representation and a certain character of representation from their presidents that, despite all the pro-president changes in the political system since the 1930s, no president can adequately meet. The result is public disillusionment, cynicism, and falling approval ratings over a president's tenure. Because presidential influence is so closely tied to popular opinion, the result is weakened presidents in a presidentially-centered political system.

Deliberative Democracy: Is Presidential Power Poison?

A reconstruction of deliberative democracy is beyond the scope of the current work. A few more words about the relationship between the presidency and deliberative democracy, however, are in order. To this point I have been somewhat critical of presidential power as it has come to be understood and celebrated since the presidency of Franklin Roosevelt. But can presidents actually have a role in the resurrection of deliberative democracy, or is presidential activity necessarily inimical to representative government based on the norm of free and reasonable public discourse within the institutional framework of the Constitution?

In certain areas, the health and perhaps even the very survival of representative government in America depends upon vigorous and independent presidential activity. As Alexander Hamilton so well demonstrated in *The Federalist*, there can be no substitute for the energetic execution of the laws. Likewise, presidential energy can be of great use in checking or slowing the progress of the national legislature. At other times the American nation depends on her presidents to act forcefully and quickly to repel invasion, to secure the interests of America abroad, or even to apply a strategic pardon in a situation in which absolute justice would be worse than allowing the guilty to go free. In all these areas presidential power is not poison, rather it is a remedy for greater defects in the political system or the international arena.

A certain spirit, however, that has inspired many of America's modern chief executives is certainly a danger to deliberative democracy. I speak here of that understanding of democratic politics that finds presidential election results to have authoritatively abolished further questions about certain public policy issues. This is the idea that Congress and other public actors should follow national election results and that presidents should be given a relatively free reign to enact their programs. This is the spirit that led FDR to threaten Congress with unilateral action and attempt to undermine the independence of the Supreme Court. It is the same basic spirit that seems to have guided some of Ronald Reagan's chief advisors in the 1981 budget battle in Congress. Reagan's budget director later described his strategy for enacting the administration's economic program: "The constitutional prerogatives of the legislative branch would have to be, in effect, suspended. Enacting the Reagan Administration's economic program meant rubber stamp approval, nothing less. The world's so-called greatest deliberative body would have to be reduced to the status of a ministerial arm of the White House."[17] It also is the same basic spirit that made it seem strangely natural that President Clinton might impugn the patriotism of those who would oppose his economic policy initiatives in 1993.[18]

This spirit, which has been legitimized by a more radical democratic ideal that became popular in certain circles during the twentieth century, is destructive to deliberative politics. It champions the quick and efficient codification and implementation of presidential initiatives rather than the slow and compromising path of legislative politics. It denies to members of Congress the representational role of mixing reason with the public mind and presidential will. It also encourages a monarchical air on the part of presidents and their administrations. Here I do not mean an understanding of the essential symbolic aspects of our elected kingship. Rather, this is a monarchical spirit of presidential will—that his is equal to the nation's and should be the rudder by which the state is guided. Such a spirit is incompatible with a complex constitutional system of representation and self-rule conceived of as the deliberate will of the public expressed through representative institutions.

I also have been critical of modern presidential rhetoric and the leadership strategy of "going public." But is there room for presidential rhetoric in a deliberative republic? Is there a presidential style of communication that would not serve to undermine the legitimacy of Congress and subvert reasoned discourse in that body? The answer must clearly be yes. There must be room for popular rhetoric in any representative democracy. The essential point is to balance the need for leadership, political education, and symbolism with the needs of independent representation and political reason.

The American Founding Fathers did not fear all political rhetoric. They did, however, have serious reservations about the effects of demagoguery, of popular leaders stirring the public passions and encouraging activities destructive to constitutional government. Likewise, not all presidential speech deserves proscription, but only that which may undermine the foundations that support deliberative democracy in America.

An essential aspect of the presidency is, and must continue to be, symbolic representation, an element of which presidential rhetoric must remain. Part of this symbolic representation is the unique place afforded our presidents to affect the public spirit. George Washington knew this place of the presidency well and in his public utterances was always mindful to set the proper tone for a free people. Presidents from Washington to the present have carried out this function to a greater or lesser degree. The president who most recently excelled at this role of the presidency was Ronald Reagan. The "Great Communicator," as he was known, was well in touch with the office as a place of moral leadership and strove to rebuild what he took to be the battered spirit of the American people as it emerged from Watergate, Vietnam, and the "malaise" of the late 1970s. From time to time in the life of a free people such secular moral leadership is essential and no other officer occupies ground from which it can be so readily provided.

Likewise, it may be the case that the presidency is the institution most capable of providing education in the constitutional morality that undergirds the American Republic. Washington and Lincoln certainly excelled at such a role for presidential speech. In his Farewell Address Washington spoke of the virtues of the national union, of the dangers of "the spirit of innovation," and of factions in a free government and counciled wariness with regard to foreign entanglements. In his Gettysburg Address, Lincoln provided to the people who remained part of the Union what he understood to be a constitutional basis for the sacrifices they had been called upon to endure in the name of preserving the Union and its fundamental compact. Such a constitutionally educative function is one that can best be provided by occupants of the presidency.

These are all rhetorical roles of the office that are not, in and of themselves at least, a danger to deliberation. The rhetorical practices of presidents that are a danger are two fold. First, presidential speech that is designed only to promote the popularity of the incumbent and thereby to increase his influence within the Washington community can do precious little good for the deliberative republic.

An even greater problem is presidential rhetoric designed specifically to circumvent the deliberative process in Congress. One such rhetorical strategy has presidents going over the heads of congressmen by speaking directly to their constituents on a specific piece of public policy and hoping to persuade these constituents to pressure congressmen to do their bidding. Such a strategy was a favorite of Ronald Reagan, particularly on areas of foreign and domestic policy with which he was ideologically committed.[19]

Other rhetorical devices used by presidents in their efforts to move Congress hold great dangers for deliberation. Andrew Jackson's chastisement of Senators for not voting according to the instructions of the legislatures that elected them is an example of one such rhetorical device.[20] Contemporary presidents simply replace Jackson's state legislatures with public opinion as the source to be heeded by members of Congress "properly" carrying out their duties. Another example is FDR's threat of unilateral action if Congress did not act as he wished.[21]

Examples of such rhetorically poisonous strategies can be found in more innocuous-appearing forms as well. Take, for example, President Bush's attempt in March 1991 to get Congress to pass his legislation dealing with transportation and crime. Bush attempted to capitalize that spring on the wildly popular war to liberate Kuwait from Iraqi control. "If our forces could win the ground war in 100 hours, then surely the Congress can pass this legislation in 100 days. Let that be a promise we make tonight to the American people."[22] The problem with such rhetoric is that it leaves no place for a freely deliberative legislative process. The limits are already set and the message is conveyed to the American people that Congress can add nothing with extra time to think, discuss, and weigh the alternatives. The lesson in constitutional morality is all wrong: the legislative process is made analogous to war, to an army carrying into effect the orders of the commander. Such is not deliberative democracy, but presidential plebiscite.

Such leadership strategies are more akin to force than persuasion. They simultaneously can constrict the deliberative process of legislative politics, undermine independent representation in Congress, and paint presidents themselves into a policy box of such gravity as may prove nearly impervious to any reasonable arguments that may still emerge from congressional deliberations and considerations of fact.

But what can a president's rhetorical role be during the legislative process? First, as the only nationally elected figures, presidents can perform an important role as the primary agenda-setter for deliberative democracy. But it should be noted that helping to establish the agenda does not necessitate the active promotion of one particular policy alternative above all others. Such a change would require a near complete revision of the dominant model of presidential leadership—of presidents leading and Congress following. This does not, however, necessitate our presidents divorcing themselves completely, even with regard to rhetoric, from the legislative process.

Rather, the needs of deliberative democracy require that presidential activity be measured, not in terms of presidential successes and failures on legislative votes, but on how they affect the deliberative aspects of representative government itself. In a deliberative republic the president's primary function, setting aside his essential roles in national security and reacting to national emergencies, is to be the chief custodian of congressional deliberation.[23]

Presidents often will be called upon to establish the agenda, to provide the grist for the legislative mill. When the nature of the concern warrants, presidents must also be prepared to remind legislators and the public of the first principles of the constitutional system as well as the underpinnings of free government and encourage the deliberative process to be carried out on such a level. In a pluralistic society and a political system categorized by some as "interest group liberalism," presidents also have a role in recalling the political dialogue to the notion of a common good. Presidents must do their part to liberate legislators from the forces of parochialism and special interests that would seek to undermine real, vital deliberation.

In the end, if presidents are to serve deliberative democracy they must contribute to the representational "space" on which it depends. Encouraging this space between special interests and those in the deliberative process is of special concern. So is the health of the space that to some degree always exists between a seated representative and his or her constituency.

A recent example of such proper executive rhetoric can be seen in the Clinton administration's public activity in favor of the North American Free Trade Agreement (NAFTA) in 1993. Particularly important was the administration's effort to create enough "space" between the special interests who opposed the agreement (e.g., labor unions) and members of Congress so the latter would have enough room to vote their consciences.

With labor unions threatening legislators with electoral defeat if they voted for the NAFTA, the administration sent Vice President Al Gore on national television to debate the agreement's chief opponent, Ross Perot. By nearly all accounts the Vice President obliterated Perot and his arguments against the treaty. With this performance they opened some space in which congressmen could oppose the special interests and intelligently defend their decision to vote for the trade accord. Despite the pressures of labor and other groups, Congress passed the North American Free Trade Agreement, which had been in serious trouble not long before.

Presidents also must allow congressmen to be separated enough from presidential will to meaningfully take part in deliberation. Presidents can use the pedagogical nature of their office to teach us to value deliberation just as much as we value efficiency and the codification of our will. And they can provide rhetorical cover for legislators who are moved by the deliberative process itself.

One Eye toward the Future:
Scholarship on Representative Government and the Presidency

In the remaining few pages I do not attempt to outline a comprehensive agenda for scholarship on the presidency or representative government. Neither do I attempt an exhaustive delineation of the consequences of this study and the perspective I have raised on these topics. Rather, I simply offer a few reflections on what I take to be the importance of this study for future scholarly research on the office and for potential reforms of the executive office and the wider political order.

Questions of democracy and representation have been central to western political theory for centuries, and they have undergone a considerable revival even over the last few years. Political theorists once again are asking fundamental questions about the structures and institutions of free government. Certain politicians and pundits, one thinks especially of 1992 independent presidential candidate Ross Perot, have even begun to urge revolutionary changes to the system of representative government that would bring it more in line with a direct democracy. Technological developments are no doubt fueling much of this trend as it becomes ever more conceivable that technology will someday soon catch up with the radically democratic vision that has inspired some in every age at least since Rousseau.

Friends of representative government cannot permit technological progress to outstrip political principles. They will have to revisit the assumptions, the needs, and even the basic justifications of representative democracy if they are to take their place in the debate on the future of the American polity. Representative government is not inevitable and it can be lost if it is not properly defended in theory as well as in practice. In none of these questions can executive power and the institution of the presidency be ignored. Toward that end, I have endeavored with this study to explore the representational aspects of the American presidency and its place in the American system of representative government. Further work will certainly need to be done in this vital area.

As I have argued, scholars should come to understand the presidency as part of the larger system of representative government. Following such a systematic perspective on the presidency, we can turn our sights to exploring presidential activity as a *process.* This would mean a restructuring of some of the basic assumptions of much of the scholarship and commentary on the office. Rather than looking at individual presidents in terms of their getting what they want from Congress, scholars could turn their attention to questions of how presidents have or have not contributed to the quality of reason in the governing and legislative processes. In this way presidents can be understood to represent in the larger process of deliberative democracy—they do not represent simply by forcing the enactment of a specific substantive policy agenda.

One should also note that serious discussion of public policy is not reserved solely for the legislature. We have considerable anecdotal evidence of the decision-making processes in various administrations. What would be useful would be more scholarly exploration of executive branch decision making with an eye toward the issues raised by concerns with representation and deliberation in government. Does real deliberation occur within the White House? Alternatively, do advisors obfuscate and avoid difficult truths dealing with options for presidential activity? How can we facilitate real discussion and argument in the White House without sacrificing the energy that is so vital to the office? How can we better allow presidents the "space" within which they can change their minds according to new evidence or reasonable arguments without incurring the wrath of an ever scrutinizing media?[24]

Another part of the literature on the presidency that is not directly addressed in this study but that holds import for these concerns are the books and articles purporting to have found a cyclical presidency or one profoundly influenced by wider circumstances in the political environment.[25] If the presidency is indeed cyclical and/or is in some way a dependent variable in regard to one or another aspect of the political environment, then the representation provided by presidents must also be cyclical and/or dependent upon prevailing circumstances. If representation is such a dependent variable, then what does that mean for representative government and democratic self-rule?

If presidents are to be considered representatives, students of the office will want to seriously consider the nature of the presidential constituency represented. Though nearly all presidents have claimed to represent some national interest or entity like "the national interest" or "the American people," scholars may want to explore the reality that may lie behind this rhetoric. Did Herbert Hoover represent the same national interest as did FDR? Did Jimmy Carter represent the same "American people" as did Ronald Reagan? How does the makeup of presidential staff affect this issue of representation? One suspects that there is a more complex story here than is normally told by our presidents and presidential watchers.

I have been critical of congressional parochialism, but it should also be noted that presidents are certainly not immune from parochial instincts. How much parochialism is there in presidential budgetary decisions that benefit a given group like the aged, farmers, or the educational establishment? How much parochialism can be seen in a president frequenting a given state and providing that state with government contracts and the like?[26] How much parochialism was there in George Bush's dropping his opposition to the development of the V-22 Osprey tilt-rotor aircraft and modernization of the Army's M-1 tank during the heat of the 1992 re-election campaign? Or how much parochialism can we attribute to his decision to sell 150 F-16 fighter jets to Taiwan, which was announced at a specially staged campaign photo-op at the General Dynamics plant where they would be built?[27] We should disabuse ourselves of the notion that only members of Congress act in such locally-biased ways. Scholars may well want to cast a serious eye in the direction of this tension between the common good and parochial and electoral concerns in the White House.

On a smaller scale than the grand debate on the future of representative government that I mentioned above, I hope this study has pointed to a much needed framework for thinking about proposed reforms of the presidency itself.[28] A myriad of reforms of the institution and aspects of the political system related to it have been forwarded over the past several decades and from the single six-year term to the abolition of the electoral college they all hold importance for presidential representation.

Most reforms that have been proposed from Woodrow Wilson to political scientists and commentators of the current hour have been formulated in the name of strengthening the hand of the president or in improving governmental efficiency and more direct democratic accountability. If we have a concern with real deliberation occurring in government, if we are to be true to the Founders' vision of a compound republic of separated institutions, then this is decidedly the wrong direction for reform. A stronger presidency will not facilitate more open discussions in Congress. A more streamlined and hierarchical legislative process will not bring the full flavor of debate to the fore.

Likewise, the siren call of much of political science, the responsible party model, is incompatible with the ideal of the process of government defended in these pages as its goal is not reasoned discussion and argument but democratic efficiency and enhanced collective cohesion of the parties. As put forward by the Committee on Political Parties of the American Political Science Association, this perspective holds that the party system should be "democratic, responsible and effective."

> An effective party system requires, first, that the parties are able to bring forth programs to which they commit themselves and, second, that the parties possess sufficient internal cohesion to carry out these programs. . . . The fundamental

requirement of such accountability is a two-party system in which the opposition party acts as the critic of the party in power, developing, defining, and presenting the policy alternatives which are necessary for a true choice in reaching public decisions.[29]

Note that the emphasis in this model is on the efficient codification of pre-established policy commitments. There is no room for real deliberation, meaningful discussions, and reasoned decision making in government. Representatives are not treated as individuals who can be moved by a careful weighing of the evidence, but are reduced to automatically carrying out their party's platform or, if in the opposition, to opposing any and all actions of the majority so that there will purportedly be a "true choice in reaching public decisions." This choice is most decidedly not the choice of a properly constituted deliberative democracy.

It is for another day or for others to more thoroughly develop proposals for institutional or constitutional reform. My purpose here is simply to lay forth the argument that any proposed reforms should be considered in light of the presidency as a representative institution and the needs of a constitutionally constrained representative democracy. As I have argued, this should include a concern to enhance or at least do no further damage to the deliberative aspects of the system. Despite the populist demogoguery of both right and left, reform should not enhance the plebiscitary elements of the system. Rather than strive to bring our representatives closer in tune with the ebbs and flows of public opinion, reforms should enhance the "space" between our representatives and our temporary judgments, but do so without denegrating the democratically essential aspects of this relationship that keeps our servants accountable for their decisions. Only if this is to occur will our representatives be positioned to use their best judgments and be moved by reason and argument to forward the national good.

Reforms also should not encourage any further movement of responsibility from the legislative to the executive branch. Rather, our representatives assembled in Congress should take responsibility for making the basic decisions of national public policy. Only in the course of legislative deliberation can the full diversity of the nation be represented and can proposed legislation be given a full airing. Though it may at times be inefficient and slow, there is no more effective, safe, and democratically legitimate method of making good law.

Though I do not advocate any specific constitutional or institutional reforms, in another way this book has been about reform. I have advocated a basic reformation on the level of the ideals and ideas that govern the contemporary American political system. At the most fundamental level, this is what is necessary to begin the process of reestablishing a more deliberative republic. Chief among the ideas should be a lowering of the expectations we have of our presidents. Fueled by presidents, presidential candidates, the media, political scientists, and the general political culture of the late twentieth century, the American people's expectations of our presidents have grown out of bounds. It is unreasonable to expect our presidents to be all things to all people. It is equally unreasonable to expect them to have an instantaneous reaction to all occurrences in the environment, to be able to swiftly enact a laundry list of programs and reforms, to be unwavering in defense of all prior commitments, or to single-handedly cure the ills of the polity. Though presidential candidates are particularly quick to encourage these expectations, presidents pay a heavy price for them as well as does representative government itself. Unfulfilled expectations mean negative publicity and news stories, falling approval ratings, and in the end can mean a delegitimized president and a disillusioned citizenry.

Hand in hand with a more realistic set of expectations for our presidents, we should come to understand representative government as a complex and mixed system of representation and responsibility. Ours is not a system geared toward the efficient representation of a single national will and we should not expect that. Rather, our Constitution helps insure that the great diversity of the nation will be represented in government. This diversity, this multiplication of voices, is not something to be overcome but is an essential engredient in deliberative politics. It is from the dialogue among these fractured representatives that good public policy and the national interest stem. The chief executive's voice is to be one among many representative voices in this system.

The presidency has always been an essential element in the American system of representative democracy. It has never been more so than at the end of the twentieth century. If we are to understand representative democracy, a task worthy of the serious concern of the scholarly community and the general public, we must think seriously about presidential activity. Executive power and presidential leadership should come to be understood in light of the needs and values of deliberation, and potential political reforms should be judged according to the standards provided by such an understanding. Such is the fundamental tension that must be achieved in a representative government of separated and independent institutions of representation.

Notes

1. George F. Will, *Restoration: Congress, Term Limits and the Recovery of Deliberative Democracy* (New York: The Free Press, 1992), 103.
2. Baron de Montesquieu, *The Spirit of the Laws*, Anne M. Cohler, Basia Carolyn Miller, and Harold Samuel Stone, trans. and eds. (Cambridge: Cambridge University Press, 1989), Book 19, Chapter 27, 325.
3. This is not to deny that deliberation can and should occur outside of government. But deliberation in political campaigns and in the normal course of life cannot substitute for meaningful dialogue among elected representatives convened for that purpose. This, no doubt, will incur the ire of those who have come to advocate some form of direct democracy in America. It is not that I have no confidence in the public. On the contrary, citizenship in a deliberative republic is a very important responsibility. It is the people alone who have the ultimate say over the outcome of the deliberative process of government and they alone who ultimately must exercise control over the makeup of representative assemblies. They are crucial members in this system—albeit in a somewhat different way than some would idealize.
4. On congressional deliberation, see George E. Connor and Bruce I. Oppenheimer, "Deliberation: An Untimed Value in a Timed Game," in Lawrence C. Dodd and Bruce I. Oppenheimer, eds., *Congress Reconsidered* (Washington, D.C.: CQ Press, 1993), 315-330.
5. For a recent and rather fine attempt to argue that deliberation does still occur in Congress see, Joseph M. Bessette, *The Mild Voice of Reason: Deliberative Democracy and American National Government* (Chicago: University of Chicago Press, 1994).
6. One should note that here I do not attempt to point to some specific "golden age" of deliberative democracy in America. Rather, my major goal is to point political scientists, the media, and the citizenry toward a certain ideal of democracy that is at once realistic as well as worthy.
7. George F. Will, *Restoration: Congress, Term Limits, and the Recovery of Deliberative Democracy* (New York: The Free Press, 1992), 172.
8. See Sidney M. Milkis, *The President and the Parties: The Transformation of the American Party System Since the New Deal* (New York: Oxford University Press, 1993), 306.

9. Theodore J. Lowi, "The State in Political Science: How We Become What We Study," *American Political Science Review* Vol. 86, No. 1 (March 1992), 5.

10. See Milkis, 1993.

11. For a history of the decline of deliberative democracy that focuses more on the internal changes in Congress, see Gerald B. H. Solomon and Donald R. Wolfensberger, "The Decline of Deliberative Democracy in the House and Proposals for Reform," *Harvard Journal on Legislation* 31 (1993), 321-370.

12. One could similarly critique the flow of responsibility to the courts during this same period. These events certainly hold import for representative government, but they are not the concern of the current volume.

13. Quoted in Andrew Taylor, "Line-Item Veto Bill Becomes Law," *Congressional Quarterly Weekly Report* (April 13, 1996), 984. Emphasis added.

14. Newt Gingrich as quoted by Representative Rick White in James G. Gimpel, *Fulfilling the Contract: The First Hundred Days* (Boston: Allyn and Bacon, 1996), 29.

15. Quoted in Katharine Q. Seelye, "Republicans Plan Ambitious Agenda in Next Congress," *The New York Times* (November 15, 1994), A1.

16. See Richard W. Waterman, ed., *The Presidency Reconsidered* (Itasca, Ill: F. E. Peacock Publishers, 1993).

17. David A. Stockman, *The Triumph of Politics: The Inside Story of the Reagan Revolution* (New York: Avon Books, 1987), 173.

18. In his televised address to the nation on February 15, 1993, President Clinton disparaged opponents of his economic proposals as "special interests" and "defenders of decline," "who've profited from the status quo." He went on, "When I was a boy we had a name for the belief that we should all pull together to build a better, stronger nation. We called it patriotism—and we still do." Not only are opponents disparaged as "defenders of decline" but opposition to the president's policy proposals is portrayed as somehow unpatriotic and thereby logically illegitimate. Speech reprinted in *Congressional Quarterly Almanac* (Vol. XLIX, 1993), 11-D.

19. In his memoirs, Reagan speaks of using this leadership strategy to promote his policies in Central America and of the frustrations he felt when it did not work. "The White House staff regularly received the results of polls that measured what Americans thought of administration policies. Time and again, I would speak on television, to a joint session of Congress, or to other audiences about the problems in Central America, and I would hope that the outcome would be an outpouring of support from Americans who would apply the same kind of heat on Congress that helped pass the economic recovery package." Ronald Reagan, *An American Life* (New York: Simon and Schuster, 1990), 479.

20. See chapter 3 above.

21. See chapter 4 above.

22. George Bush, "Address before a Joint Session of Congress on the Cessation of the Persian Gulf Conflict (March 6, 1991)," *Public Papers of the President of the United States: George Bush, 1991* (Washington, D.C.: U.S. Government Printing Office, 1992), volume 1, 221.

23. I owe this phraseology to John Alvis, "Willmoore Kendall and the Demise of Congressional Deliberation," *Intercollegiate Review* 23 No. 2 (Spring 1988), 57-66.

24. On the media's penchant to focus negatively on perceived presidential "broken promises," see Thomas E. Patterson, *Out of Order* (New York: Vintage Books, 1994).

25. See Erwin C. Hargrove and Michael Nelson, *Presidents, Politics, and Policy* (New York: Knopf, 1984); James David Barber, *The Pulse of Politics: Electing Presidents in the Media Age* (New York: W.W. Norton, 1980); Stephen Skowronek, *The Politics Presidents Make: Leadership from John Adams to George Bush* (Cambridge: Harvard University Press, Belknap Press, 1993); Ryan J. Barilleaux, "George Bush and the Changing Context of Presidential Leadership," in *Leadership and the Bush Presidency*, Ryan J. Barilleaux and Mary E. Stuckey, eds. (Westview, Conn.: Praeger, 1992), 3-23.

26. In particular, I am thinking here of President Clinton's extraordinarily frequent trips to the electorally-rich state of California during his first term as president and the series of "goodies" he was able to bring to the state.

27. John Lancaster, "Military Moves with Political Overtones," *Washington Post* (September 3, 1992), A1.

28. Elsewhere I have developed a "representational framework" for research on the presidency. See Gary L. Gregg II, "Toward a Representational Framework for Presidency Studies," *Presidential Studies Quarterly* (forthcoming).

29. American Political Science Association, *Toward a More Responsible Two-Party System: A Report of the Committee on Political Parties* (New York: Rinehart, 1950), 1-2.

Bibliography

Allen, William B., editor. *George Washington: A Collection*. Indianapolis: Liberty Fund, 1988.

Alvis, John. "Willmoore Kendall and the Demise of Congressional Deliberation." *Intercollegiate Review* (Spring 1988): 57-66.

Andrews, William G. "The Presidency, Congress, and Constitutional Theory." In *Perspectives on the Presidency*, edited by Aaron Wildavsky, pp. 24-45. Boston: Little, Brown and Company, 1975.

Arnhart, Larry. "The Deliberative Rhetoric of *The Federalist*." *Political Science Reviewer* (Spring 1990): 49-86.

Bailey, Harry A. Jr. and Jay M. Shafritz, editors. *The American Presidency: Historical and Contemporary Perspectives*. Pacific Grove, Calif.: Brooks/Cole Publishing Company, 1988.

Barber, James David. *The Presidential Character*, Second Edition Englewood Cliffs, N.J.: Prentice-Hall, 1977.

Barilleaux, Ryan J. "Toward an Institutionalist Framework for Presidency Studies." *Presidential Studies Quarterly* (Spring 1982): 154-158.

———. "Executive Non-Agreements, Arms Control, and the Invitation to Struggle in Foreign Affairs," *World Affairs* (Fall 1986): 217-228.

———. *The Post-Modern Presidency: The Office After Ronald Reagan*. New York: Praeger, 1988.

———. "George Bush and the Changing Context of Presidential Leadership." In *Leadership and the Bush Presidency*, edited by Ryan J. Barilleaux and Mary E. Stuckey, pp. 3-23. Westview, Conn.: Praeger, 1992.

————. "Liberals, Conservatives, and the Presidency." *Congress & The Presidency* (Spring 1993): 75-82.

Barilleaux, Ryan J. and Randall E. Adkins. "The Nomination Process and Patterns." In *The Elections of 1992,* edited by Michael Nelson, pp. 21-56. Washington, D.C.: CQ Press, 1993.

Barilleaux, Ryan J. and Gary L. Gregg II. "Presidential Power after the Cold War." Paper presented at the Midwest Political Science Association, Chicago, April 9-12, 1992.

Beer, Samuel H. *To Make a Nation: The Rediscovery of American Federalism.* Cambridge, Mass.: Harvard University Press, 1993.

Belz, Herman. *Lincoln and the Constitution: The Dictatorship Question Reconsidered.* Fort Wayne, Ind.: Louis A. Warren Lincoln Library and Museum, 1984.

Berns, Walter, editor. *After the People Vote: A Guide to the Electoral College.* Washington, D.C.: American Enterprise Institute Press, 1992.

Bessette, Joseph. "Deliberative Democracy: The Majority Principle in Republican Government." In *How Democratic is the Constitution?* edited by Robert Goldwin and William A. Schrambra, pp. 102-116. Washington, D.C.: American Enterprise Institute, 1980.

————. *The Mild Voice of Reason: Deliberative Democracy and American National Government.* Chicago, Ill.: University of Chicago Press, 1994.

Binkley, Wilfred E. *The Powers of the President: Problems of American Democracy.* Garden City, N.Y.: Doubleday, Doran, 1937.

————. *President and Congress,* Third Edition. New York: Vintage Books, 1962.

Birch, A. H. *Representation.* New York: Praeger, 1971.

Bonafede, Dom. "How Former Presidents Have Used the Polls." *National Journal* (August 19, 1978): 1314.

————. "Carter and the Polls—If You Live by Them, You May Die by Them." *National Journal* (August 19, 1978): 1312-1315.

————. "The Strained Relationship." *National Journal* (May 19, 1979): 830.

————. "As Pollster to the President, Wirthlin Is Where the Action Is." *National Journal* (December 12, 1981): 2184-2188.

Bork, Robert. *The Tempting of America: The Political Seduction of the Law.* New York: Basic Books, 1990.

Brace, Paul and Barbara Hinckley. *Follow the Leader: Opinion Polls and the Modern Presidency.* New York: Basic Books, 1992.

Buchanan, Bruce. *The Presidential Experience.* Englewood Cliffs, N.J.: Prentice-Hall, 1978.

Buchanan, James. *Works,* edited by John Bassette Moored. Philadelphia: J.B. Lippincott, 1908-1911.

Buckley, William F. Jr. "Agenda for the Nineties." *National Review* (February 19, 1990): 39-40.

Burke, John P. *The Institutional Presidency.* Baltimore, Md.: The Johns Hopkins University Press, 1992.

Burnham, James. *Congress and the American Tradition.* Chicago: Henry Regnery Company, 1965.

Burns, James MacGregor. *Presidential Government: The Crucible of Leadership.* New York: Avon Books, 196.

Calhoun, John C. *A Disquisition on Government and Selections from the Discourse,* edited by C. Gordon Post. New York: MacMillan, 1953.

Carey, George W., editor. *Freedom and Virtue: The Conservative/ Libertarian Debate.* Lanham, Md.: University Press of America and The Intercollegiate Studies Institute, 1984.

———. *In Defense of the Constitution,* Revised and Expanded Edition. Indianapolis: Liberty Fund, 1995.

———. *The Federalist: Design for a Constitutional Republic.* Urbana & Chicago: University of Illinois Press, 1989.

Ceaser, James W. *Presidential Selection: Theory and Development.* Princeton, N.J.: Princeton University Press, 1979.

———. *Liberal Democracy & Political Science.* Baltimore: The Johns Hopkins University Press, 1990.

Ceaser, James W., Glen E. Thurow, Jeffrey Tulis, and Joseph M. Bessette. "The Rise of the Rhetorical Presidency." *Presidential Studies Quarterly* (Spring 1981): 158-171.

Cirino, Robert. *Don't Blame the People.* New York: Random House, 1971.

Cohen, Jeffrey E. "A Historical Reassessment of Wildavsky's 'Two Presidencies' Thesis." *Social Science Quarterly* (September 1982): 549-555.

Conner, George E. and Bruce I. Oppenheimer. "Deliberation: An Untimed Value in a Timed Game." In *Congress Reconsidered,* edited by Lawrence C. Dodd and Bruce I. Oppenheimer, pp. 315-330. Washington, D.C.: CQ Press, 1993.

Corwin, Edward S. *The President: Office and Powers,* Fourth Edition. New York: New York University Press, 1957.

Covington, Cary R. "Staying Private: Gaining Congressional Support for Unpublished Presidential Preferences on Roll-Call Voting." *Journal of Politics* (August 1987): 737-755.

Cronin, Thomas. *The State of the Presidency*, Second Edition. Boston: Little, Brown, 1980.

————. "The Textbook Presidency." In *Perspectives on the Presidency: A Collection,* edited by Stanley Bach and George T. Sulzner, pp. 54-74. Lexington, Mass.: D.C. Heath, 1974.

Crovitz, L. Gordon and Jeremy A. Rabkin, editors. *The Fettered Presidency: Legal Constraints on the Executive Branch.* Washington, D.C.: American Enterprise Institute Press, 1989.

Cunliffe, Marcus. "A Defective Institution?" *Commentary* (February 1968): 27-33.

————. *American Presidents and the Presidency.* New York: American Heritage Press, 1972.

Curtis, Kenneth M. "The Presidency—An Imperfect Mirror." *Presidential Studies Quarterly* (Winter 1981): 28-31.

Dahl, Robert A. *A Preface to Democratic Theory.* Chicago: University of Chicago Press, 1956.

Davidson, Roger H. *The Role of the Congressman.* New York: Pegasus, 1967.

Deaver, Michael K. with Mickey Herskowitz. *Behind the Scenes.* New York: William Morrow and Company, 1987.

DeGrazia, Alfred. *Public and Republic: Political Representation in America.* New York: Alfred A. Knopf, 1951.

DeGrazia, Sabastian. "A Note on the Psychological Position of the Chief Executive." *Psychiatry* VIII (August 1945): 267-272.

Denton, Robert E. Jr. *The Symbolic Dimensions of the American Presidency: Description and Analysis.* Prosect Heights, Ill.: Waveland Press, 1982.

DeRosa, Marshall L. *The Confederate Constitution of 1861: An Inquiry into American Constitutionalism.* Columbia, Mo.: University of Missouri Press, 1991.

Diamond, Martin. "Democracy and *The Federalist*: A Reconsideration of the Framer's Intent." *American Political Science Review* (March 1959): 52-68.

DiClerico, Robert E. *The American President*, Second Edition. Englewood Cliffs, N.J.: Prentice-Hall, 1983.

Dowdle, Andrew. *The Protomodern Presidency*. Unpublished dissertation, Oxford, Ohio: Miami University, 1995.

Duffy, Michael and Dan Goodgame. *Marching in Place: The Status Quo Presidency of George Bush*. New York: Simon and Schuster, 1992.

Duncan, Hugh D. *Language and Literature in Society*. Chicago: University of Chicago Press, 1953.

Dye, Thomas R. "The Friends of Bill and Hillary." *PS: Political Science and Politics* (December 1993): 693-695.

Eastland, Terry. *Energy in the Executive: The Case for the Strong Presidency*. New York: The Free Press, 1992.

Easton, David. *The Political System*. New York: A. A. Knopf, 1953.

Easton, David and Jack Dennis. *Children in the Political System: Origins of Political Legitimacy*. New York: McGraw Hill, 1969.

Edelman, Murray. *The Symbolic Uses of Politics*. Urbana: University of Illinois Press, 1964.

Edwards, George C. III. *Presidential Influence in Congress*. San Francisco: Freeman, 1980.

———. *The Public Presidency: The Pursuit of Popular Support*. New York: St. Martin's Press, 1983.

———. *At the Margins: Presidential Leadership of Congress*. New Haven, Conn.: Yale University Press, 1989.

Edwards, George C. III and Stephen J. Wayne. *Presidential Leadership: Politics and Policy Making*. New York: St. Martin's Press, 1985.

Edwards, George C. III and Alec M. Gallup. *Presidential Approval: A Sourcebook*. Baltimore: The Johns Hopkins University Press, 1990.

Eidelberg, Paul. *A Discourse on Statesmanship*. Urbana, Ill.: University of Illinois Press, 1974.

Elliot J., editor. *The Debates of the State Conventions on the Adaptation of the Federal Constitution*. Philadelphia: J.B. Lippincott, 1866.

Epstein, David F. *The Political Theory of* The Federalist. Chicago: University of Chicago Press, 1984.

Evans, Joseph W. and Leo R. Wards, editors. *The Social and Political Philosophy of Jacques Maritain*. New York: Charles Scribner's Sons, 1955.

Evans, M. Stanton. *Clear and Present Dangers: A Conservative View of America's Government*. New York: Harcourt Brace Jovanovich, 1975.

Fairlie, John A. "The Nature of Political Representation." *American Political Science Review* (April and June, 1940): 236-248 and 456-466.

Farrand, Max, editor. *Records of the Federal Convention.* New Haven: Yale University Press, 1966.

Fiorina, Morris P. *Congress: Keystone of the Washington Establishment,* Second Edition . New Haven, Conn.: Yale University Press, 1989.

Fisher, Louis. *Presidential Spending Power.* Princeton, N.J.: Princeton University Press, 1975.

―――. *Constitutional Conflicts Between Congress and the President.* Lawrence, Kans.: University Press of Kansas, 1991.

―――. *Presidential War Power.* Lawrence, Kans.: University Press of Kansas, 1995.

Francis, Samuel. "Imperial Conservatives?" *National Review* (August 4, 1989): 37-38.

Franck, Thomas and Edward Weisband. *Foreign Policy by Congress.* New York: Oxford University Press, 1979.

Franklin, Daniel P. *Extraordinary Measures: The Exercise of Prerogative Powers in the United States.* Pittsburgh, Pa: University of Pittsburgh Press, 1991.

Friedrich, Carl J. "Representation and Constitutional Reform." *Western Political Quarterly* (June 1948).

―――. *Constitutional Government and Democracy.* Boston: Ginn, 1950.

Germino, Dante. *The Inaugural Addresses of American Presidents: The Public Philosophy and Rhetoric.* Lanham, Md.: University Press of America, 1984.

Goldwater, Barry. *Where I Stand.* New York: McGraw-Hill, 1964.

Grasso, Kenneth L. "Pluralism, the Public Good and the Problem of Self-Government in *The Federalist.*" *Interpretation* (May/September 1987): 323-345.

Greenstein, Fred I. "What the President Means to Americans." In *Choosing the President,* edited by James David Barber. New York: American Assembly, 1974.

―――. "Change and Continuity in the Modern Presidency." In *The New American Political System,* edited by Anthony King, pp. 45-85. Washington, D.C.: American Enterprise Institute Press, 1978.

Hargrove, Erwin C. and Michael Nelson. *Presidents, Politics, and Policy.* New York: Knopf, 1984.

Hart, Jeffrey. "The Presidency: Shifting Conservative Perspectives." *National Review* (November 22, 1974): 1351-1355.

Hart, John. *The Presidential Branch.* New York: Pergamon Press, 1987.

Hess, Robert D. and Judith V. Torney. *The Development of Political Attitudes in Children.* Garden City, N.Y.:Anchor Books, 1967.

Hess, Stephen. *Organizing the Presidency.* Washington, D.C.: The Brookings Institution, 1976.

Hinckley, Barbara. *The Symbolic Presidency: How Presidents Portray Themselves.* New York: Routledge, 1990.

Hirschfield, Robert S., editor. *The Power of the Presidency: Concepts and Controversy,* Second Edition. Chicago: Aldine Publishing Company, 1973.

Hodgson, Godfrey. *All Things to All Men: The False Promise of the Modern Presidency.* New York: Simon and Schuster, 1980.

Hogan, James. *Election and Representation.* Cork University Press, 1945.

Johnson, Lyndon B. *The Vantage Point: Perspectives of the Presidency, 1963-1969.* New York: Popular Library, 1971.

Jones, Charles O. "The Role of the Campaign in Congressional Politics." In *The Electoral Process,* edited by M. Kent Jennings and L. Harmon Ziegler, pp. 21-41. Englewood Cliffs, N.J.: Prentice-Hall, 1966.

———. *The Presidency in a Separated System.* Washington, D.C.: The Brookings Institution, 1994.

Jones, Gordon S. and John A. Marini, editors. *The Imperial Congress: Crisis in the Separation of Powers.* New York: Pharos Books, 1988.

Kaminski, John P. and Richard Leffler. *Federalist and AntiFederalist: The Debate Over the Ratification of the Constitution.* Madison, Wis.: Madison House, 1989.

Kearney, Kevin M. "Private Citizens in Foreign Affairs: A Constitutional Analysis." 36 *Emory Law Journal* 285(1987).

Kearns, Doris. *Lyndon Johnson & the American Dream.* New York: The New American Library, 1976.

Kelman, Steven. *Making Public Policy: A Hopeful View of American Government.* New York: Basic Books, 1987.

Kendall, Willmoore and George W. Carey. *The Basic Symbols of the American Political Tradition.* Baton Rouge, La.: Louisiana State University Press, 1970.

———. "The Two Majorities in American Politics." In *The Conservative Affirmation in America,* pp. 21-49. Chicago: Regnery Gateway, 1985.

———. "Equality: Commitment or Ideal?" *Intercollegiate Review* (Spring 1989): 25-33.

Kennedy, John F. *Profiles in Courage.* New York: Harper & Brothers, 1956.

Kenyon, Cecelia M. "Men of Little Faith: The Anti-Federalists on the Nature of Representative Government." *William and Mary Quarterly* (January 1955): 3-43.

Kernell, Samuel. *Going Public: New Strategies of Presidential Leadership.* Washington, D.C.: CQ Press, 1986.

Kesler, Charles R. "Woodrow Wilson and the Statesmanship of Progress." In *Natural Right and Political Right*, edited by Thomas R. Silver and Peter W. Schramm. Durham, N.C.: Carolina Adademic Press, 1984.

———. "Federalist 10 and American Republicanism." In *Saving the Revolution: The Federalist Papers and the American Founding*, edited by Charles R. Kesler, pp. 13-39. New York: The Free Press, 1987.

Ketcham, Ralph. *Presidents Above Party: The First American Presidency, 1789-1829.* Chapel Hill: The University of North Carolina Press, 1984.

King, Gary W. and Lyn Ragsdale. *The Elusive Executive.* Washington, D.C.: CQ Press, 1988.

Kingdon, John W. *Agendas, Alternatives, and Public Policies.* Boston: Little, Brown and Company, 1984.

Kirk, Russell. *A Program for Conservatives.* Chicago: Henry Regnery Company, 1954.

———. *The Conservative Mind*, Seventh Revised Edition. Chicago: Regnery Books, 1986.

———. *The Conservative Constitution.* Washington, D.C.: Regnery Gateway, 1990.

Kristol, Irving. *On the Democratic Idea in America.* New York: Harper & Row, 1972.

Kristol, William. "The Problem of the Separation of Powers, *Federalist* 47-51." In *Saving the Revolution: The Federalist Papers and the American Founding*, edited by Charles R. Kesler, 100-130. New York: The Free Press, 1987.

Leloup, Lance T. and Steven A. Shull. "Congress versus the Executive: The 'Two Presidencies' Reconsidered." *Social Science Quarterly* (March 1979): 704-719.

Leuchtenburg, William E. *In the Shadow of FDR: From Harry Truman to Ronald Reagan.* Ithaca, N.Y.: Cornell University Press, 1983.

Light, Paul C. *The President's Agenda.* Baltimore, Md.: The Johns Hopkins University Press, 1982.

Lincoln, Abraham. *Speeches and Writings.* New York: The Library of America, 1989.

Locke, John. *The Second Treatise on Civil Government.* New York: Prometheus Books, 1986.

Loss, Richard. *The Modern Theory of Presidential Power: Alexander Hamilton and the Corwin Thesis.* New York: Greenwood Press, 1990.

Lowi, Theodore J. *The End of Liberalism.* New York: Norton, 1960.

———. *The Personal Presidency: Power Invested Promise Unfulfilled.* Ithaca, N.Y.: Cornell University Press, 1985.

———. "The State in Political Science: How we Become What we Study." *American Political Science Review* (March 1992): 1-7.

Luce, Robert. *Legislative Principles.* Boston: Houghton Mifflin, 1930.

Lutz, Donald S., editor. *Union and Liberty: The Political Philosophy of John C. Calhoun.* Indianapolis, Ind.: Liberty Press, 1992.

Maass, Arthur. *Congress and the Common Good.* New York: Basic Books, 1983.

Madison, James, Alexander Hamilton, and John Jay. *The Federalist Papers*, edited by Isaac Kramnick. England: Penguin Books, 1987.

Malbin, Michael J. *Unelected Representatives: Congressional Staff and the Future of Representative Government.* New York: Basic Books, 1980.

Mansbridge, Jane J. *Beyond Adversarial Democracy.* Chicago: University of Chicago Press, 1983.

Mansfield, Harvey C. Jr. *Statesmanship and Party Government.* Chicago: University of Chicago Press, 1965.

———. "Constitutional Government: The Soul of Modern Democracy." *The Public Interest* (Winter 1982).

———. *Taming the Prince: The Ambivalence of Modern Executive Power.* New York: The Free Press, 1989.

———. *America's Constitutional Soul.* Baltimore, Md.: The Johns Hopkins University Press, 1991.

Mayhew, David R. *Congress: The Electoral Connection.* New Haven: Yale University Press, 1982.

McConnell, Grant. *The Modern Presidency*, Second Edition. New York: St. Martin's Press, 1976.

McDonald, Forrest. *The Presidency of George Washington.* Lawrence, Kans.: University Press of Kansas, 1973.

———. *Novus Ordo Seclorem: The Intellectual Origins of the Constitution.* Lawrence, Kans.: University Press of Kansas, 1985.

———. *The American Presidency: An Intellectual History.* Lawrence, Kans.: University Press of Kansas, 1994.

McWilliams, Wilson Carey. "The Anti-Federalists, Representation and party." *Northwestern University Law Review* (Fall 1989): 12-38.

Meese, Edwin III. *With Reagan: The Inside Story.* Washington, D.C.: Regnery Gateway, 1992.

Milkis, Sidney M. *The President and the Parties: The Transformation of the American Party System Since the New Deal.* New York: Oxford University Press, 1993.

Milkis, Sidney M. and Michael Nelson. *The American Presidency: Origins and Development, 1776-1990.* Washington, D.C.: CQ Press, 1990.

Mill, John Stuart. *Utilitarianism, On Liberty, Considerations on Representative Government,* edited by H.B. Acton. London: J.M. Dent & Sons, 1972.

Minnow, Newton N., John Barlow Martin, and Lee M. Mitchell. *Presidential Television.* New York: Basic Books, 1973.

Miroff, Bruce. "The Presidency and the Public Space: Leadership as Spectacle." In *The Presidency and the Political System,* Second Edition, edited by Michael Nelson, pp. 271-291. Washington, D.C.: CQ Press, 1988.

Moe, Terry M. "The Politicized Presidency." In *The Managerial Presidency,* edited by James P. Pfiffner, pp. 135-157. Pacific Grove, Calif.: Brooks/Cole, 1991.

Montesquieu, Baron de. *The Spirit of the Laws,* translated and edited by Anne M. Cohler, Basia Carolyn Miller, and Harold Samuel Stone. Cambridge: Cambridge University Press, 1989.

Morgan, Robert J. "Madison's Theory of Representation in the Tenth *Federalist.*" *The Journal of Politics* (Vol. 37 1974): 852-885.

Morgan, Ruth P. *The President and Civil Rights: Policy-Making by Executive Order.* New York: St. Martin's Press, 1970.

Muir, William K. Jr. "Ronald Reagan: The Primacy of Rhetoric." In *Leadership in the Modern Presidency,* edited by Fred I.Greenstein, pp. 260-295. Cambridge, Mass.: Harvard University Press, 1988.

Nash, George H. *The Conservative Intellectual Movement in America since 1945.* New York: Basic Books, 1976.

Neely, Richard. *How Courts Govern America.* New Haven, Conn.: Yale University Press, 1981.

Neuman, Russell W. *The Paradox of Mass Politics.* Cambridge, Mass.: Harvard University Press, 1986.

Neustadt, Richard. "The Presidency and Legislation: Planning the President's Legislative Program." *American Political Science Review* (December 1955): 980-1021.

————. *Presidential Power and Modern Presidents.* New York: The Free Press, 1990.

New Republic, The. "Swing of the Pendulum." *The New Republic* (March 27, 1971): 5-6.

Nichols, David K. *The Myth of the Modern Presidency.* University Park, Pa.: Pennsylvania State University Press, 1994.

Nixon, Richard. *Public Papers of the President of the United States: Richard Nixon, 1970.* Washington, D.C.: U.S. Government Printing Office, 1971.

Noonan, Peggy. *What I Saw at the Revolution: A Political Life in the Reagan Era.* New York: Random House, 1990.

Novak, Michael. *Choosing Our King: Powerful Symbols in Presidential Politics.* New York: MacMillan, 1974.

O'Brien, David. *Judicial Roulette: Report of the Twentieth Century Fund Task Force on Judicial Selection.* New York: Priority Press, 1988.

Padover, Saul K. "The Power of the President." *Commonweal* (August 9, 1968): 521-525.

Patterson, Bradley H. Jr. *The Ring of Power: The White House Staff and its Expanding Role in Government.* New York: Basic Books, 1988.

Patterson, Thomas E. *Out of Order.* New York: Vintage Books, 1994.

Pennock, J. Roland. "Political Representation: An Overview." In *Nomos X: Representation,* edited by J. Roland Pennock and John W. Chapman, 3-27. New York: Atherton Press, 1968.

Peppers, Donald A. "The Two Presidencies: Eight Years Later." In *Perspectives on the Presidency,* edited by Aaron Wildavsky. Boston, Little, 1975.

Peterson, Merrill D., editor. *The Portable Thomas Jefferson.* New York: Penguin Books, 1977.

Pfiffner, James P. *The Modern Presidency.* New York: St. Martin's Press, 1994.

Pious, Richard M. *The American Presidency.* New York: Basic Books, 1979.

Piper, J. Richard. "Presidential-Congressional Power Prescriptions in Conservative Political Thought since 1933." *Presidential Studies Quarterly* (Winter 1991): 35-54.

Pitkin, Hannah. *The Concept of Representation.* Berkeley, Calif.: University of California Press, 1967.

Ranney, Austin. "Turnout and Representation in Presidential Primary Elections." *American Political Science Review* (March 1972): 21-37.

Reedy, George E. *The Twilight of the Presidency.* New York: Mentor, 1972.

————. "The Presidency in the Era of Mass Communication." In *Modern Presidents and the Presidency*, edited by Marc Landy, pp. 35-41. Lexington, Mass.: Lexington Books, 1985.

Remini, Robert V. *Andrew Jackson and the Course of American Freedom, 1822-1832.* New York: Harper & Row, 1981.

————. *The Revolutionary Age of Andrew Jackson.* New York: Harper Torchbooks, 1987.

Richardson, James D., editor. *Messages and Papers of the Presidents,* Bureau of National Literature and Art, 1903.

Riemer, Neal. "James Madison's Theory of the Self-Destructive Features of Republican Government." *Ethics* (October 1954): 34-43.

Riencourt, Amaury de. *The Coming Caesars.* New York: Coward-McCann, 1957.

Rimmerman, Craig A. *Presidency by Plebiscite: The Reagan-Bush Era in Institutional Perspective.* Boulder, Colo.: Westview Press, 1993.

Roche, John P. "The Founding Fathers: A Reform Caucus in Action." *American Political Science Review* (December 1961): 799-816.

Rockman, Bert. "Presidential and Executive Studies: The One, the Few, and the Many." In *Political Science: The Science of Politics*, edited by Herbert F. Weisberg, pp. 105-140. New York: Agathon Press, 1986.

————. "The Style and Organization of the Reagan Presidency." In *The Reagan Legacy: Promise and Performance*, edited by Charles O. Jones, pp. 3-29. Chatham, N.J.: Chatham House, 1988.

Rose, Richard. *The Postmodern President: George Bush Meets the World,* Second Edition. Chatham, NJ: Chatham House, 1991.

Rossiter, Clinton. *The American Presidency*, Revised Edition. New York: Mentor, 1960.

Scanlan, James P. "The Federalist and Human Nature." *The Review of Politics* (October 1959): 657-677.

Schattschneider, E.E. *The Semi-Sovereign People.* New York: Holt, Rinehart, and Winston, 1960.

Schlesinger, Arthur M. Jr. *The Imperial Presidency.* New York: Popular Library, 1974.

Sigelman, Lee. "A Reassessment of the 'Two Presidencies' Thesis." *Journal of Politics* (November 1979): 1195-1205.

Skowronek, Stephen. *The Politics Presidents make: Leadership from John Adams to George Bush.* Cambridge: Harvard University Press and Belknap Press, 1993.

Slonim, Schlomo. "Designing the Electoral College." In *Inventing the American Presidency*, edited by Thomas E. Cronin, pp. 33-60. Lawrence, Kans.: University Press of Kansas, 1989.

Smith, Kathy B. "The Representative Role of the President." *Presidential Studies Quarterly* (Spring 1981): 203-213.

Solzhenitsyn, Alexander. "The Exhausted West." *Harvard Magazine* (July-August 1978).

Sorensen, Theodore C. *Kennedy.* New York: Bantam, 1966.

————. "Political Perspective: Who Speaks for the National Interest?" In *The Tethered Presidency: Congressional Restraints on Executive Power,* edited by Thomas N. Franck, pp. 3-20. New York: New York University Press, 1981.

Spitzer, Robert J. *President & Congress: Executive Hegemony at the Crossroads of American Government.* New York: McGraw-Hill, 1993.

Spragens, William G. *The Presidency and the Mass Media in the Age of Television.* Washington, D.C.: University Press of America, 1978.

Stanlis, Peter J., editor. *Edmund Burke: Selected Writings and Speeches.* Chicago: Regnery Gateway, 1963.

Stockman, David A. *The Triumph of Politics: The Inside Story of the Reagan Revolution.* New York: Avon Books, 1987.

Stokes, Donald E. "Political Parties in the Normative Theory of Representation." In *Nomos X: Representation*, edited by J. Roland Pennock and John W. Chapman, pp. 150-154. New York: Atherton Press, 1968.

Storing, Herbert, editor. *The Complete Anti-Federalists.* Chicago: University of Chicago Press, 1981.

Strum, Phillipa. *Presidential Power and American Democracy.* Pacific Palisades, Calif.: Goodyear Publishing Company, 1972.

Stuckey, Mary E. *The President as Interpreter-In-Chief.* Chatham, N.J.: Chatham House Publishers, 1991.

Thompson, Kenneth W. *The President and the Public Philosophy.* Baton Rouge, La.: Louisiana State University Press, 1981.

Tocqueville, Alexis de. *Democracy in America.* New York: Vintage Classics, 1990.

Truman, David B. *The Governmental Process.* New York: Knopf, 1951.

Tugwell, Rexford G. *The Enlargement of the Presidency.* New York: Doubleday, 1960.

Tulis, Jeffrey K. *The Rhetorical Presidency.* Princeton, N.J.: Princeton University Press, 1987.

————. "The Interpretable Presidency." In *The Presidency and the Political System,* Second Edition, edited by Michael Nelson, pp. 45-54. Washington, D.C.: CQ Press, 1988: 45-54.

Voegelin, Eric. *The New Science of Politics.* Chicago: University of Chicago Press, 1952.

Vogler, David J., and Sidney R. Waldman. *Congress and Democracy.* Washington, D.C.: CQ Press, 1985.

Waterman, Richard W., editor. *The Presidency Reconsidered.* Itasca, Ill.: F. E. Peacock Publishers, 1993.

Watson, Richard A., and Norman C. Thomas. *The Politics of the Presidency,* Second Edition. Washington, D.C.: CQ Press, 1988.

Wayne, Stephen J. *The Legislative Presidency.* New York: Harper & Row, 1978.

————. *The Road to the White House 1992: The Politics of Presidential Elections.* New York: St. Martin's Press, 1992.

Weber, Max. *The Theory of Social and Economic Organizations,* translated by A. M. Henderson and Talcott Persons. New York: Oxford University Press, 1947.

Weissberg, Robert. *Public Opinion and Popular Government.* Englewood Cliffs, N.J.: Prentice-Hall, 1976.

West, Thomas G. "The Rule of Law in *The Federalist.*" In *Saving the Revolution: The Federalist Papers and the American Founding,* edited by Charles R. Kesler, 150-167. New York: The Free Press, 1987.

West, William F., and Joseph Cooper. "The Rise of Administrative Clearance." In *The Presidency and Public Policy Making,* edited by George C. Edwards III, Steven Shull, and Norman Thomas. Pittsburgh: University of Pittsburgh Press, 1985.

Wildavsky, Aaron. "The Two Presidencies." In *Perspectives on the Presidency,* edited by Aaron Wildavsky, 448-461. Boston: Little, Brown and Company, 1975.

Will, George F. *Statecraft as Soulcraft.* New York: Simon & Shuster, 1983.

————. *Restoration: Congress, Term Limits and the Recovery of Deliberative Democracy.* New York: The Free Press, 1992.

Wills, Garry. *The Kennedy Imprisonment: A Meditation on Power.* New York: Pocket Books, 1981.

————. *Lincoln at Gettysburg: The Words That Remade America.* New York: Simon & Schuster, 1992.

Wilson, Woodrow. *Congressional Government.* New York: The World Publishing Company, 1967.

————. *Constitutional Government* in *The Papers of Woodrow Wilson,* Volume 18, edited by Arthur S. Link. Princeton, N.J.: Princeton University Press, 1974.

Windt, Theodore Otto, Jr. "Presidential Rhetoric: Definition of a Field of Study." *Presidential Studies Quarterly* (Winter 1986): 102-116.

Wood, Gordon S. *Representation in the American Revolution.* Charlottesville, Va.: University of Virginia Press, 1969.

————. *The Creation of the American Republic, 1776-1787.* New York: W. W. Norton, 1972.

Woodward, Bob. *The Agenda: Inside the Clinton White House.* New York: Simon & Schuster, 1994.

Index

as party leader, 36; rhetoric,
134–135, 154n28; symbolism,
21
elections, 35, 81, 126–133, 148,
151–152, 153n13, 206; *see also*
president and; Publius on
electoral college, 34–35, 44n61, 86,
127, 153n10
Executive Office of the President
(EOP), 183–187
executive orders, 179
expectations of presidents, 204–
205, 215

Federalist Papers, 36, 112, 124,
126, 159, 169, 175, 196, 198,
206; *see also* Publius
Federalists, 43n49, 128
Federal Reserve Board, 181
Ford, Gerald, 139, 143, 145, 147–
148, 177
foreign policy, *see* president and
Founding Fathers, 16, 32, 35, 36,
92, 102, 138, 141, 148,
196–197, 213; *see also*
Constitutional Convention;
Publius
Franck, Thomas M., 176

Gallup, George, 142
Germino, Dante, 23
Gerry, Elbridge, 31, 34
Gettysburg Address, *see* Lincoln,
Abraham
Gingrich, Newt, 202–204
Gore, Albert, 210
government, growth of, 199–200
Grant, Ulysses S., 39
Grasso, Kenneth, 58–59
Great Depression, 125–126, 161,
166

Great Society, *see* Johnson,
Lyndon
Greenberg, Stanley, 146–147
Greenstein, Fred, 22, 125

Haldeman, H. R., 139
Hamilton, Alexander, 20, 127–128,
168, 175, 206
Hart, Jeffrey, 111
Hart, Peter, 145
Hartley, Thomas, 31
Hepburn Act of 1906, 134
Hess, Stephen, 142, 185
Hinckley, Barbara, 5, 21, 27, 80,
148
Hodgson, Godfrey, 133
Hoover, Herbert, 38, 136, 181, 212
House of Representatives, 51, 60,
62–63, 168, 202; *see also*
Congress; legislature; Publius
Humphrey, Hubert, 129
Humphrey, William, 181
Humphrey's Executor v. U.S., 181

impeachment, 181
Impoundment Control Act, 179
I.N.S. v. Chadha, 184
interest groups, 164, 209–210
Interstate Commerce Commission,
181

Jackson, Andrew, 80–89, 94, 107;
election of, 4, 128, 113–114n5;
Jacksonian democracy, 22; as
party leader, 25, 36–37; on the
presidency, 81–84, 87; and the
public, 81–84, 124; rhetoric, 93;
on the Senate, 83, 208
Jay Treaty, 170
Jefferson, Thomas, 3–4, 22, 127–
128, 131, 165, 175

About the Author

Gary L. Gregg II is assistant professor of political science at Clarion University and Director of Academic Development at the Intercollegiate Studies Institute. He was a *cum laude* graduate of Davis and Elkins College and earned an M.A. and Ph.D. from Miami University (Ohio). A former Richard M. Weaver and Henry Salvatori Fellow with the Intercollegiate Studies Institute, he has been an award winning teacher and has published in journals such as *Perspectives on Political Science*, *Presidential Studies Quarterly*, and *The University Bookman*.

3366